WASHINGTON
2nd Edition

THE
CREAKY KNEES
GUIDE

The 100 Best Easy Hikes

SEABURY BLAIR JR.

SASQUATCH BOOKS
SEATTLE

Copyright © 2009, 2016 by Seabury Blair Jr.

All rights reserved. No portion of this book may be reproduced or utilized in any form, or by any electronic, mechanical, or other means, without the prior written permission of the publisher.

Printed in the United States of America

Published by Sasquatch Books
20 19 18 17   9 8 7 6 5 4 3 2

Cover photograph: Rob Casey
Cover design: Joyce Hwang
Interior design: Rosebud Eustace and Joyce Hwang
Interior photos: Seabury Blair Jr.
Interior maps: Marlene Blair

Library of Congress Cataloging-in-Publication Data is available.

ISBN: 978-1-63217-009-5

Sasquatch Books
1904 Third Avenue, Suite 710
Seattle, WA 98101
(206) 467-4300
www.sasquatchbooks.com
custserv@sasquatchbooks.com

IMPORTANT NOTE: Please use common sense. No guidebook can act as a substitute for experience, careful planning, the right equipment, and appropriate training. There is inherent danger in all the activities described in this book, and readers must assume full responsibility for their own actions and safety. Changing or unfavorable conditions in weather, roads, trails, snow, waterways, and so forth cannot be anticipated by the author or publisher, but should be considered by any outdoor participants. The author and publisher will not be responsible for the safety of users of this guide.

Given the potential for changes to hiking rules and regulations post-publication, please check ahead for updates on contact information, parking passes, and camping permits.

Certified Chain of Custody
Promoting Sustainable Forestry
SUSTAINABLE FORESTRY INITIATIVE
www.sfiprogram.org
SFI-01268

SFI label applies to the text stock

CONTENTS

The Chain Lakes Loop trail (#2) circles Table Mountain, center, and Herman Saddle, right.

HIKES AT A GLANCE

STROLL IN THE PARK

NO.	HIKE NAME	RATING	BEST SEASON	KIDS	DOGS
18	Tumwater Canyon Trail	🚶🚶	Spring	✔	✔
44	Takhlakh Lake Loop	🚶🚶🚶🚶	Summer, fall	✔	✔
94	Boyer Park	🚶🚶	Spring	✔	✔
95	Olympic Discovery Trail	🚶🚶🚶🚶	Summer		✔
96	Chehalis Western Trail	🚶🚶🚶	Summer		✔
97	Burke-Gilman Trail	🚶🚶🚶	Summer		✔
98	Boulevard Park	🚶🚶🚶🚶	Summer		✔
99	Apple Capital Loop	🚶🚶🚶🚶🚶	Spring, winter		✔
100	Yakima Greenway	🚶🚶🚶🚶	Spring, winter		✔

EASY WALK

NO.	HIKE NAME	RATING	BEST SEASON	KIDS	DOGS
8	Baker Lake	🚶🚶🚶	Spring	✔	✔
10	Thunder Creek Trail	🚶🚶	Fall	✔	✔
11	Lake Ann	🚶🚶🚶🚶	Summer, fall	✔	✔
13	Cutthroat Lake	🚶🚶🚶🚶	Fall	✔	✔
14	Tiffany Lake	🚶🚶	Summer, fall	✔	✔
16	Barclay Lake	🚶🚶🚶	Fall	✔	✔
17	Iron Goat Trail	🚶🚶🚶	Summer	✔	✔
21	John Wayne Trail, Cascades	🚶🚶🚶	Spring	✔	✔
22	Hyak Tunnel	🚶🚶🚶🚶	Summer, fall		✔
23	Middle Fork Snoqualmie	🚶🚶	Fall	✔	✔
29	Deer Lake	🚶🚶	Summer, fall	✔	✔
30	Tieton Meadows	🚶🚶🚶	Summer, fall	✔	✔
35	West Side Road	🚶🚶🚶	Fall, winter	✔	
48	Coldwater Lake Trail	🚶🚶🚶	Spring, summer		
49	Windy Ridge	🚶🚶🚶🚶🚶	Summer, fall	✔	
57	Dungeness Spit	🚶🚶🚶	Winter	✔	
61	Spruce Railroad Trail	🚶🚶🚶	Fall	✔	
62	Rialto Beach	🚶🚶🚶	Spring, winter	✔	✔
63	Port Gamble Trails	🚶	Fall	✔	✔
68	Ginkgo Petrified Forest Trails	🚶🚶🚶	Spring		✔

71	Cowiche Canyon Trail	🚶🚶🚶	Spring	✓	✓
74	Billy Clapp Lake Wildlife Area	🚶	Spring	✓	✓
76	Potholes Dunes	🚶🚶🚶	Spring	✓	✓
78	Klickitat Rail Trail	🚶🚶🚶	Spring	✓	✓
81	Columbia Plateau Trail North	🚶🚶🚶	Spring	✓	✓
82	Columbia Plateau Trail South	🚶🚶🚶🚶	Spring	✓	✓
83	Turnbull National Wildlife Refuge	🚶🚶🚶🚶	Spring, fall	✓	✓
87	Painted Rocks	🚶🚶🚶🚶	Spring		✓
89	Liberty Creek	🚶🚶	Spring	✓	✓
91	Centennial Trail East	🚶🚶🚶	Spring		✓
92	White Bluffs	🚶🚶🚶🚶	Fall, winter		✓

MODERATE WORKOUT

NO.	HIKE NAME	RATING	BEST SEASON	KIDS	DOGS
3	Ptarmigan Ridge	🚶🚶🚶🚶🚶	Summer, fall		✓
5	Twin Lakes Road	🚶	Summer		✓
6	Winchester Mountain Lookout	🚶🚶🚶🚶	Summer		✓
9	Sauk Mountain	🚶	Summer, fall		✓
12	Blue Lake	🚶🚶🚶🚶	Fall	✓	✓
15	Bridal Veil Falls	🚶🚶	Spring		✓
19	Little Eightmile Lake	🚶🚶	Summer	✓	
20	Rattlesnake Ledge	🚶🚶🚶	Spring, fall	✓	✓
24	Talapus Lake	🚶🚶	Fall	✓	✓
27	Naches Peak Loop	🚶🚶🚶	Summer		✓
32	Dark Meadow	🚶🚶	Summer, fall		✓
33	Yellowjacket Pond	🚶🚶🚶	Fall	✓	✓
36	Eunice Lake	🚶🚶🚶	Summer		
37	Berkeley Park	🚶🚶🚶	Summer	✓	
38	Paradise Trails	🚶🚶🚶🚶🚶	Summer, fall		
40	Spray Park	🚶🚶🚶	Summer		
41	Glacier View	🚶🚶🚶🚶	Summer		✓
45	West Fork Trail	🚶🚶🚶	Summer	✓	✓
46	Killen Creek Trail	🚶🚶🚶🚶🚶	Summer, fall		✓
47	Indian Racetrack	🚶🚶	Summer, fall	✓	✓
51	Lower Skokomish River	🚶🚶	Spring		✓
52	Spike Camp	🚶🚶	Spring	✓	
53	Dosewallips Road	🚶🚶🚶🚶	Spring	✓	✓

NO.	HIKE NAME	RATING	BEST SEASON	KIDS	DOGS
56	Camp Handy	🚶🚶🚶🚶	Spring, fall	✔	✔
59	Hurricane Hill	🚶🚶🚶🚶🚶	Summer, fall	✔	
60	Elwha Loop	🚶🚶🚶	Spring	✔	
65	Gold Creek Trail	🚶🚶	Spring, fall		✔
66	Umtanum Canyon	🚶🚶🚶🚶	Spring	✔	✔
69	John Wayne Trail West	🚶🚶	Spring		✔
70	John Wayne Trail East	🚶🚶🚶	Spring		✔
72	Ancient Lake(s)	🚶🚶🚶	Spring		✔
73	Umatilla Rock Loop	🚶🚶	Spring		✔
75	Swakane Canyon Road	🚶🚶🚶	Spring		✔
77	Hardy and Rodney Falls	🚶🚶	Spring, fall	✔	✔
79	Beacon Rock	🚶🚶🚶🚶	Spring, summer	✔	✔
85	Sullivan Lake Trail	🚶🚶🚶	Summer, fall	✔	✔
88	Dishman Hills	🚶🚶	Spring, fall		✔
90	Centennial Trail West	🚶🚶🚶🚶	Spring		✔
93	Columbia Plateau Trail	🚶🚶🚶	Spring, fall		✔

PREPARE TO PERSPIRE

NO.	HIKE NAME	RATING	BEST SEASON	KIDS	DOGS
1	Hannegan Camp	🚶🚶🚶	Summer		✔
2	Chain Lakes Loop	🚶🚶🚶	Summer, fall		✔
4	Heliotrope Ridge	🚶🚶🚶🚶🚶	Summer, fall		✔
7	High Pass	🚶🚶🚶🚶	Summer, fall		✔
25	Snow Lake	🚶🚶🚶🚶	Fall	✔	✔
26	Squaw Lake	🚶🚶🚶🚶	Summer, fall		✔
28	Noble Knob	🚶🚶🚶🚶	Summer		✔
31	Hogback Ridge	🚶🚶	Fall		✔
34	Walupt Creek	🚶🚶🚶	Summer, fall	✔	✔
39	Pinnacle Saddle	🚶🚶🚶	Fall		
40	Spray Park	🚶🚶🚶	Summer		
42	Comet Falls	🚶🚶	Summer, fall		
43	Bird Creek Meadows	🚶🚶🚶	Summer, fall	✔	✔
50	Norway Pass	🚶🚶🚶🚶🚶	Summer, fall		
58	Maiden Peak	🚶🚶🚶🚶	Summer, fall		
64	Green Mountain Trail	🚶	Spring, fall		✔
84	Shedroof Mountain	🚶🚶🚶🚶	Summer, fall		✔
86	Columbia Mountain	🚶🚶🚶🚶🚶	Summer, fall		✔

KNEE-PUNISHING

NO.	HIKE NAME	RATING	BEST SEASON	KIDS	DOGS
38	Paradise Trails	𝀀𝀀𝀀𝀀𝀀	Summer, fall		
54	Mount Townsend	𝀀𝀀𝀀𝀀	Summer, fall		✔
55	Marmot Pass	𝀀𝀀𝀀𝀀	Summer, fall		✔
67	Manastash Ridge	𝀀	Spring		✔
80	Dog Mountain	𝀀𝀀𝀀𝀀	Spring		✔

Climbing into the hills toward Doris, John Wayne Trail East (#70).

ACKNOWLEDGMENTS

My wife, Marlene (B. B. Hardbody to my three readers), gets many thanks for her help and encouragement in bringing this edition to reality. She created the maps here and walked many of these trails with me while—unlike me—keeping a full-time, legitimate job.

Thanks, too, to the authors of the guidebooks that directed me to many of the trails in this book: James P. Johnson, Ron C. Judd, Rich Landers, Mike McQuaide, Dan A. Nelson, and Craig Romano. Each helped me find pathways I'd never hiked before, and all gave me accurate and timely information to decide whether they might be included here. Although distance prevents me today from joining them nearly as often as I wish, I continue to owe thanks to The Ladies and Two Guys for slowing down to walk trails with me. The Ladies include Jean Cornwell, Karen Johnson, Tamae Johnson, Joyce Kimmel, Gayla Perini, Ann Richey, and Linda Weinacher. The Two Guys are Gary Larson and my good friend Jim Drannan, the Gnarly Dude.

Finally, I thank Christy Cox, Gary Luke, Haley Stocking, and all the good people at Sasquatch Books for the opportunity to show you some of my favorite joint-friendly hikes.

INTRODUCTION

I've only recently remembered what slipped my feeble mind around four decades ago: we who live in Washington State reside on an extremely rare piece of real estate. If I didn't care about the hundreds of scolding letters I'd receive from all of you who respect the English language, I'd suggest that our state is "almost" unique. Pitifully few places in this country—or on earth—pack such variety and beauty into such a small package. Where else can you walk from ocean to glacier in one day? Where else can you drive from rain forest to desert in a few hours?

Few places give us such diversity. Walk into the Olympic Peninsula rain forest to find trees that were saplings hundreds of years before Columbus landed on America's shores. Wander sage-dotted coulees etched by rivers of ice that covered the continent millions of years ago. Wonder that in the middle of a land where rainfall totals less than five inches every year, cool lakes stretch for miles. Climb in less than an hour to the still-steaming maw of a volcano, so close the sulfur sneaks into your senses. Bask in the sunshine of Wenatchee or Yakima or Spokane, the warm light that draws thousands of moss-draped Westsiders. One of the most powerful rivers in the nation splits our state in two; the greatest ocean on the planet washes our shores; our mountains embrace more living glaciers than any in the Lower 48.

Little wonder, then, that a place of such geologic diversity would spawn such a splendid variety of animals and plants who share this small corner of our nation with us. The largest mammal in North America cruises the wetlands and forests of northeastern Washington, while the smallest rodent harvests hay on the slopes of Mount Rainier. Keeping company with the moose and the pika is an array of wildlife few earthly zoos could match: Herds of two elk species graze from the Olympic Peninsula to the Blue Mountains; mountain goats and sheep climb along the high, lonely ridges; foxes, coyotes, and wolves sing to us from the edge of forest and desert. Even the grizzly bear, the icon of free, wild North America, calls this state home.

And don't get me started on plants, largely because I don't know a helluva lot about them. Suffice it to say that once I hiked the hills of Eastern Washington and climbed the canyons of the Columbia River Gorge, I realized I'd need something other than my trusty *Wildflowers of Mount Rainier* to identify those purple and yellow blossoms popping up everywhere. Likewise, I found I might fill two distinctly different life lists with all those winged creatures in the sky, trees, and sage.

Despite the territorial dichotomy created by Washington's Cascade Mountains, I found the pedestrians who ply our pathways from west to east and north to south are pretty much the same. They all know and love the country at their back door—be it forest or flatland, mountain or meadow, desert or river. In checking the trails for this guide, I met a ninety-five-year-old hiker walking a Mount Baker trail, a fifty-two-year-old woman jogging through pines along the Spokane River, and Real Mountain Climbers toting a football to the summit of Mount Adams for a pickup game. All told me about their favorite trail or hike and spoke about the beauty of the country around them.

From the college kids climbing out of the Salmo-Priest Wilderness to the eighty-nine-year-old hiker on the Chain Lakes Trail, all the people I met who hike the wild pathways of Washington will tell you the same thing: walking is the best thing you can do for your soul and your body—especially if you are surrounded by the beauty you can find around our neck of the woods. Age and physical condition are simply not as important to them as getting outside to see what surprises Mother Nature plans for them. It is in that spirit that I offer this guide to all of you.

Sooner or later, we all realize that "easy hike" is a relative term. What might be an easy hike when you are twenty-two years old, so full of vim and vigor, is not likely to merit that same adjective when you are fifty-two and the vigor has morphed to varicose veins. So while the one hundred hikes outlined in this guide are all labeled "easy," you are likely to find yourself wondering at least once if I am already senile. If you feel—as I often do when trying to keep up with my wife, B. B. Hardbody—like a leaking hydration pack, I'll be happy. In fact, if you don't curse your humble correspondent at least once while sweating up a hill or limping back to the trailhead, I have failed in my mission. Don't be fooled by the title. Unless you are a retired Olympic athlete or can still jog a dozen miles in under an hour, you'll find plenty of hikes in this guide to keep your heart rate up and your lungs sucking harder than a Dyson.

I've been lucky in my more than seven decades on this planet to stay healthy enough to keep walking, and in those years, I have met hundreds of people on the trail who aren't as fortunate as me. My recent hiking partners include The Ladies and Two Guys, a group of women and—not surprisingly—two men who take regular Wednesday walks of four to six miles up a nearby hill. One of the Ladies speeds through the forest on an artificial hip; nearly all of these folks are older than me, and most leave me behind, panting like an asthmatic jackass in the woods. The Ladies and Two Guys are members of the Monday Hikers, a loosely organized group of Kitsap County outdoors folk who—as you may have guessed—go hiking every Monday. They split into three groups: the Walkers, the Hikers, and the Mountain Goats. I went on a couple of hikes with the Mountain Goats, who are all my age, and had hammie cramps for several weeks afterward. At least six of the eight Monday Hikers leave me a quivering mass of flab and sweat on the trail. On the other hand, I have walked with younger folk who wonder why they can't keep up with that old bald man with the bouncing belly he calls Stummick. The important thing, it seems to me (and Stummick), is that regardless of age or physical condition, you try one of the trails outlined here, sharing the trail with rare beauty and solitude.

USING THIS GUIDE

The beginning of each trail description is intended to give you quick information that can help you decide whether that specific day hike is one that interests you. Here's what you'll find:

TRAIL NUMBER AND NAME

Trails are numbered in this guide following the main highway corridors in each geographical region in the state: the north, central, and south Cascades; Mount Rainier; Olympic and Kitsap peninsulas; central Washington; Columbia River Gorge; Spokane and northeastern Washington; and southeastern Washington. I've also included what I feel are the seven best urban trails in the state.

OVERALL RATING

Rating these hikes was difficult for me. "In the first place," I asked the very wise and generous editor, "why would anyone want to take a hike I rate with only one star? A guidebook should only outline hikes that are worth taking, not dung-heap trails you wouldn't recommend to a psycho killer."

He replied: "True, but you must distinguish between the very best trails—with five stars—and the trails that aren't quite so good—with one to four stars." The trails that really suck (and I paraphrase here because editors are much too refined to use that word) won't be outlined here. Some hikes may not be as good as others, but they are all better than the ones that really bite.

Another problem I had was attempting to be objective in rating the trails. I'm a pushover for hikes above timberline, where the wildflowers wave in gentle summer breezes, where mountains claw the clouds, where cooling snowfields linger through summer. So I may have rated these trails higher than you might rate them.

If you're a hiker who loves walking along rattling rivers or past forested lakes, or padding on rain-forest trails softened by mosses, I'd suggest you add one star to every lowland hike and subtract one star from every alpland hike in this guide.

Finally, objective criteria such as trail conditions, trail length, and obstacles such as creek crossings can affect the overall rating. On the other hand, you can forget all that junk and just take my word for it.

DISTANCE

The distance listed is round-trip, exclusive of any side trips mentioned along the way. If these excursions off the main trail are longer than 0.2 mile or so, I'll mention that in the description of the hike.

In an effort to prove that trails are indeed getting longer as I grow older, I packed a GPS on some trails and carried my trusty Fitbit on others. I learned, to my disappointment, that trails aren't getting longer—although there are notable exceptions—and that I might have equipped myself better by carrying my own oxygen supply instead of a bloody GPS unit that is allergic to fir and pine forests.

HIKING TIME

This is an estimate of the time it takes the average hiker to walk the trail round-trip. Since none of us are average hikers, you may feel free to ignore this entry.

For the most part, I calculated the pace on the trail to be between 1.5 and 2 miles per hour. I assumed the pace might slow on trails with significant elevation gain or loss and tried to err on the conservative side. It's my hope that many of you will wonder what sort of trail slug came up with such ridiculously long hiking times.

ELEVATION GAIN

This is a calculation of the total number of feet you'll have to climb on the trail. Don't assume, as one fool early in his hiking days did (I have since learned better), that all of the elevation will be gained on the way to your destination. Some of these trails actually lose elevation on the way and gain it on the return, or alternately gain and lose elevation along the way. It has always been a source of wonder to me that on a round-trip hike, you always gain the same amount of elevation that you lose.

HIGH POINT

This is the highest point above sea level you'll reach on any given hike. In cases like the ocean beach walks, it is often at the trailhead.

EFFORT

This was another tough one for me. I've been hiking for so many years that it was a task to remember what it was like to take some of these hikes as a novice. My good friend Grizzly Hemingway once turned back from a hike after encountering a footlog that was too high to cross—a log I had forgotten also scared the pee out of me the first time I crossed it.

So again, I tried to be conservative in judging the effort it would take to finish each hike. Whereas other guides discuss the overall difficulty of the trail, I thought the energy expended to hike out and back might be more meaningful. A hike might be difficult, for example, if you had to walk that footlog, but the rest of the trail could be flat as a pancake griddle, requiring no more effort than a stroll in the park. Thus you'll find the following categories:

A **Stroll in the Park** will serve up few, if any, hills to climb and is generally between 1 and 3 miles long round-trip, a hike suitable for families with small children.

On a hike rated as an **Easy Walk**, you might expect to find longer, but still gently graded, hills and trails around 2 to 4 miles long round-trip.

A hike described as a **Moderate Workout** would be one with longer grades and elevation changes greater than about 500 feet from beginning to high point, hikes between 3 and 6 miles long round-trip.

A hike rated as **Prepare to Perspire** is one that will make your deodorant fail you, no matter your excellent physical condition. It will have sustained steep climbs of at least 1 mile, with elevation gain and loss greater than 1,500 feet, and is about 7 to 10 miles long round-trip.

A **Knee-Punishing** hike is one that will challenge your physical abilities beyond what you might expect you can accomplish, one that will send you rushing to the anti-inflammatory shelf in your medicine cabinet upon your return.

BEST SEASON

Here is my suggestion for the season I think you'd most enjoy this hike, as well as whether the path will be free of snow throughout the year.

PERMITS/CONTACT

This entry will tell you whether you need a Northwest Forest Pass and who to contact for information. In the case of Olympic and Mount Rainier national parks, I've included general fee information. Hikers who are fortunate enough to have been on earth 62 years or longer qualify for a Interagency Senior Pass, which, at $10 for life, gets you onto just about any federally managed trail and gives you half-price camping at National Forest campgrounds.

MAPS

I've tried to include the USGS quadrangle maps for every hike in the guide, plus Green Trails maps where available, as well as Custom Correct maps for Olympic Peninsula trails.

TRAIL NOTES

Here are some regulations specific to each hike you'll most likely want to know: whether leashed pets can accompany you; whether you'll encounter mountain bikes, equestrians, or ATVs on the trail; whether your children might like this hike. If there are circumstances about the hike you might like to know, such as whether you'll fry if you hike the trail in summer, I'll mention it here.

THE HIKE

This is an attempt to convey the feel of the trail in a sentence or two, including the type of trail and whether there's a one-way hiking option.

GETTING THERE

Here's where you'll either find out how to get to the trailhead or, if I've screwed up, become hopelessly lost. You'll learn the elevation at the trailhead and—assuming my GPS didn't sniff any firs or pines—the coordinates for the trailhead.

As I mentioned, all of the hikes are organized according to the major highway corridors you'll follow to get to the National Forest or Park roads leading to the trailhead. I've tried to indicate starting points along those corridors, such as cities or towns, or major highway junctions.

THE TRAIL

Here's where you'll get the blow-by-blow, mile-by-mile description of the trail. I've tried to stick to information your feet will find useful and apologize if, every now and then, I look up to recognize an awesome view or rhapsodize about something absolutely without redeeming social or cultural value. I'm guessing you'll recognize these features without much coaching.

GOING FARTHER

Many of you might find some of these hikes too easy, while others will be ready to turn around before they reach my recommended spot. For that reason, I've included suggestions for extending many hikes from the same trailhead—or from a nearby trailhead that can be accessed before your heart rate decreases or your joints stiffen.

BE CAREFUL

It is all too easy on a warm, sunny day on the trail to forget most of the stuff you ought to be carrying in your pack. Day hikers, especially, are likely to leave that extra fleece sweater or that waterproof, breathable parka in the trunk. Some folks even forget that First Essential: a hiking partner.

Never hike alone.

Virtually all the time, day hikers who forget one or two of the basic rules for safe wilderness travel return to the trailhead smiling and healthy. No trail cop is going to cite you for negligent hiking if you have only nine of the Ten Essentials, or if you hit the trail without registering or telling someone where you're going.

I dislike preaching safety—if you looked in my pack on a good-weather day hike, you might find my extra clothing consists of a spare do-rag and my map clearly shows the hike I took last week. Perhaps the only weighty argument anyone can make to convince other day hikers to follow the rules for safe travel in the out-of-doors is to remind them of the annual, avoidable tragedies that occur when hikers ignore those rules.

THE TEN ESSENTIALS

First—no matter the distance or difficulty of the hike—please carry the Ten Essentials in your pack. With no apologies to those credit card people: don't leave home without them.

- A topographic map of the area.

- A compass, and the ability to use it in conjunction with the map. While excellent aids to navigation, portable GPS units are no substitute for a compass that does not require batteries or satellite reception.

- Extra clothing, which should consist of a top and bottom insulating layer and a waterproof, windproof layer. A hat or cap is absolutely essential: mountaineers will tell you that when your feet are cold, put on your hat. It works.

- Extra food. To avoid grazing on my extra food, I try to pick something I would only eat if I were starving. Stuff like freeze-dried turnips or breakfast bars that taste like pressed sawdust fire starters. In fact, some of my extra food can be used as emergency fire starters.

⚹ A flashlight with extra batteries and bulbs. I carry a headlamp because it allows me to swat at the moths that fly into the light without dropping the bloody flashlight. Many of these lights have spare bulbs built in. Lithium batteries and LED lights, though more expensive, weigh less and make excellent spare batteries because their shelf life is longer than yours.

⚹ A first-aid kit. You can buy these already assembled, and they are excellent. Consider one thing, however: the type of injury that is likely to incapacitate a day hiker is likely to be different than that suffered by a backpacker. If your first-aid kit doesn't include wraps for sprains, add an ankle support, at the very least. Blister treatment for day hikers is another essential.

⚹ Matches in a waterproof case. Although butane lighters are often carried as a substitute, both altitude and temperature can affect their performance.

⚹ A fire starter. Candles work well, along with a variety of lightweight commercial fire starters.

⚹ A pocket knife. In addition to the all-important corkscrew, my Swiss Army knife has 623 blades, including a tiny chain saw.

⚹ Sunglasses and sunscreen.

In addition to these items, most day hikers never hit the trail without toting some toilet paper in a plastic bag and perhaps some type of bug repellent on summer hikes. A loud emergency whistle is a lightweight addition. Binoculars may help you find your route if you become lost and are worth the weight simply for watching wildlife.

WEATHER

Every region in Washington demands we pay attention to a different facet of the weather. In the Olympic Mountains, a dry change of clothing in the pack or car is always a good idea because rain can sneak up on you. In the dry canyons of Yakima, an extra liter of water would be a better idea.

No matter where you're hiking, learn to read the clouds and wind and learn the general rules that may keep you safer or more comfortable. Winds from the southwest often bring storms. Northerlies often herald better weather. Afternoons in the high country are more likely to be stormy. I like to think of Mother Nature as a schizoid who is most often a friendly, generous old lady who bakes cookies and bread for you, but when you least expect it, puts on a goalie's mask and whacks at you with an icicle or lightning bolt.

So be prepared, Scouts.

WATER

You'll find plenty of opportunities to refill your water bottle on many of the hikes outlined in this book, especially on the wet west side of the Cascades. Treat all water as if it were contaminated, although this is not as great an issue in Washington wilderness as it is often suggested by those who might be held liable if you were to contract a waterborne illness. The most worrisome problem with the water might be a little critter called *Giardia lamblia,* which can give you a case of the trots that you'll never forget. The most noticeable symptom of giardiasis is "explosive diarrhea." Need I say more? I think not.

Thankfully, there is an easy way to ensure that the water you take from mountain streams and lakes is safe to drink. When used properly, filter pumps eliminate at least 99.9 percent of *Giardia* and other dangerous organisms from the water. A recent and far more convenient substitute for filter pumps, especially for day hikers, is a relatively inexpensive water bottle equipped with its own filter. You simply fill the bottle from the stream (taking extreme care not to contaminate the mouthpiece or drinking cap), drop the filter into place, and screw on the top, and you're ready to drink filtered water. Another system purifies water with ultraviolet, and perhaps the most effective water treatment is with chemicals such as iodine; the trade-off is processing time.

WILDLIFE

The first time I saw a black bear, half a mile from the trailhead, I snapped a shaky picture of it and considered shedding my pack on the spot so it would eat my lunch and not bother making lunch of me. Since that time, I have come to regard most animals and plants that share our Washington home as benign, for the most part.

Day hikers certainly needn't fear black bears, but they must realize these are wild animals that can cause serious injury if provoked. While there are but a few grizzlies to worry about in Washington, research indicates that a black bear attack—though extremely rare—may lead more often to a fatality. Respect a bear's personal space, in short, and never get between a cub and its mother. If you encounter a black bear on the trail, make certain it knows you're there by addressing it in a calm voice (it will probably run off at this point), give it a wide berth, and count yourself fortunate for seeing it. Some few bears have learned that humans carry food in their packs, but this is a far greater concern for backpackers, and you'll find warnings or closure signs at the trailhead.

A greater potential danger might be from cougars. Until recently, I've regarded myself lucky to have seen a cougar once in the Cascade Mountains and discovered I was once tracked by an unseen cougar through 5 miles of Olympic snow. But there is growing evidence to suggest that day hikers should treat cougar sightings as extremely dangerous encounters with predators who it appears may sometimes hunt humans for food. Shortly before setting out to check the trails in an earlier guide, I read Jo Deurbrouck and Dean Miller's excellent book *Cat Attacks*. It convinced me that—though the odds of being attacked by a cougar are on the order of winning the lottery while being struck by lightning—I should be more aware of the animals to whom the wilderness belongs, particularly the ones that are quite capable of hunting you down and killing you.

Trailhead signs will tell you how to respond if you are confronted by a cougar. Generally, you must face the animal down. Don't turn your back on it or bend down to get something to throw at it. Shouting may help. Barking like a dog may send the animal off into the woods. But most importantly: Maintain eye contact at all times.

Most unsettling is the fact that most cougar attacks upon humans don't occur as a result of the kind of encounter described above. Most people who were attacked by cougars in the past decade—attacks have increased significantly in the past 10 years—were struck from behind and were not aware of the cougar's presence until the attack.

How can a hiker defend such an attack? Given that the odds of an encounter are extremely remote and an attack less likely still, author Deurbrouck suggests hikers simply be aware of places where cougars are most likely to wait in ambush. She says that while trail-running, she tries to think like a deer, the cougar's main prey. In other words, be watchful of banks above the trail and places where the trail rounds hillside corners. In most cases, cougars attack from ambush, above and behind their prey.

Above all, cougar attacks in the past decade have given greater weight to the unbreakable rule against solo hiking. When attacking, cougars appear to be so focused on their prey that they completely ignore other people. Even when those people open a big can of whup-ass on that kitty, they are most likely to escape a retaliatory attack. Those attacked by cougars can be saved by companions who most likely won't suffer injury from the animal—and I'm hoping that is by far and away more than you want or will ever need to know about cougars.

Another Northwest mammal to respect is the mountain goat. Though usually shy, goats in some areas like Olympic National Park have become aggressive. One goat gored a hiker to death several years ago. As with information about bears and cougars, you will find tips on avoiding goats at trailheads.

Less dangerous but more common hazards to day hikers might include stinging and biting pests such as yellow jackets—particularly in late summer and early autumn—blackflies, mosquitoes, and deerflies. Liberal doses of insect repellent can take care of the mosquitoes and deerflies but probably won't keep those nasty yellow jackets away. My technique for protection from yellow jacket stings is to send my hiking partners ahead about 100 feet: if they get stung as they pass a nest, I wait until things settle down, then bypass the area carefully.

Poison oak and ivy grow in some areas, particularly on the east side of the state, but are easily avoided by learning to identify the plants. A more common plant pest is stinging nettle, which grows along many trails on both the wet and dry side of the state, but it can be recognized and avoided most of the time.

Snakes are common on the sunny side of Washington; you have only to keep a watch out for them to enjoy a safe, bite-free hike. If only I had taken that advice before I stepped on that snake on the Umtanum Canyon Trail. Neither the snake nor I stuck around long enough to find out if either of us was poisonous.

Waterfalls tumble down cliffs above the trail to Hannegan Camp (#1).

THE CASCADES

S cratching clouds sweeping off the Pacific Ocean, the Cascade Mountains stretch from the Canadian border to the Columbia River and beyond. They catch storms toting rivers of water that in the high country yield avalanches of snow—more than 90 feet of the white stuff in one year at some locations. And they serve up some of the finest mountain scenery and alpine hiking to be found anywhere.

Several major highways give us access to the trails that climb into these mountains, the crystal lakes they hold, and the rivers that race to the ocean, carving canyons and cliffs and feeding forests along the way. From the north to the south, you can reach trails by following the Mount Baker Highway (State Route 542), the North Cascades Highway (State Route 20), and Stevens Pass Highway (US Highway 2). You can take hikes on either side of Interstate 90 at Snoqualmie Pass or find trails farther south at Chinook Pass Highway (State Route 410) and White Pass Highway (US Highway 12).

No matter which of these highways you follow, you'll find at least one thing Cascade trails have in common: the farther east you travel from the Cascade crest, the dryer the trail. If finding sunshine on your hike is important to you, head east. If forested shade and cooler weather are high on your priority list, and you don't mind a greater risk of sharing your trail with rainfall, stay on the west side of the mountains.

The Ptarmigan Ridge trail (#3) stretches toward Mount Baker.

MOUNT BAKER HIGHWAY (STATE ROUTE 542)

1. Hannegan Camp

RATING	🚶 🚶 🚶
DISTANCE	7.2 miles round-trip
HIKING TIME	4 hours, 30 minutes
ELEVATION GAIN	1,600 feet
HIGH POINT	4,740 feet
EFFORT	Prepare to Perspire
BEST SEASON	Summer
PERMITS/CONTACT	Northwest Forest Pass required/Mount Baker-Snoqualmie National Forest, (360) 599-2714; www.fs.usda.gov/mbs
MAPS	USGS Mount Sefrit; Green Trails Mount Shuksan
NOTES	Leashed dogs welcome

THE HIKE

This is a high-country walk with expansive mountain views, tremendous wildflowers, waterfalls, and alpine forests.

GETTING THERE

From Interstate 5 in Bellingham, drive east on State Route 542 to the Hannegan Pass Road (Forest Road 32) and follow it for 5.3 miles to the end, staying left at the fork 1.3 miles from the highway. The trailhead is 3,106 feet above sea level. GPS trailhead coordinates: N48°54.610′; W121°35.516′

THE TRAIL

The Hannegan Pass Trail was one of the first I hiked in the north Cascades, a backpack of epic proportions to Middle Lake, beyond Whatcom Pass. The upper reaches of the trail were so rough and rugged it inspired my first wife, Old Iron Knees, to propose her own version of D. F. Crowder and Roland Tabor's *Routes and Rocks: Hiker's Guide to the North Cascades*, published by The Mountaineers in 1965. She would call her version *Roots and Rocks of the North Cascades*, and it would be a guide to stumbling and tripping over all of the boulders and roots Mother Nature conspired to place in our footpath.

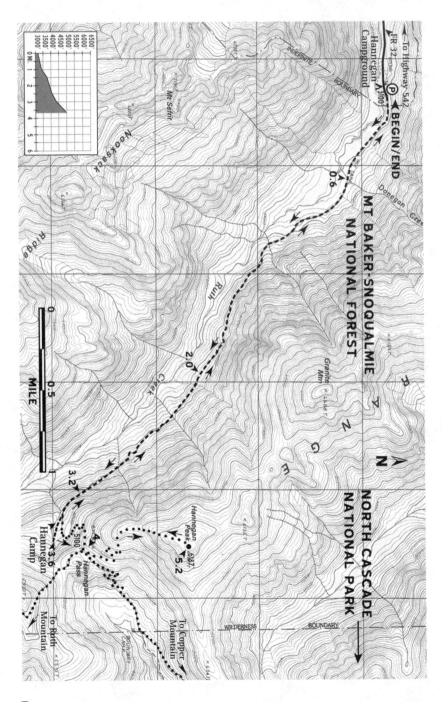

The lower part of this hike is anything but rocky or full of roots. It wanders, barely climbing, through a subalpine forest of silver fir, alongside noisy Ruth Creek. Open meadows of cow parsnip wave greetings, while stinging nettles reach for your legs, and mountains lean over from above on either side of the valley. Cross Donegan Creek at 0.6 mile and continue to climb through forest and open meadows. Cross two more creeks, possibly dry by autumn, and at about 2.0 miles, begin to climb more steeply as the creek below tumbles down the mountain. The Ruth Creek valley narrows, and cliffs above shine with snowmelt.

Your real workout begins 3.2 miles from the trailhead, where the route begins a series of steep, rocky switchbacks on a path bordered by broken granite and views reaching all the way down Ruth Creek to its confluence with the North Fork of the Nooksack River. Vine maple blasts scarlet foliage from the side of the trail. Climb for another 0.4 mile to the flat meadows of Hannegan Camp to the right, your picnic and turnaround spot.

GOING FARTHER

It's another steep 0.5 mile and 300 vertical feet to 5,100-foot Hannegan Pass, which is surrounded by forest and not as pleasant as the camp below. If you decide to climb up there, I'd suggest you continue climbing along the Hannegan Peak Trail. It's 1.2 miles and 1,100 feet to the broad summit, but you needn't go all the way for the exceptional views of Mounts Baker and Shuksan and Ruth Mountain—a popular late-spring backcountry ski destination.

2. Chain Lakes Loop

RATING	🚶 🚶 🚶
DISTANCE	6.0 miles round-trip
HIKING TIME	4 hours, 30 minutes
ELEVATION GAIN	1,900 feet
HIGH POINT	5,400 feet
EFFORT	Prepare to Perspire
BEST SEASON	Late summer, early fall
PERMITS/CONTACT	Northwest Forest Pass required/Mount Baker–Snoqualmie National Forest, (360) 599-2714; www.fs.usda.gov/mbs
MAPS	USGS Shuksan Arm; Green Trails Mount Shuksan
NOTES	Leashed dogs welcome

THE HIKE

You'll get just about everything on this walk—a good bit of exercise past clear alpine lakes with fine alpine vistas of Mounts Baker and Shuksan, huckleberry-picking stops, and wildflowers all over the place.

GETTING THERE

From Interstate 5 in Bellingham, drive east on State Route 542 for about 55 miles, past the Mount Baker Ski Area to the Heather Meadows Visitor Center on the right. A number of trails radiate from the center, 4,400 feet above sea level. GPS trailhead coordinates: N48º51.267′; W121º41.129′

THE TRAIL

You can start this hike farther up the road, at a higher elevation, which means you'll face a steep climb at the end of the hike instead of the beginning. So start here and get your climbing in early by following the Upper Wild Goose Trail at the end of the upper visitor center parking area. The trail is just underneath part of the road to Artist Point, which is often blocked by snow until July or later.

The trail climbs above the Bagley Lakes Basin and reaches the Artist Point parking area and trailhead 0.8 mile from your trailhead. Cross the parking lot and follow the Ptarmigan Ridge/Chain Lakes Loop Trail as it drops into forest at the west end of the parking area. It emerges onto a

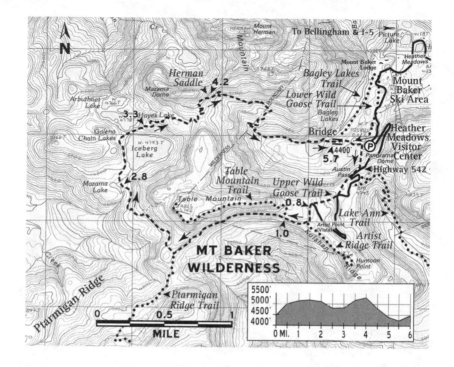

south-facing meadow and at 1.0 mile arrives at a junction with the Table Mountain Trail. Stay left and continue under the southern cliffs of Table Mountain to a saddle and a second junction. The Ptarmigan Ridge Trail heads to the left; stay right and descend nearly 500 feet past Mazama Lake, at 2.8 miles. Next in the chain are Iceberg Lake, which—by no strange coincidence—is pretty darn cold, and Hayes Lake, at 3.3 miles, a good spot for a picnic and rest.

To continue, begin a steady climb to the broad Herman Saddle, a popular destination for backcountry skiers in the winter, 4.2 miles from the trailhead. There's a great view of the Bagley Lakes Basin below; Mount Shuksan towers to the east. Begin a 1.5-mile descent into the Bagley Lakes Basin, then cross a rock bridge across the inlet stream at 5.7 miles, and climb out of the valley to the visitor center.

GOING FARTHER

You can add another 1.5 miles and at least one more leg cramp to your hike by following the Bagley Lakes Loop down and back up to the visitor center. The loop begins and ends at the rock bridge across the Bagley Lakes inlet stream.

3. Ptarmigan Ridge

RATING	🚶 🚶 🚶 🚶 🚶
DISTANCE	4.0 miles round-trip
HIKING TIME	2 hours, 30 minutes
ELEVATION GAIN	900 feet
HIGH POINT	6,000 feet
EFFORT	Moderate Workout
BEST SEASON	Late summer, early fall
PERMITS/CONTACT	Northwest Forest Pass required/Mount Baker–Snoqualmie National Forest, (360) 599-2714; www.fs.usda.gov/mbs
MAPS	USGS Mount Baker; Green Trails Mount Shuksan
NOTES	Leashed dogs welcome

THE HIKE

If you have time for only one hike in the Mount Baker area, make it this one. The views are incredible, the hike is not too difficult, and the wildflower variety is amazing.

GETTING THERE

Follow State Route 542 from Bellingham for 58 miles, passing the Mount Baker Ski Area (check out the great raven sculpture at the entrance) and climbing to the end of the road at Artist Point, 5,100 feet above sea level. GPS trailhead coordinates: 48°50.783′; W121°41.573′

THE TRAIL

This hike tends to draw crowds, although not for the typical reasons, but because the road to the trailhead is open to Artist Point only a few months each year. So everyone who wants to take this above-timberline walk without hiking several miles of road waits until late July before hitting the trail. Even so, hikers in late August 2008 had to negotiate a steep snowfield to get onto the trail from the parking area.

Don't let a little snow deter you from trying this outing. The beginning of this hike is along a south-facing hillside, so most of the white stuff has melted out. The view of Mount Baker barely gets better from the parking area, but the trail drops in a short, steep switchback (or snowfield) into a

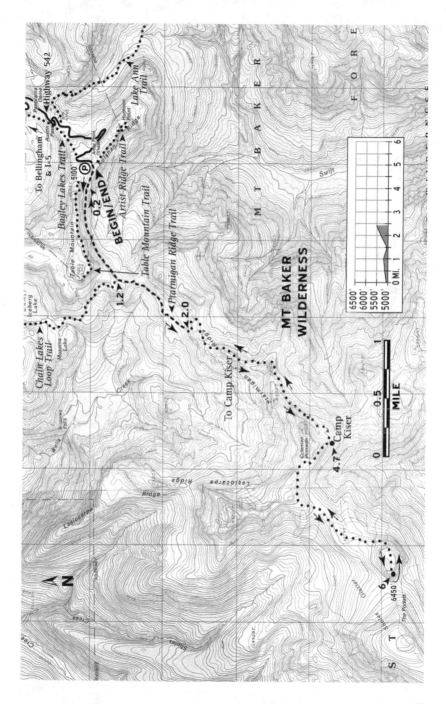

forest of moss-draped alpine trees, emerging in a few hundred yards onto a wide, steep meadow etched by scree fields. In 0.2 mile find a junction with the Table Mountain Trail, climbing to the right. Stay left and cross this distinctive mountain just under its south-facing cliffs, and look down into meadows frequented by mountain goats.

Reach a low, rocky saddle where the resident marmot population will certainly raise the alarm at about 1.0 mile, and in another 0.2 mile, find a trail junction with the Chain Lakes Loop Trail. Stay left and first descend, then climb on a traverse on the north side of Ptarmigan Ridge. At 2.0 miles you'll cross the ridge in a wide, flat meadow, a great spot for a feast, both on the views and whatever it is you brought for your picnic.

GOING FARTHER
The Ptarmigan Ridge Trail continues for another 2.7 miles to Camp Kiser under Coleman Pinnacle, climbing mostly along the south side of Ptarmigan Ridge. The trail traverses the south side before climbing to the end of the maintained trail, 6 miles from the trailhead.

4. Heliotrope Ridge

RATING	🥾 🥾 🥾 🥾 🥾
DISTANCE	6.0 miles round-trip
HIKING TIME	4 hours, 30 minutes
ELEVATION GAIN	1,900 feet
HIGH POINT	5,600 feet
EFFORT	Prepare to Perspire
BEST SEASON	Summer, early fall
PERMITS/CONTACT	Northwest Forest Pass required/Mount Baker–Snoqualmie National Forest, (360) 599-2714; www.fs.usda.gov/mbs
MAPS	USGS Groat Mountain; Green Trails Mount Baker
NOTES	Leashed dogs welcome

THE HIKE

Expect company on this popular climb to alpine meadows along a trail leading to the toe of the Coleman Glacier, which gouges the north face of Mount Baker.

GETTING THERE

From Bellingham, take State Route 542 west past the Glacier Public Service Center and turn right onto Glacier Creek Road (Forest Road 39). Follow it for 8 miles as it climbs to the trailhead parking area, 3,700 feet above sea level. GPS trailhead coordinates: N48°48.129′; W121°53.752′

THE TRAIL

This is one of the most popular hikes in the north Cascades and with good reason: it leads to an up-close-and-personal view of a real, live glacier. Except for a couple of trails in Mount Rainier National Park and at Mount Adams, you can't get any closer to a massive, moving river of ice.

Begin by dropping to a new footlog across Grouse Creek, then start your climb along one of the most historic maintained trails in the Mount Baker–Snoqualmie National Forest. You'll share the trail with real mountaineers, who begin their climb of Mount Baker from the end of a way trail leading to the Coleman Glacier. This adds significant wear and tear

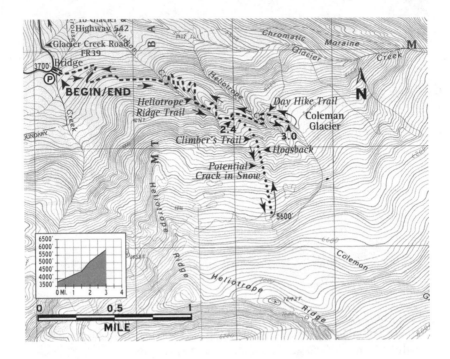

to the trail, leading to muddy patches and exposed roots—but volunteers and Forest Service trail workers keep it in good shape.

The trail climbs up a forested ridge in switchbacks, from which you'll be able to hear hikers talking both above and below you climbing or descending. The hikers and climbers coming down are likely the noisiest because they won't be as breathless as those ascending the path. At **1.0** miles from the trailhead, you'll ford the first of several creeks where a set of trekking poles or a walking stick might come in handy for balance. Savvy hikers take this walk early in the morning, when these tumbling creeks aren't so full of water. Those who don't like to get up at dawn should schedule this hike in early fall, when the water volume is lowest.

After a steep climb and another creek crossing, **1.6** miles from the trailhead, you'll get a brief rest at the site of the old Kulshan Cabin, once a campsite and retreat for Western Washington University mountaineers and hikers. Just beyond, about **2.4** miles, you'll find yourself on a steep meadow hillside chock-full of wildflowers with views above of Mount Baker. A climber's trail turns right and continues to climb; you cross left into a meadow and rock-hop across Heliotrope Creek, where the views of the Coleman Glacier icefall are most spectacular. Cop a squat. Dig the scenery. Join the marmots in chorus.

5. Twin Lakes Road

RATING	🏃
DISTANCE	5.0 miles round-trip
HIKING TIME	3 hours, 30 minutes
ELEVATION GAIN	1,600 feet
HIGH POINT	5,200 feet
EFFORT	Moderate Workout
BEST SEASON	Summer
PERMITS/CONTACT	Northwest Forest Pass required/Mount Baker–Snoqualmie National Forest, (360) 599-2714; www.fs.usda.gov/mbs
MAPS	USGS Mount Larrabee; Green Trails Mount Shuksan
NOTES	Incredibly strong mountain bikers and leashed dogs welcome

THE HIKE

You are likely to be offered a ride by one of the brave motorists headed up to Twin Lakes in an SUV. Believe me, you'll appreciate the walk and the view from the road more on foot than from a rocking, rolling four-wheel-drive vehicle.

GETTING THERE

From Interstate 5 in Bellingham, follow State Route 542 east for about 46 miles to Twin Lakes Road (Forest Road 3065); turn left and follow it 4.5 bumpy miles to the Yellow Aster Butte/Tomyhoi Lake trailhead, 3,600 feet above sea level. GPS trailhead coordinates: 48°56.616'; W121°39.725'

THE TRAIL

This trail is in fact a road, frequented mostly by Real Men and Real Women who pilot Real SUVs up steep, rocky switchbacks and across deep washouts beyond the end of the maintained road at the Yellow Aster Butte trailhead. On the day I was there, I saw two dead Hummers and was forced to put a severely injured Range Rover out of its misery. This is no road for wimpy two-wheel-drive vehicles—but if you decide to try it, make sure it's a rental car.

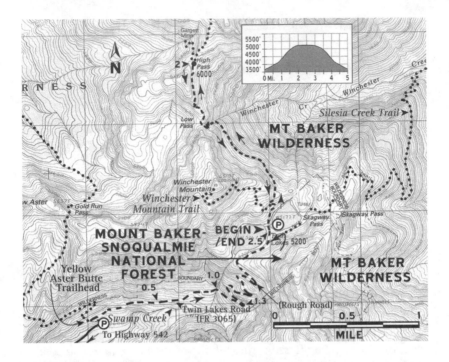

The route climbs along an open hillside past a sign noting the end of the maintained road and advising you to proceed at your own risk. In 0.5 mile, it crosses the first of several rocky washouts, easily navigated on foot; perhaps less so by long-wheelbase vehicles. The route alternately climbs through forest and steep meadow, crossing the outlet stream (usually dry by August) from Twin Lakes at 1.0 mile from the trailhead.

The road switches back at 1.3 miles, the first of five sharp hairpins as it climbs toward the lakes along the Twin Lakes outlet. As you emerge from trees near the last switchback, look down to the Yellow Aster Butte trailhead and all those tiny cars below. The road finally takes a broad turn and traverses north into an alpine saddle that cups splendid Twin Lakes. You'll find campsites and big parking areas for picnics.

GOING FARTHER

The road continues around the north Twin Lake and turns into a trail that climbs through Skagway Pass in 0.5 mile, then drops steeply down to Winchester Creek. If you've decided to drive up the road and are wearing clean underwear, I'd suggest the 3.2-mile round-trip climb up to the Winchester Mountain Lookout (hike #6 in this guide).

6. Winchester Mountain Lookout

RATING	🚶 🚶 🚶 🚶
DISTANCE	3.2 miles round-trip
HIKING TIME	2 hours
ELEVATION GAIN	1,350 feet
HIGH POINT	6,510 feet
EFFORT	Moderate Workout
BEST SEASON	Summer
PERMITS/CONTACT	Northwest Forest Pass required/Mount Baker–Snoqualmie National Forest, (360) 599-2714; www.fs.usda.gov/mbs
MAPS	USGS Mount Larrabee; Green Trails Mount Shuksan
NOTES	Leashed dogs welcome; extremely rough road access

THE HIKE

This is a steep but short climb to an old fire lookout with stupendous alpine views that more than make up for the nerve- and auto-racking drive to the trailhead.

GETTING THERE

From Interstate 5 in Bellingham, follow State Route 542 east for about 46 miles to Twin Lakes Road (Forest Road 3065); turn left and follow it 4.5 bumpy miles to the Yellow Aster Butte/Tomyhoi Lake trailhead, 3,600 feet above sea level. The Forest Service road maintenance ends here; the 2.5-mile road is narrow and steep, with sharp switchbacks and several washout crossings where a short-wheelbase or high-clearance vehicle will come in handy. Still, at least two front-wheel-drive sedans were at the trailhead, 5,200 feet above sea level, on the day I checked this hike. GPS trailhead coordinates: N48°57.096′; W121°38.111′

THE TRAIL

Begin your hike at the isthmus of the Twin Lakes, which—by no strange coincidence—look pretty much the same: clear, cold mountain lakes with views that'll make you wonder if the vistas up the trail will be any better. Trust me: they are.

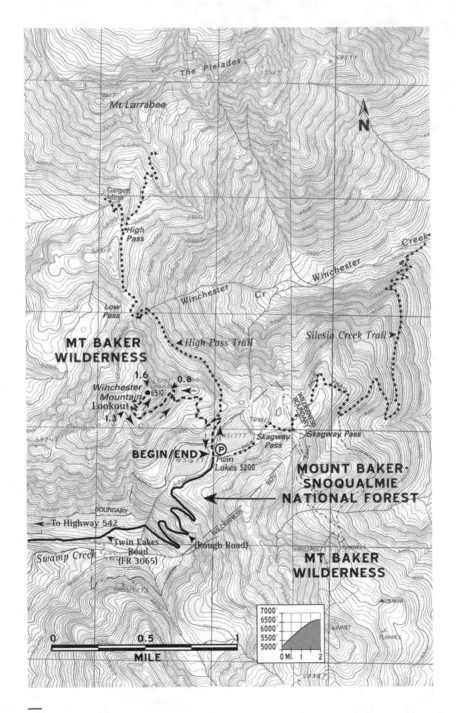

You'll start climbing right at the get-go, traversing the lower reaches of Winchester Mountain to the west, arriving at a junction with the High Pass Trail at **0.3** mile from the trailhead. Stay left here, and switchback more steeply up the eastern ridge of Winchester Mountain through alpine meadows dotted with snow-stunted trees. Turn south at about **0.8** mile and cross the eastern face of the mountain, about 6,200 feet above sea level. Look down to Twin Lakes and across to Mounts Shuksan and Baker.

This gentle uphill traverse ends at about **1.3** miles, where the trail takes a no-nonsense, 0.25-mile climb in switchbacks to the summit and Winchester Mountain Lookout, maintained by a number of hardy volunteers from the Mount Baker Hiking Club. The views expand to the west, to Yellow Aster Butte and Tomyhoi Peak and Lake. You'll see mountains in just about every direction: American Border Peak to the north (which—by no strange coincidence—is located just about on the Canadian-American border) and the remote Picket Range to the south, beyond Mount Baker. Choose your viewing seat, and be prepared for the neurosis that occurs when you have such incredible 360-degree views you don't know where to look first.

GOING FARTHER

There are two ways to further punish your joints on this hike: begin by parking at the Tomyhoi Lake trailhead or take the High Pass trail (hike #7 in this guide). The first option would add 5 round-trip miles and about 1,600 vertical feet; the second, 4 miles and 1,400 vertical feet.

7. High Pass

RATING	🚶 🚶 🚶 🚶
DISTANCE	4.0 miles round-trip
HIKING TIME	3 hours, 30 minutes
ELEVATION GAIN	1,400 feet
HIGH POINT	6,000 feet
EFFORT	Prepare to Perspire
BEST SEASON	Summer, early fall
PERMITS/CONTACT	Northwest Forest Pass required/Mount Baker-Snoqualmie National Forest, (360) 599-2714; www.fs.usda.gov/mbs
MAPS	USGS Mount Larrabee; Green Trails Mount Shuksan
NOTES	Leashed dogs welcome; extremely rough road access

THE HIKE

Expect some solitude on this up-and-down alpine walk along a mountainside, with long wildflower-gazing pauses in the summer and huckleberry-picking stops in early fall. This hike might be a good choice for a foggy day because there's more to see besides the exceptional vistas.

GETTING THERE

From Interstate 5 in Bellingham, follow State Route 542 east for about 46 miles to the Twin Lakes Road (Forest Road 3065); turn left and follow it 4.5 bumpy miles to the Yellow Aster Butte/Tomyhoi Lakes trailhead, 3,600 feet above sea level. The Forest Service road maintenance ends here; the 2.5-mile road is narrow and steep, with sharp switchbacks and several washout crossings where a short-wheelbase or high-clearance vehicle will come in handy. Still, at least two front-wheel-drive sedans were at the trailhead, 5,200 feet above sea level, on the day I checked this hike. GPS trailhead coordinates: N48°57.096´; W121°38.111´

THE TRAIL

You'll start your hike at the trailhead between Twin Lakes, which—by no strange coincidence—comprises two lakes. Begin on the Winchester Mountain Lookout Trail and climb for about 0.25 mile to a junction with the High Pass Trail. Turn right and climb to a saddle about 0.4 mile

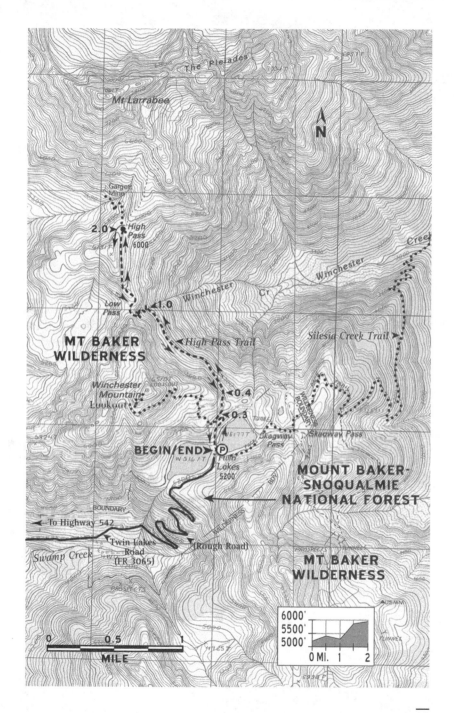

from the trailhead. That rocky jumble of peaks to the east is the Pleiades; Mount Larrabee dominates the view to the north.

The trail drops steeply over the saddle—making a 300-foot vertical climb on your return—and then traverses across alpine meadows blanketed by enough wildflowers to send a botanist into fits of uncontrollable babbling, mostly in Latin. This traverse ends at 1.0 mile, with steep but short switchbacks up a rocky hillside to Low Pass, which—not entirely without coincidence—is about 400 vertical feet lower than High Pass. Despite its lowly stature, it affords splendid views to the peaks of British Columbia and Tomyhoi Peak. This might make an excellent picnic and turnaround spot for families with younger hikers.

To continue, walk north through forest and meadow above the Winchester Creek valley, alternately climbing and descending for another mile to High Pass. This 6,000-foot-high saddle is directly below the south face of Mount Larrabee.

GOING FARTHER

Two way trails lead about 0.5 mile from the end of the maintained trail. The first climbs a southerly ridge toward Mount Larrabee to the right; the second takes you around the ridge to the left and about 400 feet down to the old Gargett Mine. If you'd like additional servings of ibuprofen, other options include the climb to Winchester Mountain Lookout (hike #6 in this guide) or beginning this walk at the Tomyhoi Lake trailhead (hike #5 in this guide).

The Baker River rolls south under a footbridge on the Baker Lake trail (#8).

NORTH CASCADES HIGHWAY (STATE ROUTE 20)

8. Baker Lake

RATING 🚶 🚶 🚶
DISTANCE 4.1 miles round-trip
HIKING TIME 2 hours, 30 minutes
ELEVATION GAIN 200 feet
HIGH POINT 960 feet
EFFORT Easy Walk
BEST SEASON Spring; open year-round
PERMITS/CONTACT Northwest Forest Pass required/Mount Baker–Snoqualmie National Forest, (360) 856-5700; www.fs.usda.gov/mbs
MAPS USGS Mount Shuksan; Green Trails Lake Shannon
NOTES Leashed dogs welcome; good family hike

THE HIKE

This marvelous lowland forest walk offers something similar hikes don't: fine mountain vistas and a chance to ice swollen joints in frigid Baker Lake on the way home.

GETTING THERE

Follow State Route 20 east from Sedro-Woolley for about 15 miles to Baker Lake Road; turn left and climb past Baker Lake for 26 miles to road's end at the Baker River trailhead, 773 feet above sea level. GPS trailhead coordinates: N48°45.010′; W121°33.340′

THE TRAIL

The views from the river and along the sandbars below the trail make the occasionally rough drive to the trailhead worthwhile. You'll begin with a gentle walk along the Baker River Trail through an old forest of cedar and Douglas fir, accompanied by the rush and shuffle of the Baker River nearby. The pathway meanders around massive tree trunks and some areas that could be wet or muddy in the spring for 0.5 mile to a junction with the Baker Lake Trail 610. Turn right here and cross a splendid laminated wood-beam bridge over the Baker River.

The bridge is a good spot to pause and look back and up to the ridges of Mount Baker above and the clear waters of Baker River rolling down

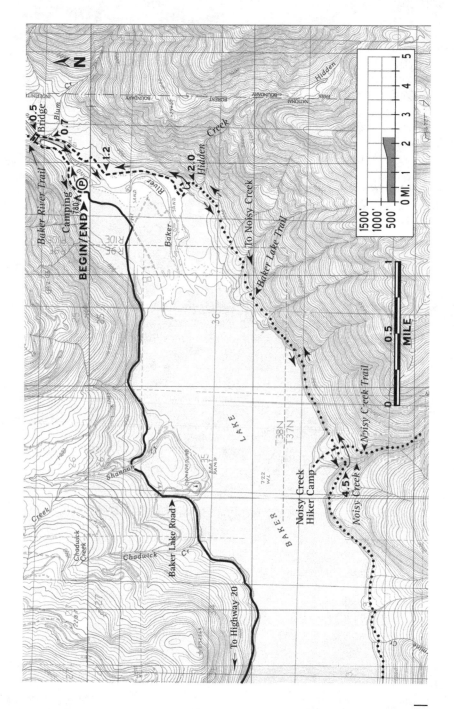

to Baker Lake. Once across the bridge, turn right and follow the trail as it traces a route through the forest along the river's edge. The trail alternately climbs and drops in little chunks as it follows the river downstream, crossing chattering Blum Creek on another fine bridge at 0.7 mile.

Beyond, the trail continues to climb and drop through the evergreens in sections that look as if they could be slippery during the wet months. You'll get great views up and down the river from a rocky point 1.2 miles from the trailhead. Continue along the river in the forest to a spot where you can hear Hidden Creek plunging down the mountainside, and begin a switchback climb to a bridge that crosses Hidden Creek, at just a bit over 2.0 miles.

GOING FARTHER

You can hike another 2.5 miles one-way to the Noisy Creek hiker camp on Baker Lake, a good picnic area for day hikers. If the bridge remains closed and you'd like to extend your walk, return to the Baker River trail junction and hike upstream for 1.5 miles to the North Cascades National Park boundary, where hikers with leashed dogs should turn around. The dog-deprived may continue another 0.5 mile to Sulphide Creek.

9. Sauk Mountain

RATING	🧍
DISTANCE	4.2 miles round-trip
HIKING TIME	3 hours
ELEVATION GAIN	1,200 feet
HIGH POINT	5,500 feet
EFFORT	Moderate Workout
BEST SEASON	Summer, fall
PERMITS/CONTACT	Northwest Forest Pass required/Mount Baker–Snoqualmie National Forest, (360) 856-5700; www.fs.usda.gov/mbs
MAPS	USGS Sauk Mountain; Green Trails Lake Shannon
NOTES	Leashed dogs welcome

THE HIKE

The mile-high summit of Sauk Mountain is an excellent spot to see everything from Mount Rainier to the snow giants of Mounts Baker and Shuksan and the crags of the north Cascades.

GETTING THERE

Take State Route 20 for 7 miles east of Concrete (watch for the speed trap!) and turn left on Sauk Mountain Road (Forest Road 1030). Follow it for 7.5 miles to a junction, keep right, and drive another 0.2 mile to the trailhead, 4,350 feet above sea level. GPS trailhead coordinates: N48°31.276′; W121°36.441′

THE TRAIL

Expect company on this climb, especially on summer weekends when the sun shines and views are expansive from the trail, almost entirely above timberline. The trail begins with a traverse across the lower slopes of Sauk Mountain, directly above, to a steep meadow about 0.3 mile from the trailhead. From here, you'll climb in more than a dozen short switchbacks up the wildflower-filled meadow, where, when you're ready for a rest, you can look south to the confluence of the Sauk and Skagit rivers. You'll pass what accounts for forest view-blockers at about 0.4 mile, then continue to climb switchbacks up the steep hillside.

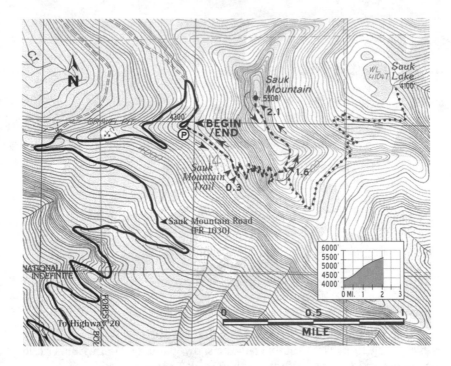

The switchbacks end as you round the south shoulder of Sauk Mountain, more than 800 feet above the trailhead. Just beyond, at 1.6 miles, you'll find a junction with the Sauk Lake Trail. Stay left here, and continue climbing for 0.5 mile to a saddle underneath Sauk's rocky summit. This is a good turnaround point, although you can follow a rough way trail a bit farther east. Surrounding peaks at peaks include Mounts Baker and Shuksan, as well as summits in British Columbia to the north, the Olympic Mountains to the southwest, and Mount Rainier to the south.

GOING FARTHER

For a significantly tougher workout, return to the junction with the Sauk Lake Trail and descend a steep 1.2 miles and 1,200 vertical feet to Sauk Lake—keeping in mind that you'll have to climb out of that cirque 1,200 vertical feet and 1.2 miles on your return.

10. Thunder Creek Trail

RATING	🚶 🚶
DISTANCE	4.0 miles round-trip
HIKING TIME	2 hours
ELEVATION GAIN	200 feet
HIGH POINT	1,400 feet
EFFORT	Easy Walk
BEST SEASON	Fall; open year-round
PERMITS/CONTACT	Northwest Forest Pass required/North Cascades National Park, (360) 873-4500; www.nps.gov/noca
MAPS	USGS Ross Dam; Green Trails Diablo Dam
NOTES	Leashed dogs welcome; good family hike

THE HIKE

Walk along rumbling, tumbling Thunder Creek, which—not entirely without coincidence—sometimes makes noises like thunder, with views above of the rocky summits of the north Cascades.

GETTING THERE

Drive 10 miles east of Newhalem on State Route 20 to the Colonial Creek Campground and turn right, following the signs to the Thunder Creek trailhead, 1,200 feet above sea level. GPS trailhead coordinates: N48°41.115′; W121°05.568′

THE TRAIL

This hike begins by passing the campground amphitheater and a kiosk with a map and interpretive signs, then follows the western shore of Thunder Arm for 0.2 mile to a junction with the Thunder Woods Nature Trail. (The climb into and descent from the hillside forest on the Thunder Woods Trail is best saved for your return, to add a mile to your hike.) Stay left and continue along the nearly level trail as the Thunder Creek canyon narrows around Thunder Arm. At about 0.7 mile, braided Thunder Creek enters the lake, and at 1.0 mile, you'll cross a footbridge to the other side of the canyon and creek. Families with young children might want to turn around here after a creekside picnic.

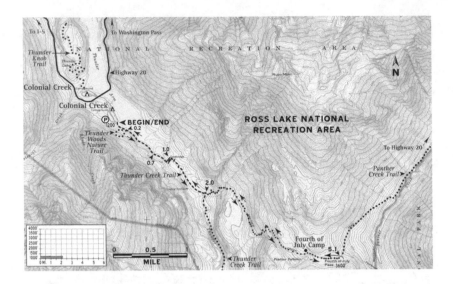

Beyond, the trail climbs above the creek, occasionally negotiating those muddy spots filled by that type of glacial goo that can (and, in my case, often does) cause interesting pratfalls. The trail follows the sidehill for 0.8 mile to a junction with a side trail to Thunder Creek Camp. Continue on the main trail, and at **2.0** miles you'll find a junction with the Fourth of July Pass Trail. Turn right and walk a few hundred feet to a creek crossing and your turnaround point.

GOING FARTHER
The Thunder Creek Trail can be followed along the narrowing canyon for another mile or more as it parallels the creek, yielding round-trip hikes of 5 to 7 miles. For a more strenuous trek, return to the Fourth of July Pass Trail junction and switchback steeply up for 2.6 miles and 2,000 vertical feet to Fourth of July Camp.

11. Lake Ann

RATING	🥾 🥾 🥾 🥾
DISTANCE	3.6 miles round-trip
HIKING TIME	2 hours, 30 minutes
ELEVATION GAIN	655 feet
HIGH POINT	5,475 feet
EFFORT	Easy Walk
BEST SEASON	Summer, fall
PERMITS/CONTACT	Northwest Forest Pass required/Okanogan National Forest, (509) 996-4003; www.fs.usda.gov/okawen
MAPS	USGS Washington Pass; Green Trails Mount Logan
NOTES	Leashed dogs welcome; great family hike; State Route 20 closed in winter

THE HIKE

Climb a well-trodden trail to a quiet alpine lake with great views of the surrounding north Cascades, as well as its own island, formed from the debris of huge winter avalanches that swept down from Maple Pass, 1,400 feet above.

GETTING THERE

Follow State Route 20 to the Rainy Pass Picnic Area, 37 miles east of Newhalem, and continue to the Lake Ann–Maple Pass parking area, 200 yards beyond. The trailhead is 4,800 feet above sea level. GPS trailhead coordinates: N48°30.738′; W120°44.075′

THE TRAIL

The first time I visited Lake Ann, I waded across it to the island at the southwest end for a great picnic away from the crowds. I got a big surprise when I was joined by a deer that swam to the island, perhaps in search of food or to get away from swarms of blackflies.

Begin this hike by climbing along a hillside and switching back above the parking area for about 0.2 mile, then turning and climbing more steeply along a forested gully, rounding a ridge to the south and switching back again about 1.0 mile from the trailhead, above wetland

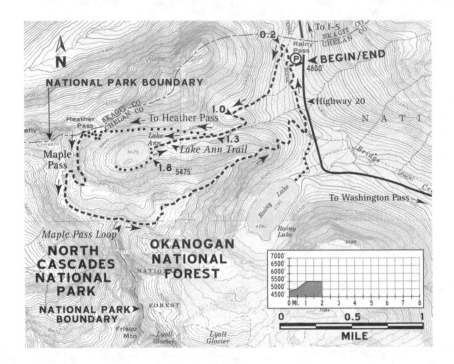

meadows. At 1.3 miles, you'll find a junction with the Maple Pass Trail. Stay left and contour, dropping slightly, into the wet cirque that holds beautiful Lake Ann, at 1.8 miles. You can scramble along the lake's southern shore toward the island. In the late summer the lake is about 5 feet deep at its narrowest point near the island, if you want to wade to this remnant of the mountain.

GOING FARTHER

You can add 1.8 gentle miles to your hike by returning to the trailhead and following the Rainy Lake Trail to the lake. A more strenuous hike would be to climb to Heather Pass, 2 miles and 500 feet above Lake Ann on the Maple Pass Trail. For an even more cramp-filled adventure, continue past Heather Pass to Maple Pass and follow the Maple Pass Loop Trail back to the parking area. The entire loop is 7.2 miles, with an elevation gain and loss of 2,150 feet.

12. Blue Lake

RATING	🚶 🚶 🚶 🚶
DISTANCE	4.4 miles round-trip
HIKING TIME	3 hours
ELEVATION GAIN	1,050 feet
HIGH POINT	6,250 feet
EFFORT	Moderate Workout
BEST SEASON	Fall
PERMITS/CONTACT	Northwest Forest Pass required/Okanogan National Forest, (509) 996-4003; www.fs.usda.gov/okawen
MAPS	USGS Washington Pass; Green Trails Washington Pass
NOTES	Leashed dogs welcome; good family hike; State Route 20 closed in winter

THE HIKE

Climb under the icons of the north Cascades—Early Winter Spires and Liberty Bell—to a splendid alpine lake ringed by cliffs and alive with fall colors, including golden larches set against dark mountainsides.

GETTING THERE

Take State Route 20, turning south to the trailhead 0.5 mile east of milepost 161. This parking area is 0.8 mile west of Washington Pass, 5,200 feet above sea level. GPS trailhead coordinates: N48°31.388′; W120°39.995′

THE TRAIL

This hike begins with a gentle climb through a spruce forest that parallels the North Cascades Highway for about 0.3 mile, then takes a broad switchback around a ridge several hundred feet above the trailhead. You'll switchback again and climb in increasingly open hillside underneath a wide cirque directly below Early Winter Spires. This hillside is littered with huge boulders that make good slalom gates for skiers and snowboarders who climb to the saddle below the peaks when the North Cascades Highway opens in the late spring.

The trail continues to climb in switchbacks and at 1.7 miles strikes a junction with a climbers' way trail to the Spires and Liberty Bell. Stay right and contour toward the Blue Lake outlet stream, switching back

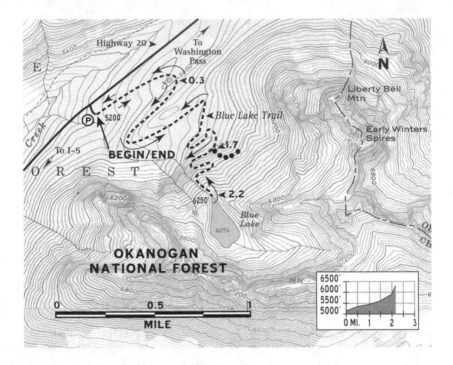

several times before turning and climbing directly to the lake, tucked in a rocky cirque and ringed by mountain larches.

GOING FARTHER

The trail ends at Blue Lake, although you can scramble around the lakeshore or climb to a tiny tarn on a bench west of the lake. If you have a sense of adventure and are comfortable traveling off-trail, return to the climbers' trail and climb steeply to the 7,000-foot saddle west of Early Winter Spires. This is the beginning of the "Birthday Route," a backcountry ski adventure that descends to Early Winters Creek and rejoins the North Cascades Highway at the big switchback underneath Liberty Bell.

13. Cutthroat Lake

RATING	🚶 🚶 🚶 🚶
DISTANCE	4.0 miles round-trip
HIKING TIME	2 hours, 30 minutes
ELEVATION GAIN	450 feet
HIGH POINT	4,953 feet
EFFORT	Easy Walk
BEST SEASON	Fall
PERMITS/CONTACT	Northwest Forest Pass required/Okanogan National Forest, (509) 996-4003; www.fs.usda.gov/okawen
MAPS	USGS Washington Pass; Green Trails Washington Pass
NOTES	Leashed dogs welcome; good family hike; State Route 20 closed in winter

THE HIKE

If you're looking for an easy hike to a beautiful alpine lake ringed by cliffs and golden larches in the fall, this is it. If you have time for only one hike in the north Cascades, this is the one I'd suggest.

GETTING THERE

Take State Route 20 to Forest Road 400, 4 miles east of Washington Pass and 25 miles west of Winthrop, and turn west. Follow the road 1 mile to the trailhead, 4,500 feet above sea level. GPS trailhead coordinates: N48°33.373'; W120°39.299'

THE TRAIL

I have a confession: before writing this book I had never hiked the trail to beautiful Cutthroat Lake. I have skied the trail a couple of times and am pretty certain that at least once, I was only a few feet above the trail. The access road, FR 400, is a groomed cross-country ski trail in the winter and, combined with the highway—closed in the winter at Silver Star Creek—makes for a fine outing.

Anyway, I am certain I found the beginning of the trail by crossing a nice log bridge and climbing gently along Cutthroat Creek on a wide trail through an open forest that includes tamarack and fir. Look ahead and above for peekaboo views of Cutthroat Peak and the rocky ridge

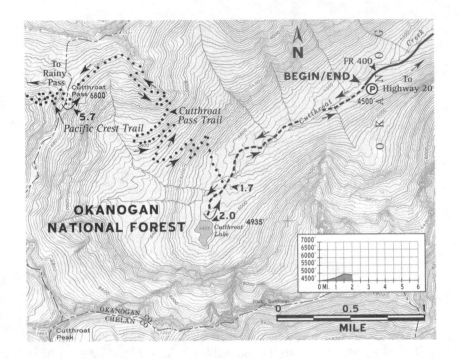

that stretches to the southwest. The trail follows the creek for 1.4 miles before turning and climbing more steeply to the north along a gully. It turns and traverses back to the creek and at **1.7** miles, strikes a junction with the Cutthroat Pass Trail. Stay left, cross Cutthroat Creek, and climb to a bench above the lake, **0.3** mile from the trail junction. The lake is cupped in an ancient glacier-carved cirque decorated with larches, and if you've waited until after the first frost for this hike, you'll enjoy a bug-free picnic.

GOING FARTHER

It is a tough 4-mile climb from the Cutthroat Pass Trail junction to the pass, 1,800 vertical feet above. Another alternative for those who have two autos is to meet at Cutthroat Pass for a picnic and a key exchange. Park the first car at the Rainy Pass trailhead and follow the Pacific Crest Trail as it climbs 5 miles east to Cutthroat Pass. Both parties would hike about 10.7 miles.

14. Tiffany Lake

RATING	🚶 🚶
DISTANCE	3.6 miles round-trip
HIKING TIME	2 hours, 30 minutes
ELEVATION GAIN	800 feet
HIGH POINT	7,144 feet
EFFORT	Easy Walk
BEST SEASON	Summer, fall
PERMITS/CONTACT	Northwest Forest Pass required/Okanogan National Forest, (509) 996-4003; www.fs.usda.gov/okawen
MAPS	USGS Tiffany Mountain
NOTES	Equestrians and leashed dogs welcome

THE HIKE

This short hike to a sparkling alpine lake is a must-do for families with young children.

GETTING THERE

From the community of Conconully, drive around the south shore of the lake on West Fork Road (County Road 2017) for 3.5 miles to the junction with Forest Road 37. Turn right on FR 37 and drive 16.5 miles to FR 39; turn right and drive 7 miles to the Tiffany Springs Campground. The trailhead is across the road, 6,780 feet above sea level. GPS trailhead coordinates: N48°42.009´; W119°57.240´

THE TRAIL

What makes this long drive on forest roads worth the effort is beautiful Tiffany Lake, cupped underneath Tiffany Mountain in subalpine forest less than a mile from the trailhead. Better still, that mile is downhill, making it a great walk for families with younger children. The lake serves up pan-sized brook trout that are easy to catch, and the woods around the lake and down the outlet stream provide plenty of room for exploration.

The trail follows an open sidehill as it angles down toward the lake, passing Tiffany Springs about 0.1 mile from the trailhead. It enters subalpine forest and continues down to the lake basin, then follows the

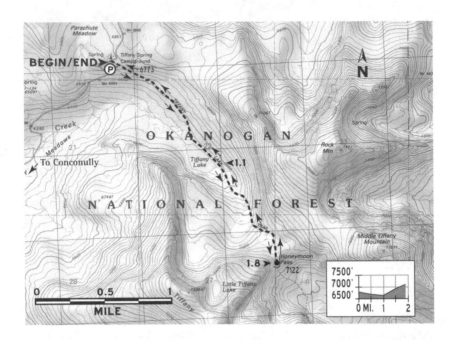

eastern shore around the lake. Several campsites can be found beside the trail or on the knoll at the south end of the lake. At the lake's north end, 1.1 miles, the trail begins a steep climb in switchbacks along the inlet stream to the lake, passing alpine meadows and mini-waterfalls. You'll continue to climb to a wide saddle—Honeymoon Pass—with views north down Boulder Creek. This area was burned in the Tiffany Mountain wildfire several years ago.

GOING FARTHER

Several options for a longer hike are available. You can turn off the trail to the left at Honeymoon Pass and climb to the summit of Middle Tiffany Mountain or follow way trails that climb along the wide ridge to the right, dropping into Little Tiffany Lake in about 0.6 mile. The lake is a beautiful rockbound tarn underneath Tiffany Mountain, favored by fly anglers for its population of cutthroat trout.

For a real workout, follow the trail north as it drops down Boulder Creek to a junction with the Tiffany Mountain Trail. Turn right, cross the creek, and climb steeply underneath the north side of Tiffany to a rocky ridge that climbs to the summit. The round-trip hike to Tiffany Mountain using this route is about 8 miles; an easier hike to the peak follows the Freezeout Ridge Trail.

The Iron Goat Trail (#17), lined with daisies, is a gentle climb toward Stevens Pass.

STEVENS PASS HIGHWAY (US HIGHWAY 2)

15. Bridal Veil Falls

RATING	🚶 🚶
DISTANCE	4.2 miles round-trip
HIKING TIME	2 hours, 30 minutes
ELEVATION GAIN	1,000 feet
HIGH POINT	1,600 feet
EFFORT	Moderate Workout
BEST SEASON	Late spring
PERMITS/CONTACT	Northwest Forest Pass required/ Mount Baker–Snoqualmie National Forest, (360) 677-2414; www.fs.usda.gov/mbs
MAPS	USGS Index; Green Trails Index
NOTES	Leashed dogs welcome

THE HIKE

This crowded climb leads to what has to be one of the most spectacular waterfalls in the central Cascades, best visited when the veil is fresh and full in the spring.

GETTING THERE

Drive 21 miles east of Monroe on US Highway 2 and turn right on Mount Index Road (Forest Road 6020). Drive 0.3 mile to FR 6020-109 and turn right to the trailhead, just ahead at 607 feet above sea level. GPS trailhead coordinates: N47°48.550′; W121°34.408′

THE TRAIL

Expect company on this climb, especially on weekends when hikers are headed for the falls or Lake Serene, which—by no strange coincidence—is a quiet and peaceful body of water. It is also the lake that supplies the rumble and tumble of Bridal Veil Falls at its outlet.

The trail follows an old logging road to the south through a damp forest up a gully and under a sharp ridge for about 400 vertical feet, then swings east around a low hill, 1.3 miles from the trailhead. Here, the path leaves the old road to the right and climbs around a gully to a junction with the Lake Serene Trail at 1.8 miles. Stay right at the junction and continue climbing toward the rush and roar of the falls, directly ahead.

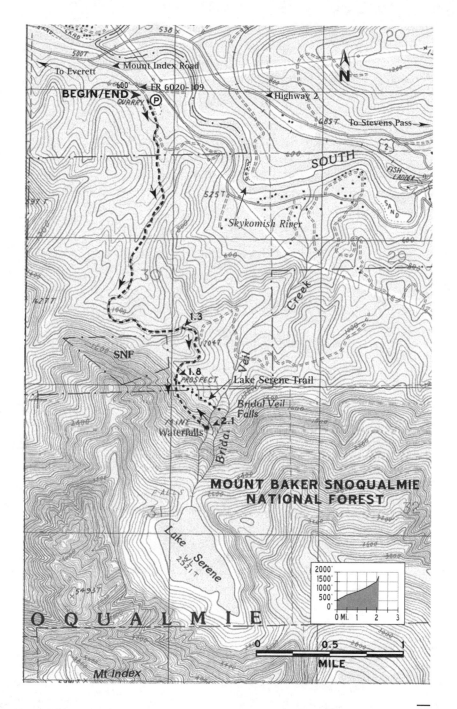

The forest opens near the ruins of an old miner's cabin, then climbs up a series of wood-framed steps. It crosses a perpetually wet and muddy hillside to the falls, which crash over a cliff 100 feet above you, splash across a ledge, and plunge over a cliff 100 feet below you. The rock and viewpoint are often slippery; keep a tight rein on dogs and children.

GOING FARTHER

For a longer and much more strenuous hike, return to the Lake Serene Trail junction and turn right. The trail traverses the forested hillside below the falls, crosses Bridal Veil Creek on a bridge, then climbs in steep switchbacks for 2 miles on wood-framed steps to the lake, cupped under the cliffs of Mount Index.

16. Barclay Lake

RATING	🚶 🚶 🚶
DISTANCE	4.4 miles round-trip
HIKING TIME	3 hours
ELEVATION GAIN	450 feet
HIGH POINT	2,422 feet
EFFORT	Easy Walk
BEST SEASON	Fall
PERMITS/CONTACT	Northwest Forest Pass required/Mount Baker–Snoqualmie National Forest, (360) 677-2414; www.fs.usda.gov/mbs
MAPS	USGS Baring; Green Trails Monte Cristo
NOTES	Leashed dogs welcome; good family hike

THE HIKE

The walk to this beautiful subalpine lake underneath the granite cliffs of Mount Baring is best saved for the autumn, when the crowds have thinned a bit and the lake may seem a bit more remote and wild.

GETTING THERE

Follow US Highway 2 for 6 miles east of Mount Index and turn left on Barclay Creek Road (Forest Road 6024), which climbs 4.5 miles to the parking area at road's end, 2,291 feet above sea level. GPS trailhead coordinates: N47°47.531′; W121°27.562′

THE TRAIL

Begin by dropping along a gentle grade through a shaded lowland forest to Barclay Creek, which carves a broad, flat valley to the east toward the lake. The trail meanders along the creek; muddy sections in the spring may be drier in the fall. At about 1.0 mile, find the first of several plank boardwalks. Mother Nature frequently conspires to make these wooden highways quite slippery when they get wet, so a good pair of hiking boots will likely work better than flip-flops.

The trail turns north and crosses Barclay Creek 1.5 miles from the trailhead, then climbs more steeply as the canyon narrows. Ford a small stream, which may be dry in the fall, at 2.0 miles, then traverse the north shore of the lake.

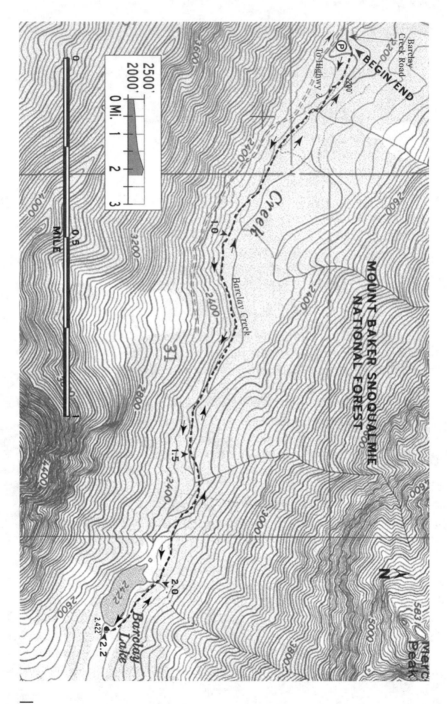

17. Iron Goat Trail

RATING	🚶 🚶 🚶
DISTANCE	6.0 miles round-trip
HIKING TIME	3 hours
ELEVATION GAIN	200 feet
HIGH POINT	3,100 feet
EFFORT	Easy Walk
BEST SEASON	Summer
PERMITS/CONTACT	Northwest Forest Pass required/Mount Baker–Snoqualmie National Forest, (360) 677-2414; www.fs.usda.gov/mbs
MAPS	USGS Scenic; Green Trails Stevens Pass
NOTES	Leashed dogs welcome; good family hike

THE HIKE

This downhill walk along an old railroad grade will take you back in time to a piece of Northwest history, through old snow sheds and past long-abandoned tunnels, with an opportunity for a one-way hike and key exchange.

GETTING THERE

Follow US Highway 2 east to the summit and Stevens Pass Ski Area. Turn across the highway and drive west on Highway 2 just beyond the first bend to the old Stevens Pass Highway, which turns in a hard right off the shoulder between concrete barriers. Drive down the old highway in switchbacks for 2.8 miles and turn right at the junction with Forest Road 50 to the Wellington trailhead parking area, 3,134 feet above sea level. GPS trailhead coordinates: N47º44.832'; W121º07.648'

THE TRAIL

The worst rail disaster in Washington State history took place right here, almost 100 years ago. Nearly 100 passengers were killed when a massive avalanche swept down Windy Mountain and buried their train, delayed by the heavy blizzard that triggered the slide. The Great Northern Railway later abandoned the route in favor of a new, longer tunnel. The area around Stevens Pass is notorious for big backcountry avalanches,

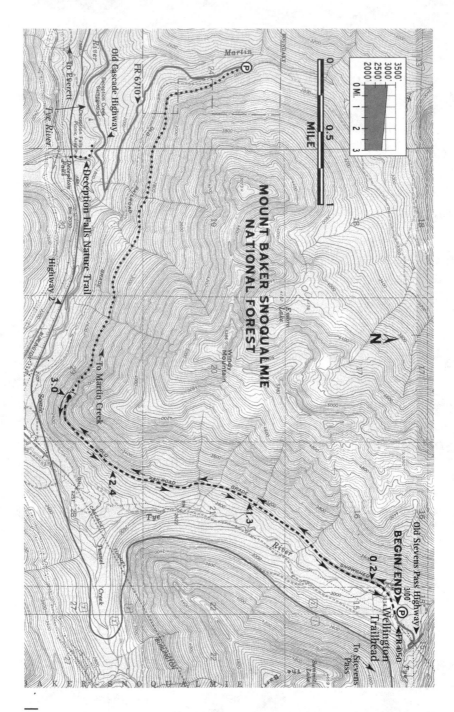

evidenced in the summer by the broad open slopes clean of all timber but slide alder and vine maple.

The history of that disaster and the golden days of railroading are spelled out in a series of fascinating trailside interpretive signs and displays. Begin by walking down the wide, gently graded path fringed with daisies past the remains of old railroad equipment; at **0.2** mile, enter the first of several snow sheds along the route. These sturdy structures built into the side of the mountain protected the trains and in the winter saved days of labor keeping the rails open and free of snow and avalanche debris; today, they'll keep you relatively dry on rainy days. This first shed is about 0.6 mile long and emerges onto a slope where, **1.3** miles from the trailhead, you'll pass another shed crushed by Old Man Winter's hammer.

The route continues to descend very gently, passing a rest area and an overlook of the Skykomish River valley and the Stevens Pass Highway below and across the valley, at **2.4** miles. The pathway then rounds the broad ridge climbing to Windy Mountain, above you to the north. At **3.0** miles, you'll find the Windy Point Tunnel, a good turnaround and picnic spot.

GOING FARTHER

Hikers who can convince another group to park 3 miles farther down the trail and hike uphill to meet at Windy Point Tunnel for a picnic and key exchange can enjoy another 3 miles to the Martin Creek trailhead. The group hiking uphill from Martin Creek won't need too much supplementary oxygen, however: the entire 6 miles climbs only 700 feet.

18. Tumwater Canyon Trail

RATING	🚶 🚶
DISTANCE	2.4 miles round-trip
HIKING TIME	2 hours
ELEVATION GAIN	140 feet
HIGH POINT	1,450 feet
EFFORT	Stroll in the Park
BEST SEASON	Spring
PERMITS/CONTACT	Northwest Forest Pass required/ Wenatchee National Forest, (509) 548-6977; www.fs.usda.gov/okawen
MAPS	USGS Leavenworth; Green Trails Leavenworth
NOTES	Leashed dogs welcome; good family walk

THE HIKE

Use this walk to smooth out the winter hitches in your get-along or to work off that pint of porter and German sausage (*mit brochen!*) you gobbled in Leavenworth.

GETTING THERE

Follow US Highway 2 over Stevens Pass to a parking area 3 miles west of Leavenworth, 0.4 miles east of milepost 97 on Highway 2. The parking area is a sharp right off the highway at river's edge, 1,400 feet above sea level. GPS trailhead coordinates: N47°35.036′; W120°42.540′

THE TRAIL

When preparing this book, I figured I'd check this trail out early in the spring, when the Wenatchee River was in full fettle. The fettle proved fuller than I anticipated, and I ended up returning in late summer for a better look at this riverside walk.

You'll begin by walking upstream a bit on this old Great Northern right-of-way to the metal trestle, part of a pipeline that charged the turbines supplying power to the electric engines toting freight and passengers through the Cascade Tunnel. Cross the bridge and turn upstream, where the trail meanders along the rushing Wenatchee River. You'll be climbing over rocks that were once part of the Icicle Ridge above, decorated by a

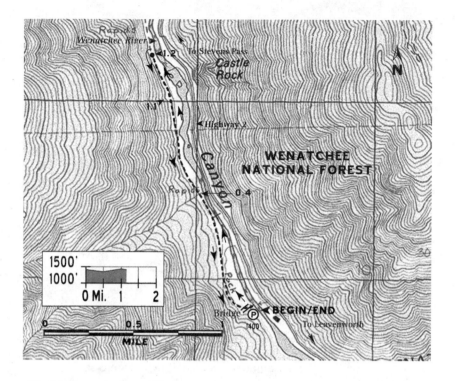

silver forest of snags left by a number of past wildfires. Rusty parts of the old pipeline can be seen along sections of the trail.

At 0.4 mile, you'll encounter the fettle that turned me back in the spring: a creek that plunges from the Tumwater Canyon wall and was significantly kinder and gentler in late summer. Cross this creek and continue upstream on the path that rarely climbs more than 20 feet from the river's edge. Eddies and pools on the river form little sandy bays for cliff-watching and sunbathing in the summer, and flat rocks invite you to sit down and watch the river rush past.

At 1.1 miles, you'll find a field of large boulders to be navigated, making upstream travel more difficult, and another 0.1 mile beyond, you'll find a good turnaround spot. That big rock above and across the river is Castle Rock, which—by no strange coincidence—looks something like a castle. It sometimes *is* a castle to peregrine falcons, which nest here, and to rock climbers, who don't.

19. Little Eightmile Lake

RATING	🚶 🚶
DISTANCE	5.6 miles round-trip
HIKING TIME	3 hours, 30 minutes
ELEVATION GAIN	1,020 feet
HIGH POINT	4,404 feet
EFFORT	Moderate Workout
BEST SEASON	Summer
PERMITS/CONTACT	Northwest Forest Pass required/ Wenatchee National Forest, (509) 548-6977; www.fs.usda.gov/okawen
MAPS	USGS Cashmere Mountain; Green Trails The Enchantments
NOTES	Dogs prohibited; good family hike; hot in summer

THE HIKE
Climb through a fire-scarred, logged forest with excellent views of neighboring mountains to a tiny alpine lake, a cooling welcome as nice as the wildflower show in summer.

GETTING THERE
From Leavenworth, follow Icicle Road at the west end of town for 8.5 miles to Forest Road 7601. Turn left and follow the steep, bumpy road for 3 miles to the Eightmile Lake trailhead, 3,423 feet above sea level. GPS trailhead coordinates: N47°32.128'; W120°48.799'

THE TRAIL
You may not have heard of the clandestine hiking club, GetOffMy Trail, which charges dues of $5,000 per year. There were 65 members the last time I checked, and they use the membership dues to operate a washboarding machine on various Forest Service roads throughout the state. You've never seen the washboarding machine, because the club operates under cover of darkness, but I'm certain you've experienced the results of their work. The washboarding machine turns roads into a series of parallel ruts that run perpendicular to your direction of travel. When you drive over the ruts, you risk losing your dentures, peeing your

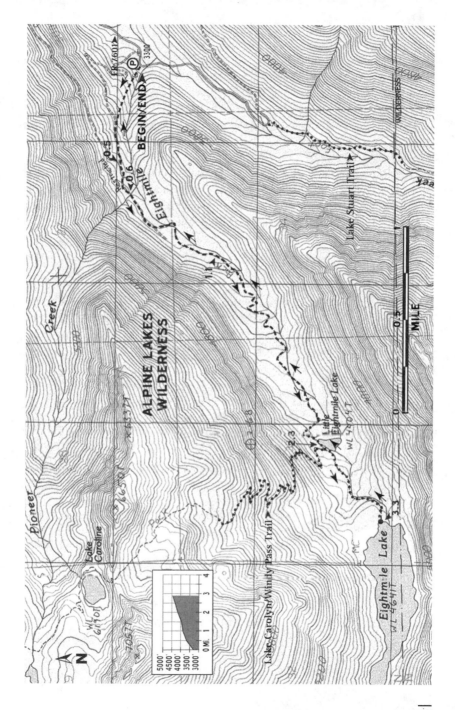

pants, dislodging your contact lenses, or shattering every weld in your SUV. GetOffMyTrail members use the washboarding machine to discourage other hikers from using the roads, thus reducing the impact on their favorite hiking trails. I drove Forest Road 7601, the Eightmile Lake Road, only days after the club had treated it with the washboarding machine. Please feel free to check my research on this topic.

The climb to Little Eightmile Lake begins in a forest where views have been opened by several wildfires. The downside is that the trail lacks the shade provided by a mature forest; the upside is that the view of the surrounding countryside is improved. The trail climbs steeply for the first 0.5 mile, then joins an abandoned logging road, where the grade eases a bit. Cross Pioneer Creek in another 0.1 mile and continue climbing, never far from the sight or sound of Eightmile Creek.

You'll climb through what is likely to become a silver forest in a few decades—gnarled snags of trees burned in wildfires nearly two decades ago—at 1.1 miles from the trailhead. Beyond, the Eightmile canyon narrows a bit, and the trail switches back several times and gets slightly steeper. The trail alternates between flower-filled meadows and recovering forest for the next mile, climbs, then drops slightly to Little Eightmile Lake, at 2.8 miles. This calm mountain tarn makes a good turnaround point and picnic spot.

GOING FARTHER

Larger (and probably more crowded) Eightmile Lake is another 0.5 mile and 200 vertical feet farther up Eightmile Creek. Another option for substantial joint destruction is to climb from the trail junction at Little Eightmile Lake to the right, up the Lake Caroline Trail. This is a steep, take-no-prisoners hike that switchbacks nearly 2,000 vertical feet in 3 miles, one that should only be attempted by iron-jointed hikers and members of the GetOffMyTrail Club.

A beautiful timber suspension bridge spans the Middle Fork of the Snoqualmie River (#23) near the trailhead.

SNOQUALMIE PASS (INTERSTATE 90)

20. Rattlesnake Ledge

RATING	🚶 🚶 🚶
DISTANCE	4.0 miles round-trip
HIKING TIME	2 hours, 30 minutes
ELEVATION GAIN	1,100 feet
HIGH POINT	2,079 feet
EFFORT	Moderate Workout
BEST SEASON	Spring, fall
PERMITS/CONTACT	Discover Pass/Department of Natural Resources South Puget Sound Region, (360) 825-1631; www.dnr.wa.gov
MAPS	USGS North Bend; Green Trails Rattlesnake Mountain
NOTES	Leashed dogs welcome; good family hike

THE HIKE

This is not a hike for acrophobes, like me, who can barely stand there and watch all those fools, like you, who have no regard for the power of gravity and stand on the edge of a 1,000-foot-high cliff, watching all those people below. One of the worst things about acrophobia is that you transfer your fear to everyone, so you are needlessly frightened for others as well as for yourself. Hold tight to kids and pets—even in-laws—if you have any regard for their safety.

GETTING THERE

Drive east on Interstate 90 from Seattle to exit 32 in North Bend. Turn south on 436th Avenue SE, which turns into Cedar Falls Road SE, and drive for 2.7 miles up to the trailhead parking area, 954 feet above sea level. GPS trailhead coordinates: N47º26.051′; W121º46.066′

THE TRAIL

This and the Mount Si Trail across the valley are the closest hikes to Seattle that have a hint of wilderness to them. Expect crowds as well as great views of all of the hikes that await you farther east in the central Cascades, plus an incredible and thrilling sight of Rattlesnake Lake so very far below. No worries, mate: nobody has spotted a rattlesnake around these parts in years, if ever. Actually, the lake got its name when

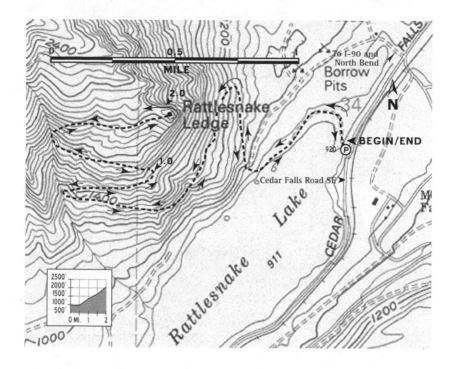

an unknown prankster tied a baby rattle to a stuffed boa constrictor and placed it on the rocks along the ledge. Feel free to check my research on this point.

Start your hike along a wide, flat path that circles the north end of the lake under a shaded lowland forest of alder and, once around the lake, begins climbing gently. The trail here was rebuilt in the last decade to eliminate steep switchbacks that, curiously, many hikers cut in their hurry to the summit. The new trail is far more gentle, thanks to the work of volunteers and Seattle Public Utilities staffers. At 1.0 mile from the trailhead, you get a peekaboo look at the Cedar River Watershed Education Center above the southeast shore of Rattlesnake Lake, already several hundred feet below. Beyond, to the south, is Mount Rainier.

The forest hides the view once again, and your climb continues in long switchbacks up the southern face of Rattlesnake Mountain. At 2.0 miles, you'll find a junction with the Rattlesnake Mountain Trail. Stay right and (cautiously) walk out onto the exposed, rocky ledge for expansive views of the Cascade Mountains to the east, Rainier to the south, and Mount Si to the north. Tell all those fools to get back from the ledge, grab a big handful of solid rock, and look down 1,100 feet to the lake below.

21. John Wayne Trail, Cascades

RATING	🚶 🚶 🚶
DISTANCE	6.0 miles round-trip
HIKING TIME	4 hours, 30 minutes
ELEVATION GAIN	240 feet
HIGH POINT	1,140 feet
EFFORT	Easy Walk
BEST SEASON	Spring; open year-round
PERMITS/CONTACT	Discover Pass/Washington State Parks, (360) 902-8844; www.parks.wa.gov
MAPS	USGS North Bend; Green Trails Rattlesnake Mountain
NOTES	Bicyclists and leashed dogs welcome; good family walk

THE HIKE

This gentle climb along an old railroad grade through dense forest is perfect for an early-season tune-up, to get those joints working after a winter hibernation.

GETTING THERE

Drive east on Interstate 90 from Seattle to exit 32 in North Bend. Turn south on 436th Avenue SE, which turns into Cedar Falls Road SE, and drive for 2.7 miles up to the trailhead parking area, bearing left to the upper lot, 975 feet above sea level. GPS trailhead coordinates: N47°25.928'; W121°45.998'

THE TRAIL

This gentle walk follows a portion of the Iron Horse State Park, a linear giant that stretches from North Bend all the way to the Columbia River along the route of the old Chicago, Milwaukee, St. Paul, and Pacific Railroad. Like the growing number of rail trails in Washington and elsewhere, it makes excellent hiking for those whose knees and other joints don't work as well as they once did. Hikers without those worries should be able to develop them simply by adding rocks to their packs or running a few extra miles up and down the trail.

Begin the hike by climbing around the lower reaches of the Snoqualmie foothills and at 0.5 mile, find the junction with the Cedar Butte Trail.

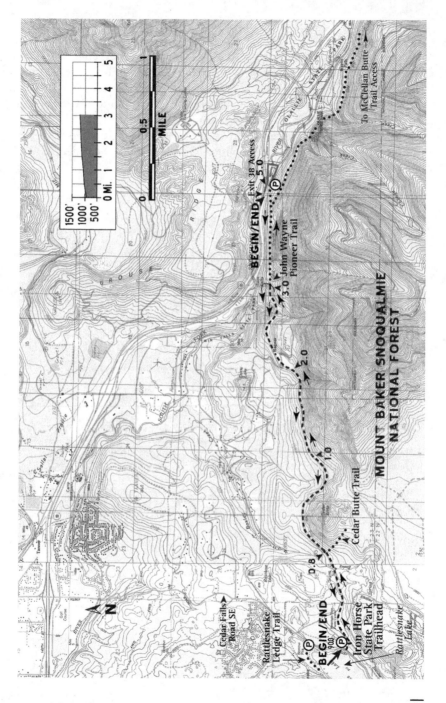

Stay left and continue climbing ever so gently underneath the steep hillside of Cedar Butte. The trail contours under steeper cliffs in trees that sometimes permit views of the Snoqualmie Valley and Mount Si, but do little to hide the sound of Interstate 90 traffic below. Pretend it is the sound of rushing water.

At 1.0 mile, swing around a wide forested canyon and traverse under cliffs, turn northwesterly, and cross a second wide gully to climb to a promontory overlooking the valley and I-90 corridor, 2.0 miles from the trailhead. Make a turn east, and climb another mile to the junction with the Twin Falls Trail to your left, your turnaround spot.

GOING FARTHER
The best way to extend this hike is to turn downhill on the Twin Falls Trail and follow it steeply downhill for about 0.5 mile to Twin Falls, which you certainly won't be surprised to find has an upper and lower tier.

22. Hyak Tunnel

RATING	🚶 🚶 🚶 🚶
DISTANCE	5.2 miles round-trip
HIKING TIME	3 hours
ELEVATION GAIN	100 feet
HIGH POINT	2,600 feet
EFFORT	Easy Walk
BEST SEASON	Summer, fall
PERMITS/CONTACT	Discover Pass/Iron Horse State Park, (360) 902-8844; www.parks.wa.gov
MAPS	USGS Snoqualmie Pass; Green Trails Snoqualmie Pass
NOTES	Bicyclists and leashed dogs welcome; carry powerful headlamps or headlights, extra batteries, and rain gear

THE HIKE

This is a virtually flat, unusual hike *under* a mountain along the roadbed of the old Chicago, Milwaukee, St. Paul, and Pacific Railroad, now part of the John Wayne Pioneer Trail.

GETTING THERE

From Snoqualmie Pass, drive east on Interstate 90 for 2 miles to exit 54. Turn right at the exit and immediately left on the spur 906 road, signed "Snoqualmie Tunnel." Drive 0.5 mile and turn right at the Hyak trailhead, 2,600 feet above sea level. GPS trailhead coordinates: N47°23.529'; W121°23.550'

THE TRAIL

Two perfect times come to mind for this hike: Halloween night and the hottest day of the year. The tunnel is traditionally open from May through October, although early snows might cause Washington State Park staffers to close the tunnel sooner. Still, a nighttime hike any time of year would be a great adventure. For an even scarier time, try walking the distance with only candlelight (and, of course, good headlamp backup) to show your way through this 2.3-mile tunnel.

If a midnight hike in total darkness doesn't appeal to you, save this walk for a hot summer day. As you round the bend on the old railroad grade

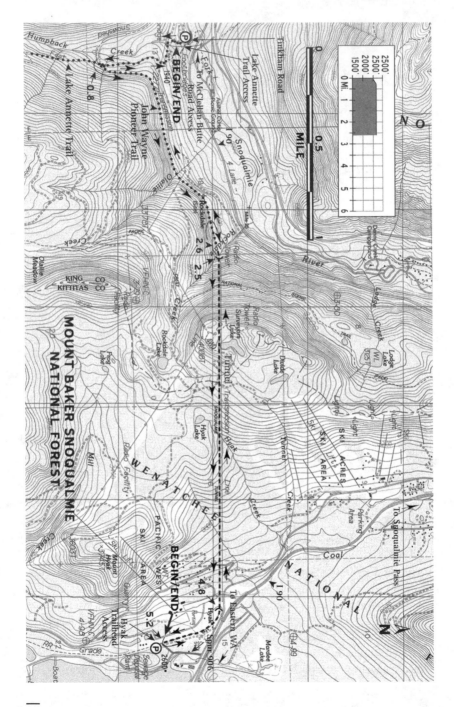

0.2 mile from the trailhead, you'll feel a gentle cooling breeze that intensifies as you near the tunnel entrance. This chill wind almost always blows from west to east, the difference between cool marine air to the west and dry, warm air to the east. You couldn't find a more comfortable walk on a hot day, unless you could find a 2.0-mile hike under a waterfall.

On this walk you'll *feel* like you're hiking 2 miles under a waterfall, which in a sense is what you are doing. The instant you enter the tunnel, at 0.3 mile, you'll hear and feel the drip-drop of water from above. That's the water from the 4,000-foot-high peak over your head, which cups Surveyors and Hyak lakes in its arms. Guess where the water from those lakes and snowfields percolates? (If your answer is the top of your noggin, go to the head of the class.)

So carry rain gear and wear a good pair of water-resistant boots or shoes, as well as warm clothing. Once inside the tunnel, the light from the entrance fades rapidly, and since the tunnel is straight as a ruler, you might glimpse the pinpoint of light at the other end, 2.3 miles away. For a real thrill, walk 0.5 mile into the tunnel, turn your headlamp off, and see how far you can go before you run into the side of the tunnel. If you're like me, you'll zigzag your way from one side of the tunnel to the other.

The west end of the tunnel makes a good turnaround point. Warm up, drink hot chocolate, dry off, and head back the other way.

GOING FARTHER

For a longer hike, continue west for 1.5 miles to a junction with the Lake Annette Trail, turn right, and descend Humpback Creek for 0.7 mile to the Annette Lake trailhead, a good spot for a snack and to turn around. That would make your hike 9.6 miles round-trip.

23. Middle Fork Snoqualmie

RATING	🚶 🚶
DISTANCE	6.0 miles round-trip
HIKING TIME	3 hours, 30 minutes
ELEVATION GAIN	350 feet
HIGH POINT	1,150 feet
EFFORT	Easy Walk
BEST SEASON	Fall; open year-round
PERMITS/CONTACT	Northwest Forest Pass required/Mount Baker–Snoqualmie National Forest, (425) 888-1421; www.fs.usda.gov/mbs
MAPS	USGS Lake Philippa; Green Trails Mount Si and Skykomish
NOTES	Leashed dogs welcome; bicyclists welcome on odd-numbered days; good family hike

THE HIKE

This pleasant river walk heads through valley and canyon along the tumbling Snoqualmie, shaded by huge second- and third-growth evergreens that make this a good choice on hot days.

GETTING THERE

From Seattle, follow Interstate 90 east to North Bend and take exit 34. Turn left on 468th Avenue SE and continue about 0.8 mile, passing the Seattle Truck Plaza to the Middle Fork Road (Forest Road 56). Stay left at the first junction, although both roads rejoin in about a mile. Drive 11.6 miles on FR 56 to the trailhead on the right, 1,020 feet above sea level. GPS trailhead coordinates: N47°32.902′; W121°32.212′

THE TRAIL

For a hike in the ever-popular Interstate 90 corridor, the Middle Fork Snoqualmie is fairly serene, especially on weekdays in the fall or early winter. Parts of this trail during these times can get muddy and slippery, further discouraging hikers who don't want to dirty their Vibrams. Begin on a wide, flat trail leading to the Gateway Bridge, a beautiful laminated-wood-trussed span that may well be the highlight of this walk for engineers and architects.

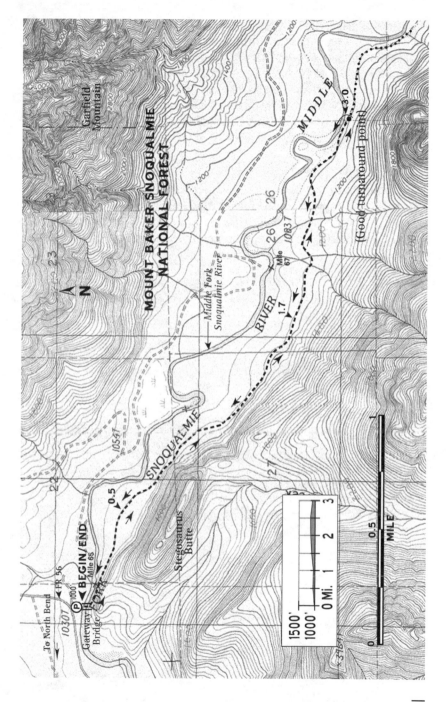

Turn left and follow the trail upstream with views above to 4,900-foot Mount Garfield and nearby springtime sights of sprouting trillium, skunk cabbage, and salmonberry. The trail climbs for 0.5 mile from the trailhead along the rocky hillside of Stegosaurus Butte, which—by no strange coincidence—might resemble an ancient dinosaur's back to some.

Continue back into the forest to an abandoned railroad grade, at 1.7 miles. The route now meanders through the forest before dropping back to the river at 3.0 miles, your picnic and turnaround spot.

GOING FARTHER

The route continues upriver for another 11 miles to Dutch Miller Gap. But a wiser choice—given the fact that you may find yourself navigating numerous blowdowns—would be to continue another 2.8 miles one-way to the Dingford Creek Trail, which crosses the river and makes a round-trip hike of 11.6 miles.

24. Talapus Lake

RATING	🚶 🚶
DISTANCE	4.4 miles round-trip
HIKING TIME	2 hours, 30 minutes
ELEVATION GAIN	800 feet
HIGH POINT	3,400 feet
EFFORT	Moderate Workout
BEST SEASON	Fall
PERMITS/CONTACT	Northwest Forest Pass and free Alpine Lakes Wilderness permit required/Mount Baker–Snoqualmie National Forest, (425) 888-1421; www.fs.usda.gov/mbs
MAPS	USGS Bandera; Green Trails Bandera
NOTES	Leashed dogs welcome; good family hike

THE HIKE

This is a moderate climb up a wide, often rough forest trail to a subalpine lake with good views of the surrounding mountains and a chance to cool off in the lake.

GETTING THERE

From North Bend, drive 14 miles east on Interstate 90 to exit 45 and turn north. Turn left on Forest Road 9030 and bear right at the junction in 1 mile. Continue climbing for 2.4 miles to the end of the road at the trailhead, 2,606 feet above sea level. GPS trailhead coordinates: N47º24.067'; W121º31.117'

THE TRAIL

I'd rate this hike higher, except for the fact that solitude is difficult to find throughout the summer and autumn weekends. If possible, plan this walk on a fall weekday, and you might enjoy some privacy. If, on the other hand, you don't mind sharing this wild subalpine lake with others, disregard my advice and hit the trail.

Talapus Lake is the first of a number of subalpine and alpine lakes along this trail, which forms a long loop by joining the Pratt Lake Trail at Olallie Lake. That's a mite too far for day hikers, so settle back, lace up

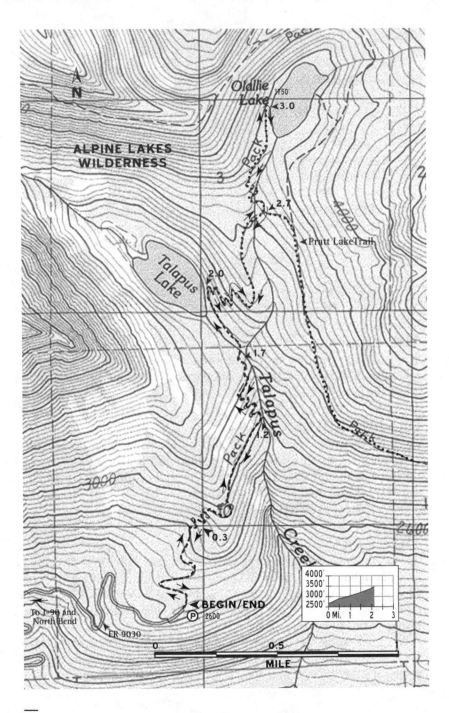

those Vibrams, and begin by issuing yourself an Alpine Lakes Wilderness permit at the trailhead.

Start your hike on a wide forested path that is well worn and decorated with trip-roots that, when I first hiked this trail in 1968, were just as prominent. Sections of the trail are on boardwalk, which can get slippery in wet weather. Though you'll see plenty of hikers on this trail wearing lightweight jogging shoes or trail-runners, hiking shoes will serve you better on slippery planks and the occasional mud patch.

After a series of steeper switchbacks at 0.3 mile, you'll traverse into the gully that carries Talapus Creek in the crook of its arm. At the creek, 1.2 miles from the trailhead, begin another series of steeper switchbacks, climbing about 200 feet in less than 0.25 mile. At 1.7 miles, you'll enter the Alpine Lakes Wilderness and stay right at the trail junction signed "Main Trail." Beyond, you'll cross Talapus Creek and stay left at the junction with a side trail, then contour to the lake, where you'll find open shoreline and good picnic spots.

GOING FARTHER

The hike to Olallie Lake from Talapus adds 1.4 miles round-trip to your hike—but it is a significantly tougher climb than the trail you've just hiked. It climbs nearly 400 feet in 0.5 mile before striking a junction with the Pratt Lake Trail. Stay left and climb another 0.25 mile to scenic Olallie Lake.

25. Snow Lake

RATING	🚶 🚶 🚶 🚶
DISTANCE	6.0 miles round-trip
HIKING TIME	4 hours
ELEVATION GAIN	1,700 feet
HIGH POINT	4,400 feet
EFFORT	Prepare to Perspire
BEST SEASON	Fall
PERMITS/CONTACT	Northwest Forest Pass and free Alpine Lakes Wilderness permit required/Mount Baker–Snoqualmie National Forest, (425) 888-1421; www.fs.usda.gov/mbs
MAPS	USGS Snoqualmie Pass; Green Trails Snoqualmie Pass
NOTES	Leashed dogs welcome; good family walk

THE HIKE

Join the crowds on this climb to one of the largest alpine lakes in the central Cascades, a cliff-bound crystal of exceptional beauty.

GETTING THERE

Take exit 52 from Interstate 90 at Snoqualmie Pass, 21 miles east of North Bend, turning left under the interstate and right on the Alpental Road. Drive 1.5 miles to the upper Alpental parking area, 3,142 feet above sea level. The trail begins on the right, above the parking area. GPS trailhead coordinates: N47°26.684'; W121°25.410'

THE TRAIL

This was my first hike in the Cascades, waaaay back in 1961. Because the trail was about 3 miles longer in those days, I didn't get to the lake, but rather pigged out on huckleberries on the ridge above the lake. I returned in 1967 on one of my first overnight backpacks, using a plastic Army mattress cover for a tent and a ratty old Army wool blanket for a sleeping bag. It rained all night, and in the morning I woke up in about 2 inches of water and slogged out of there at first light. I have since spent far more enjoyable days at this scenic destination.

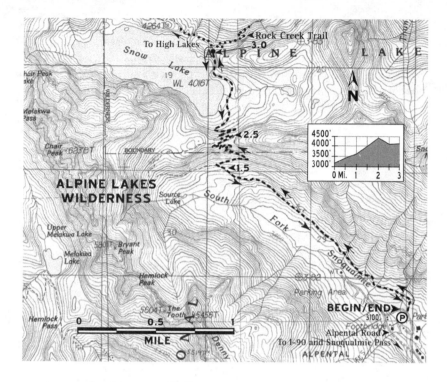

The trail climbs on a series of steps to gain the old trail, which traverses under cliffs that shine with waterfalls. You'll emerge from alpine forest to look across the infant South Fork of the Snoqualmie River to the Alpental ski area, Denny and Chair peaks. Cross talus slopes on a gentle climb to a junction at 1.5 miles. The old trail continued to the left and climbed above tiny Source Lake, then turned back in a wide switchback that traversed a big, steep snowfield. Your route turns right at the junction and begins a series of steep switchbacks to the low saddle, 2.5 miles from the trailhead, on the east ridge of Chair Peak. This is the Alpine Lakes Wilderness boundary and yields excellent views of the surrounding peaks and the South Fork valley. Look north across the Snow Lake basin to the Middle Fork Snoqualmie River valley.

From the saddle, the trail descends in switchbacks to the lake. Portions of the lake were once private property, and the remains of an old cabin stood above the south end of the lake. In the late summer and early fall, the huckleberries are so thick they'll stain your boots.

GOING FARTHER

You can add 4 round-trip miles and 1,600 feet of elevation gain and loss to your hike by heading past Snow Lake and dropping briefly from the outlet stream to a junction with the Rock Creek Trail. Stay left here and begin climbing to aptly named Gem Lake, a great picnic destination and turnaround for strong hikers who leave most of the crowds behind at Snow Lake.

26. Squaw Lake

RATING	🚶 🚶 🚶 🚶
DISTANCE	5.0 miles round-trip
HIKING TIME	4 hours, 30 minutes
ELEVATION GAIN	1,100 feet
HIGH POINT	4,841 feet
EFFORT	Prepare to Perspire
BEST SEASON	Late summer, early fall
PERMITS/CONTACT	Northwest Forest Pass required/ Wenatchee National Forest, (509) 852-1100; www.fs.usda.gov/okawen
MAPS	USGS Mount Daniel; Green Trails Stevens Pass
NOTES	Leashed dogs welcome

THE HIKE

You'll welcome the cold waters of this alpine lake after climbing here on a hot summer day. Enjoy wide-open views of the Cle Elum River valley below and the eastern Cascades across the valley. This is one of the best hikes in the central Cascades.

GETTING THERE

Drive east of Snoqualmie Pass on Interstate 90 to exit 80 and cross the freeway to the north. Drive 2.8 miles to Salmon La Sac Road (Highway 903) and turn left. Drive 16.7 miles to Salmon La Sac Campground and turn right on Forest Road 4330. This rough road climbs 12.3 miles to Tucquala Meadows, the trailhead and end of the road, 3,142 feet above sea level. GPS trailhead coordinates: N47°26.684′; W121°25.410′

THE TRAIL

B. B. Hardbody and I first visited Tucquala Meadows on our mountain bikes, riding about 16 miles from Copper Lake, across the Cle Elum River valley. The road from Salmon La Sac seemed shorter on the bike than it did when I bounced along in a car while preparing this book. On that first visit, we helped push a pickup truck out of a creek crossing after the driver couldn't get up the bank on the opposite side. A concrete trough has since been added to make the crossing easier.

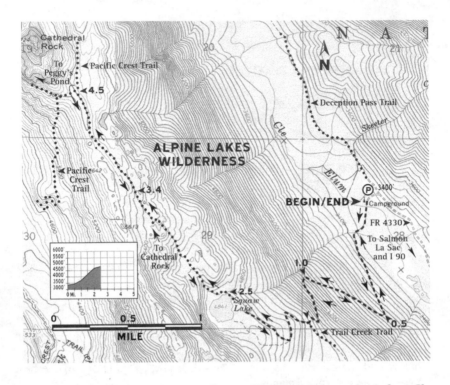

The trail heads west across a flower-filled meadow to the infant Cle Elum River, crosses the river on a bridge, and enters a shady forest of cedar and fir. Don't let this gentle section fool you; the path begins climbing in several hundred yards along a forested hillside with peekaboo views of the Wenatchee Mountains to the east and the valley below. You'll climb steadily for about 0.5 mile before switching back and continuing to climb at a pace that is guaranteed to either get your ticker ticking or—if you are as out of shape as I am—stop it altogether. Climb another 0.5 mile to the gully that carries the outlet creek from Squaw Lake, directly above, then switchback and take a brief rest as the grade levels a bit before getting steeper again to a fourth switchback. After another short, steep climb and switchback, you'll arrive at a junction with the Trail Creek Trail, which is signed "Michael Lake," 1.8 miles from the trailhead.

Stay right, and climb in two more switchbacks up an open ridge with views to the valley and meadows below. Cross a broad ridge to the north and at 2.5 miles find Squaw Lake, nestled in a cliffside cirque. Wide meadows near the outlet and along the southern shore make great picnic spots.

The Noble Knob (#28).

CHINOOK PASS HIGHWAY (STATE ROUTE 410)

27. Naches Peak Loop

RATING	🥾 🥾 🥾
DISTANCE	3.2 miles round-trip
HIKING TIME	2 hours, 30 minutes
ELEVATION GAIN	650 feet
HIGH POINT	5,850 feet
EFFORT	Moderate Workout
BEST SEASON	Summer
PERMITS/CONTACT	Northwest Forest Pass required; free self-issue wilderness permit at William O. Douglas Wilderness boundary/Naches Ranger District, (509) 653-1400; www.fs.usda.gov/okawen
MAPS	USGS Mount Rainier East; Green Trails Mount Rainier East
NOTES	Leashed dogs welcome to park boundary

THE HIKE
This is a grand loop hike, almost entirely in alpine country, with nice views of the eastern Cascades and Mount Rainier.

GETTING THERE
Follow State Route 410 from Enumclaw past Crystal Mountain Boulevard and through Mount Rainier National Park to its junction with Highway 123; turn left and climb past Tipsoo Lake over Chinook Pass. Two parking areas are available: one on the right just over the pass and the second about 200 feet downhill on the left. The trailhead is at the log overpass entrance to Mount Rainier National Park and heads southeast into the William O. Douglas Wilderness, 5,430 feet above sea level. GPS trailhead coordinates: N146°52.352′; W121°30.957′

THE TRAIL
Begin by climbing to the trail that crosses above the highway on the log overpass, then turns easterly through alpine forest and, in less than 0.1 mile, enters the William O. Douglas Wilderness, where you will find a free self-issue permit box. The route climbs gently underneath the east side of Naches Peak, passing a calm mountain tarn ringed

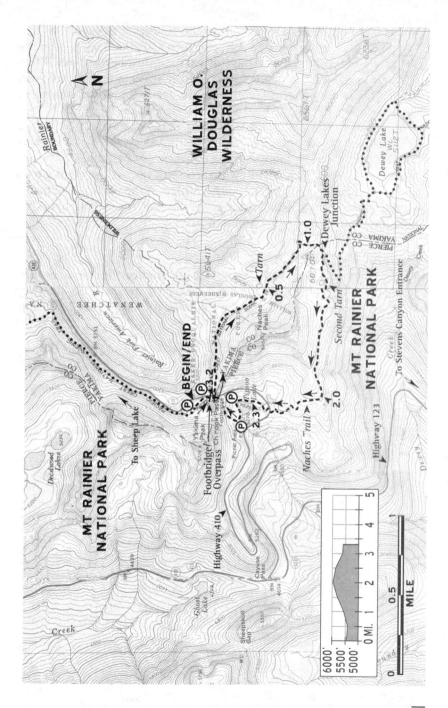

by huckleberry fields, 0.5 mile from the trailhead. Beyond, the trail continues to climb across a rocky area, then switches back and briefly climbs more steeply to a little pass, at 1.0 mile. Just beyond, you'll find a junction with the Pacific Crest Trail, which drops to the left to Dewey Lakes. This is the point where hikers with dogs should turn around or continue down the Pacific Crest Trail to Dewey Lakes.

To continue, stay right and traverse under the west face of Naches Peak, rounding a ridge at 2.0 miles and getting an eyeful of Mount Rainier. The trail descends more steeply from here past an alpine tarn just above the Chinook Pass Highway, then crosses the highway and circles Tipsoo Lake to the north, at 2.3 miles. Walk past the parking and picnic areas at the lake and climb under the west face of Tipsoo Peak over Chinook Pass, descending to the trailhead parking area.

GOING FARTHER
To add another 3 round-trip miles and 400 vertical feet to your hike, turn left on the Pacific Crest Trail and descend a steep hillside to Dewey Lakes, where you can rest up for the climb back to the Naches Peak Loop.

28. Noble Knob

RATING	🚶 🚶 🚶 🚶
DISTANCE	7.0 miles round-trip
HIKING TIME	4 hours
ELEVATION GAIN	800 feet
HIGH POINT	6,011 feet
EFFORT	Prepare to Perspire
BEST SEASON	Summer
PERMITS/CONTACT	Northwest Forest Pass required/White River Ranger District, (360) 825-6585; www.fs.usda.gov/mbs
MAPS	USGS Noble Knob; Green Trails Lester
NOTES	Bicyclists and leashed dogs welcome

THE HIKE

Walk along a sunny ridge blanketed by purple lupine to a splendid view of the east side of Mount Rainier and the icy stretch of the Emmons Glacier.

GETTING THERE

Drive 13.3 miles south of Greenwater on State Route 410 to Forest Road 7174, on the left. Turn left on FR 7174 and follow it to Corral Pass, about 6 miles on a steep, rough dirt road. Take the left fork of the road at Corral Pass for the Noble Knob trailhead or, for more parking, continue to the right 0.2 mile to the large parking area at the Corral Pass Campground. The trailhead is 5,650 feet above sea level. GPS trailhead coordinates: N47°00.883′; W121°28.008′

THE TRAIL

Save this hike for a late-summer day when you can see forever, because you can definitely see forever along this trail. OK, maybe "forever" is a slight exaggeration, but with the number of close-up views, there's no need to strain your eyes. Look west to Mount Rainier and the Emmons Glacier, where with the naked eye you can see climbing routes etched into the ice and with binoculars watch climbers negotiating the massive crevasse at the top of the route.

Or take the hike to Noble Knob on a day when you can't see any of that stuff. Wildflowers are showier in the diffuse light provided by fog, and the

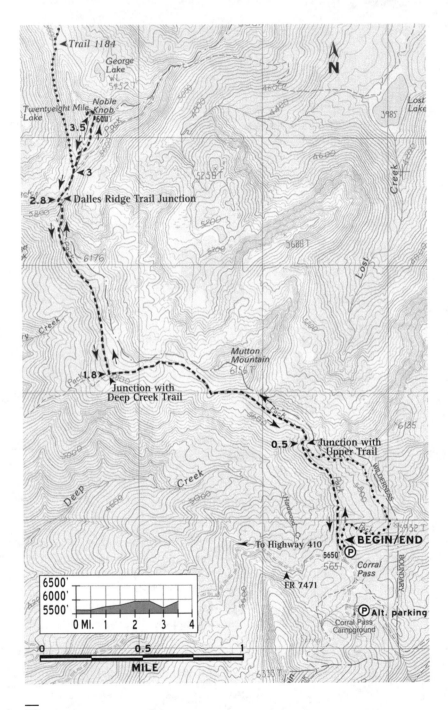

squadrons of horseflies won't trouble you. Either way, find the trail at the north end of the Noble Knob parking lot, or, if you are in the mood for an immediate climb to the broad ridge above, begin by following the old road to the east. Both trails join 0.5 mile north—but the trail that climbs east gains and loses several hundred feet and is longer by 0.5 mile, while the northerly trail simply traverses the mountainside.

The first 0.6 mile of the northerly trail traverses through a shady alpine forest before striking the junction with the upper trail. Keep left and walk on open hillside for 1.8 miles to the junction with the Deep Creek Trail. Stay right and hike along the ridge; drop to a wide, flat saddle; climb a steep hillside; and round another ridge to traverse to a rocky peak directly south of Noble Knob.

The trail rounds the peak and drops steeply to a switchback and junction with the Dalles Ridge Trail, 2.8 miles from the trailhead. Keep right and drop to the flat saddle below Noble Knob, directly to the north.

At 3.0 miles you'll find a junction with two trails at the flat saddle. Stay right at the first fork and, in 10 feet, left at the second fork. The trail to Noble Knob briefly climbs the west shoulder before switching back and, in a climbing traverse, circles the peak to the east and arrives at the summit from the north in 0.5 mile.

Just below the rocky summit there's a wide, flat campsite for picnics with a great mountain view, complete with a 10-foot rock scramble to the Knob itself.

GOING FARTHER

George Lake, directly below Noble Knob to the north, is the closest of several spots to cool off on a hot day. Follow the trail back to the three-way trail junction and turn right on the George Lake Trail, which traverses under the west side of Noble Knob.

At about 0.6 mile from the trail junction, look for a way trail leading right in 0.2 mile to the lake.

A great spot to read along the Tieton Meadows trail (#30).

WHITE PASS (US HIGHWAY 12)

29. Deer Lake

RATING	🚶 🚶
DISTANCE	4.2 miles round-trip
HIKING TIME	2 hours
ELEVATION GAIN	570 feet
HIGH POINT	5,000 feet
EFFORT	Easy Walk
BEST SEASON	Late summer, fall
PERMITS/CONTACT	Northwest Forest Pass required/Wenatchee National Forest, (509) 653-1401; www.fs.usda.gov/okawen
MAPS	USGS White Pass; Green Trails White Pass
NOTES	Leashed dogs welcome; great family hike; popular equestrian trail

THE HIKE

Expect to find a bunch of hikers with purple hands and faces on this forested walk, victims of huckleberry craving. This walk makes a pleasant destination and introduction to the Pacific Crest Trail.

GETTING THERE

From US Highway 12 at White Pass, drive east to an unsigned road just east of the White Pass parking strip on the north side of the highway. Turn north and follow the road to a junction with a road to the horse camp. Stay left and find the trailhead on the right at the south end of Leech Lake and the primitive White Pass Campground. The trailhead is 4,432 feet above sea level. GPS trailhead coordinates: N46°38.696'; W121°22.947'

THE TRAIL

While Leech, or White Pass, Lake is a popular destination for fly and catch-and-release anglers, little Deer Lake might be a great place for younger anglers who would like to catch-and-cook. The lake serves up both cutthroat and brook trout, although the best time to catch them—midsummer—is also the best time to be caught by the squadrons of

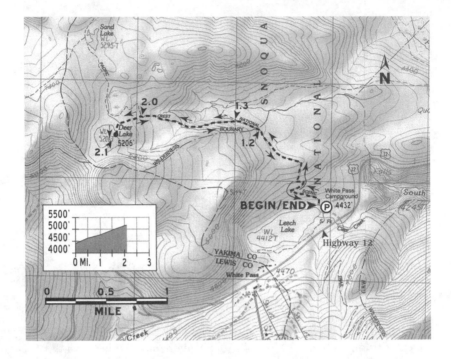

mosquitoes and blackflies that patrol the lake. For a bug-free hike, wait until the first frost, usually in early September.

The trail—the Pacific Crest Trail—climbs northeasterly through the forest at a moderate grade and makes several long switchbacks. You'll gain about 350 feet in the first mile before turning to the northwest and entering the William O. Douglas Wilderness, 1.2 miles from the trailhead. At 1.3 miles, you'll pass a junction with a path leading down to Dog Lake. Stay left and keep climbing gently through the evergreen forest and bushels of huckleberries. At 2.0 miles, you'll find a junction with the Deer Lake spur. Turn left and drop down to the lake, 2.1 miles from the trailhead. Campsites and good picnic spots are at the northwest end of the lake.

GOING FARTHER

The Pacific Crest Trail can take you all the way to Canada from here, but you likely won't be able to make it in a day. So if you want more exercise, I'd suggest you follow the trail another 0.9 mile and 300 feet to Sand Lake, a popular backcountry ski destination in winter. The round-trip distance would be 5.8 miles, with an elevation gain of 850 feet.

30. Tieton Meadows

RATING	🚶 🚶 🚶
DISTANCE	3.8 miles round-trip
HIKING TIME	2 hours
ELEVATION GAIN	200 feet
HIGH POINT	3,600 feet
EFFORT	Easy Walk
BEST SEASON	Summer, fall
PERMITS/CONTACT	Northwest Forest Pass required/Wenatchee National Forest, (509) 653-1401
MAPS	USGS White Pass; Green Trails White Pass
NOTES	Leashed dogs welcome; great family hike

THE HIKE

Tieton Meadows is among the easiest-reached backcountry alpine gardens in the Cascades, full of wildflowers in the summer and a quiet spot for watching wildlife in the fall.

GETTING THERE

From White Pass, drive east on US Highway 12 to Clear Lake Road (Forest Road 1200) and turn right. Drive 3 miles around Clear Lake to the North Fork Tieton Road (FR 1207). Turn right and follow it for 5 miles to the end of the road and the trailhead, 3,355 feet above sea level. GPS trailhead coordinates: N46°34.690′; W121°39.938′

THE TRAIL

It is difficult to imagine that the view just below the trailhead on the road is going to get any better, but it does. You're looking into the heart of the Goat Rocks Wilderness at Old Snowy Mountain, which—by no strange coincidence—holds snow on its northeasterly bowls through much of the summer, making it a popular destination for ski and snowboard diehards.

Wilderness pedestrians, on the other hand, will enjoy this hike in the summer for the wildflowers and in the fall for the chance to see or hear the Rocky Mountain elk that head for the low country (and feeding station) west of Naches. The meadows make an excellent destination for

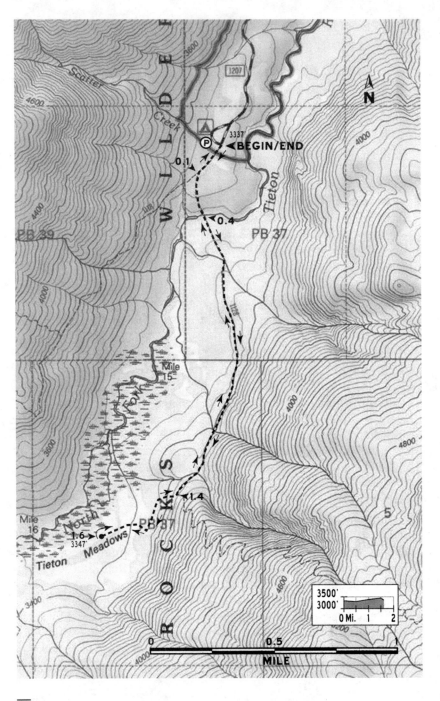

families with younger children who would like to spend a fall Saturday or Sunday getting acquainted with one of the most majestic animals on the planet.

The hike begins with a footbridge crossing and traverse through forest beside the North Fork of the Tieton River into a grassy meadow and trail junction, 0.1 mile from the trailhead. Stay left at the junction and ignore a faint way trail leading upstream. Follow the Tieton Meadows Trail No. 1128 as it drops gently to cross the North Fork on a footlog at 0.2 mile. Spring floodwaters sometimes wash the footlog crossing away, but it's usually replaced by fall; in any event, the stream here is easily forded.

Once across, the trail climbs a sidehill to the south and skirts the valley wetlands where you are likely to spot dozens of bird species and a mess of four-legged critters, from coyotes to the aforementioned elk. The trail traverses the hillside for about 1.4 miles, then turns left and begins a series of steep switchbacks to the south. Here is where you leave the main trail and continue to the right on a way trail that contours above the wetlands for 0.2 mile, then drops down to the riverside meadows. The trail disappears in the meadow, but you can walk upstream several hundred yards.

GOING FARTHER

If you're looking for exercise, return to the Tieton Meadows Trail and turn right. You'll get exercise until your calf muscles reach out and grab you by the throat, threatening to strangle you if you don't stop. The trail climbs in seemingly endless switchbacks for 3.4 miles and 2,800 vertical feet to a broad saddle above the Bear Creek valley—a lofty goal for hardbodies. The route then turns west and continues another 3 miles to Bear Creek Mountain, a round-trip killer hike of 16.6 miles.

31. Hogback Ridge

RATING	🚶 🚶
DISTANCE	8.0 miles round-trip
HIKING TIME	5 hours
ELEVATION GAIN	2,000 feet
HIGH POINT	6,400 feet
EFFORT	Prepare to Perspire
BEST SEASON	Fall
PERMITS/CONTACT	Northwest Forest Pass required/Gifford Pinchot National Forest, (360) 497-1100; www.fs.usda.gov/giffordpinchot
MAPS	USGS White Pass; Green Trails White Pass
NOTES	Leashed dogs welcome

THE HIKE

Here's a tough climb to a great viewpoint looking into the Goat Rocks Wilderness and east to the Tieton River valley and beyond, best hiked in the fall to avoid hordes of mosquitoes big enough to suck the blood from a full-grown elephant.

GETTING THERE

From US Highway 12 at White Pass, drive east to the east end of the White Pass winter sports area parking strip and turn right just beyond at a poorly marked road leading several hundred feet to the trailhead parking lot, 4,478 feet above sea level. GPS trailhead coordinates: N46°38.606'; W121°22.719'

THE TRAIL

There are two seasons to hike this trail, but only one if you aren't a cross-country skier. Once the autumn evening frost has driven the mosquitoes away, this trail to the high country around White Pass and the gateway to the splendid Goat Rocks Wilderness is a winner. Start as the Pacific Crest Trail 2000 crosses a stream on a footbridge and begins climbing through a mixed evergreen forest in switchbacks bordering the White Pass winter sports area. You'll climb to a low saddle as the forest thins and the trail drops slightly to tiny Ginnette Lake, 1.8 miles from

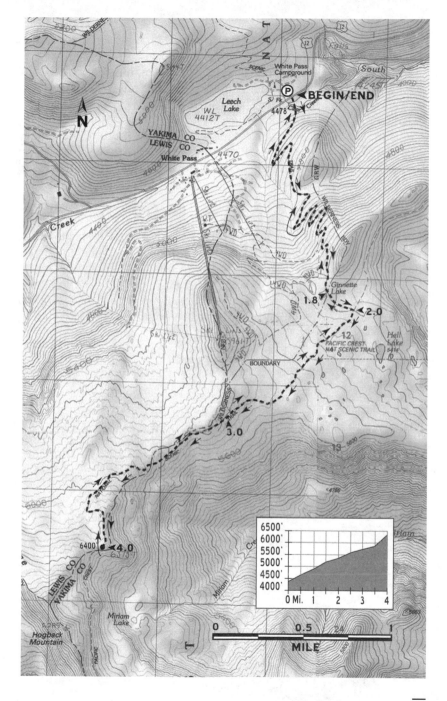

the trailhead. At **2.0** miles, you'll reach a junction with the Three Peaks Trail. Stay right and turn to the southwest through bear grass meadows and evergreens festooned with bright green lichens.

In 1.0 mile, you'll emerge on steep, rocky slopes to the south and find a way trail leading to the top of the express chair at White Pass. Stay to the left and walk along the crest of Hogback Ridge, just inside the boundary of the Goat Rocks Wilderness, to a 6,373-foot-high promontory and turnaround spot at **4.0** miles. Look to the south to Old Snowy Mountain and the Goat Rocks Wilderness, to the east to the Tieton River valley and Clear and Rimrock lakes, and beyond, to the apple orchards of Naches and Yakima.

GOING FARTHER
The Pacific Crest Trail heads south into Oregon and California before ending at the Mexican border, but it isn't likely you'll want to go that far in a day. Strong hikers might want to continue a mile or so along the Hogback Ridge to Hogback Mountain, 5.3 miles from the trailhead. For an even longer hike, continue another 1.2 miles to Shoe Lake, which—by a considerable stretch of the imagination—looks something like a shoe.

32. Dark Meadow

RATING	🧍 🧍
DISTANCE	6.0 miles round-trip
HIKING TIME	4 hours
ELEVATION GAIN	600 feet
HIGH POINT	4,400 feet
EFFORT	Moderate Workout
BEST SEASON	Summer, fall
PERMITS/CONTACT	Northwest Forest Pass required/Gifford Pinchot National Forest, (360) 497-1100; www.fs.usda.gov/giffordpinchot
MAPS	USGS McCoy Peak; Green Trails McCoy Peak
NOTES	Leashed dogs welcome

THE HIKE

This popular path is among the best wildflower hikes in the south Cascades, starting in deep forest and emerging in an alpine meadow with views to the surrounding snow giants of Mounts Adams and Rainier.

GETTING THERE

From US Highway 12 in Randle, turn south on Forest Road 25 and drive 1 mile to FR 23. Follow this mostly paved road for more than 24 miles to the junction with FR 2325. Turn right on FR 2325 and follow it 5.3 miles to the unmarked trailhead on the left, 3,950 feet above sea level. GPS trailhead coordinates: N46°16.537′; W121°44.611′

THE TRAIL

The toughest part of this hike is the first 0.5 mile, which climbs almost 600 feet on a poorly defined trail in the forest to a junction with a developed and maintained ridge crest trail about 4,600 feet above sea level. Turn right here, and follow the ridge trail another 0.5 mile to a junction with the Boundary Trail. Stay right on the Boundary Trail.

The final mile of this hike contours northerly under the steeper slopes of Dark Mountain to the west, rounds a sharp ridge, and drops into Dark Meadow. Acres of wildflowers put on a colorful show in the summer, and

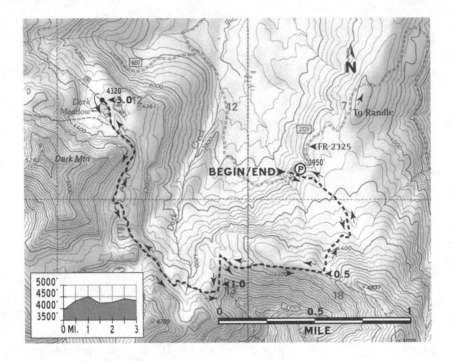

the trail meanders through the meadow for 0.5 mile before beginning to climb again—your opportunity for a picnic and turnaround.

The big mountains around you include Mount Adams to the east and Mount Rainier to the north.

GOING FARTHER

You can continue another 2.6 miles north on the Boundary Trail, climbing around 1,400 feet to the Dark Divide and following the ridge crest to Jumbo Peak, 5,801 feet above sea level.

33. Yellowjacket Pond

RATING	🚶 🚶 🚶
DISTANCE	4.4 miles round-trip
HIKING TIME	3 hours
ELEVATION GAIN	800 feet
HIGH POINT	4,640 feet
EFFORT	Moderate Workout
BEST SEASON	Fall
PERMITS/CONTACT	Northwest Forest Pass required/Mount St. Helens Volcanic Monument, (360) 247-3900; www.fs.usda.gov/mountsthelens
MAPS	USGS McCoy Peak; Green Trails McCoy Peak
NOTES	Leashed dogs welcome; good family hike

THE HIKE

This is a climb underneath a gnarly peak to a quiet mountain tarn surrounded by forest glades, below a high mountain pass.

GETTING THERE

From Cougar, 27 miles east of Interstate 5 on Highway 503, follow Forest Road 90 to its junction with FR 93 at the Lewis River Campground. Turn left on FR 93 and follow it to its junction with FR 9341. Turn right and follow FR 9341 to the trailhead on the left, 4,200 feet above sea level. GPS trailhead coordinates: N46°14.883'; W121°48.927'

THE TRAIL

Begin by climbing up the valley carved by Snagtooth Creek, which splashes off the trail below you on the left. After 0.25 mile, the trail swings to the east to climb more steeply through a wide forested gully, turning northwest 0.5 mile from the trailhead. The trail rounds a ridge and continues to climb around the rock-strewn northeast face of Snagtooth Mountain, above you to the left. Here are some terrific views of the big snow giants to the north and east.

You'll begin a descending traverse to a wide saddle to the north before climbing again underneath Hat Rock to the north and, at 1.8 miles, joining the Langille Ridge Trail. Turn left and climb a steep gully to the

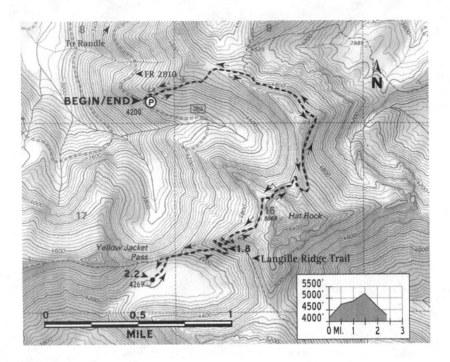

south, emerging at a flat meadow about 200 feet below Yellowjacket Pass. Look to the left for a short way trail leading to an unnamed pond, your turnaround point.

GOING FARTHER

For a longer hike, two options are possible: climb to Yellowjacket Pass and follow the trail 1.1 miles beyond to Craggy Peak, where you may see mountain goats; or return to the junction with the Langille Ridge Trail and walk up to 4 miles north, with views on the return of Mounts St. Helens and Adams.

34. Walupt Creek

RATING	🚶 🚶 🚶
DISTANCE	7.0 miles round-trip
HIKING TIME	4 hours, 30 minutes
ELEVATION GAIN	940 feet
HIGH POINT	4,800 feet
EFFORT	Prepare to Perspire
BEST SEASON	Summer, fall
PERMITS/CONTACT	Northwest Forest Pass required/Gifford Pinchot National Forest, (360) 497-1100; www.fs.usda.gov/giffordpinchot
MAPS	USGS Walupt Lake, Hamilton Butte; Green Trails Walupt Lake, Blue Lake
NOTES	Equestrians and leashed dogs welcome; great family hike

THE HIKE

Walk along the shore of a beautiful alpine lake and scramble along a tumbling creek before climbing to berry-filled meadows along the Pacific Crest Trail.

GETTING THERE

Turn south on Forest Road 25 off US Highway 12 in Randle and in 1 mile, turn left onto FR 23. Follow FR 23 to its junction with FR 21, about 2.5 miles south of Blue Lake Creek Campground. Turn left on FR 21 and follow it to FR 2160. Turn right and follow FR 2160 to the trailhead at Walupt Lake Campground, 3,940 feet above sea level. GPS trailhead coordinates: N46°25.387′; W121°28.277′

You can also reach the trailhead by turning south on Johnson Creek Road (FR 21) 2 miles west of Packwood on Highway 12 and driving 19 miles south to FR 2160—but this road is much rougher.

THE TRAIL

One of the nicest parts of this hike is the Walupt Lake Campground at the trailhead, which I think is one of the best campgrounds in Gifford Pinchot National Forest. Though few of the spots are right on the lakefront,

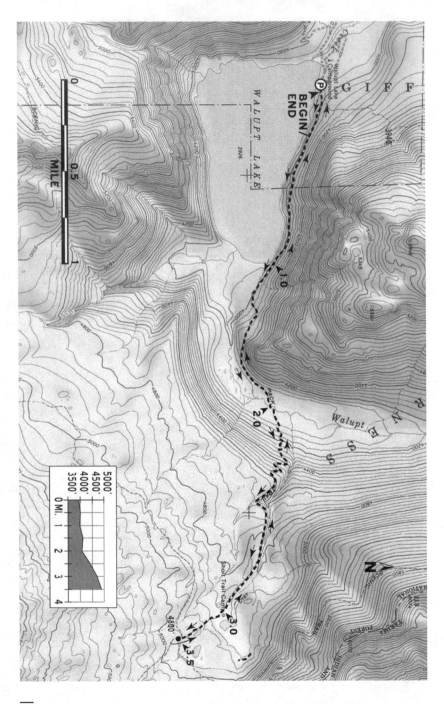

none are so far you'll blister your bare feet walking to the beach day-use area for a swim, a kayak or canoe paddle, or a float tube chase after a wily trout.

The trail follows the north shoreline of the lake for about 1.0 mile, passing several walk-in tent sites along the way. At the end of the lake, you'll climb under the steep south face of Nannie Ridge for another mile, crossing Walupt Creek at **2.0** miles. The climb gets steeper here, and the creek crossing might make a good turnaround spot for families with younger children. You'll switchback a couple of times above a steep gully, then climb into open meadows at **3.0** miles, heading southwest to a junction with the Pacific Crest Trail, **3.5** miles from the trailhead.

GOING FARTHER
The Pacific Crest Trail heads north for 4 miles to splendid Sheep Lake, although you needn't hike that far—walk as far as your legs and lungs want to go. In the event you do reach Sheep Lake, you might as well descend to the Walupt Lake trailhead by turning left on the Nannie Ridge Trail No. 98 and walking 4.4 miles. The Walupt Creek–Pacific Crest Trail–Nannie Ridge loop hike is 12 miles, with an elevation gain and loss of 1,800 feet.

Mount Rainier overlooks the trail to Berkeley Park (#37).

MOUNT RAINIER

Tahoma (the original Native American name for Mount Rainier) towers above all else in Washington, being the highest mountain in the state at 14,411 feet. A satellite survey a few years back generously gave the mountain another foot. Mount Rainier decorates our official license plate, although I would much rather see an image of the Columbia River, which better defines both sides of the state. The mountain is contained by one of the oldest national parks, established in 1899.

The hikes outlined here will give you different views of this snow giant and are the best you'll find in the park. Since pets are prohibited on park trails, I've included several hikes that serve up the flavor of the park without the bitter taste of the rule prohibiting dogs on park trails. You'll find them here and in the Chinook Pass Highway and White Pass Highway subsections within The Cascades section of this book.

A hiker pauses along the West Side Road (#35).

MOUNT RAINIER

35. West Side Road

RATING	🚶 🚶 🚶
DISTANCE	7.2 miles round-trip
HIKING TIME	3.5 hours
ELEVATION GAIN	675 feet
HIGH POINT	3,550 feet
EFFORT	Easy Walk
BEST SEASON	Fall, winter
PERMITS/CONTACT	Entrance fee/Nisqually Entrance Station, (360) 569-2211; www.nps.gov/mora
MAPS	USGS Mount Wow; Green Trails Mount Rainier West
NOTES	Bicyclists welcome; good family walk

THE HIKE

Walk up a gentle road to trailheads leading to the wild, remote side of the Big Mountain.

GETTING THERE

Drive 1 mile up Longmire-Paradise Road from the Nisqually Entrance Station and turn left onto West Side Road. Follow it 3.3 miles to the spot where a locked cable gate closes the road to the public, 2,875 feet above sea level. GPS trailhead coordinates: N46º46.053'; W121º52.697'

THE TRAIL

Though used frequently by park staff in cars, West Side Road is closed to the public because of safety concerns. Park officials say mudflows and floods so frequently spit from the South Tahoma Glacier that there is a danger of private vehicles and their passengers being trapped on the wrong side of a washout.

But here's the good news about West Side Road:

🚶 It makes a great hike for the whole family.

🚶 You can ride a mountain bike on the road for at least 7.5 miles one-way to trails that climb into alpine meadows of stunning beauty.

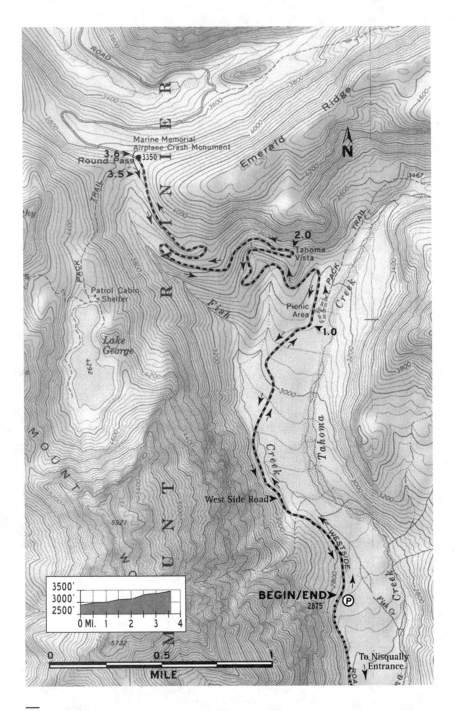

🏃 In winter, the road is gated just beyond its intersection with the Longmire-Paradise Road. When the snow level is below 2,000 feet, West Side Road provides an excellent family snowshoe or cross-country ski outing. When the snow level is higher, it would be difficult to find a quieter, more scenic winter walk.

The road climbs gently from the gate, first crossing a huge culvert and quarter-mile-long section of road built in 2000 after Fish Creek carved a new canyon down the middle of the old road. Just beyond the new road is a spectacular view of Mount Rainier and the Sunset Amphitheater, courtesy of the last tree-killing flood and mudflow from the South Tahoma Glacier. This is the best view of Mount Rainier you'll get on this hike.

The road continues to climb gently past a picnic area 1.0 mile from the parking area. This was the site of an old auto campground and trailhead to Emerald Ridge and Indian Henry's Hunting Ground. The way now switches back and begins climbing only slightly more steeply to Tahoma Vista, at the 2.0-mile mark. Today, Tahoma Vista fails to live up to its name because the forest has grown and obliterated the view of Rainier.

Continue climbing along the road past two more switchbacks to a huge parking area and turnaround spot at the Lake George trailhead, at 3.5 miles. You can walk another 0.1 mile on the road to view the Marine Memorial Airplane Crash Monument.

GOING FARTHER

Hikers seeking a longer walk can follow the Lake George Trail another mile to the lake or continue hiking the road another 0.7 mile to the South Puyallup trailhead, which leads in a very steep 4.8 miles to St. Andrews Park.

Strong, fast hikers and mountain bikers can continue past the South Puyallup trailhead for another 3.3 miles to the St. Andrews Ranger Station and trailhead, which leads uphill to splendid Klapatche Park in 2.6 steep miles.

Bicyclists can continue another 2 miles to Klapatche Point, where the road was closed more than three decades ago. The road originally continued 2 miles beyond Klapatche Point to the North Puyallup River, where a beautiful old stone bridge crosses the river to a former auto campground.

36. Eunice Lake

RATING	🚶 🚶 🚶
DISTANCE	4.4 miles round-trip
HIKING TIME	2 hours, 30 minutes
ELEVATION GAIN	620 feet
HIGH POINT	5,400 feet
EFFORT	Moderate Workout
BEST SEASON	Summer
PERMITS/CONTACT	Entrance fee/Carbon River Ranger Station, (360) 829-9639; www.nps.gov/mora
MAPS	USGS Carbon River; Green Trails Mount Rainier West
NOTES	Expect weekend crowds

THE HIKE

This walk to beautiful alpine meadows around a clear alpine lake could be one of the finest hikes in the park, except that part of the foot-worn trail is in horrid condition.

GETTING THERE

Take State Route 165 for 9 miles south of Wilkeson to its junction with Carbon River Road and follow it to the right. This road climbs in about 19.6 miles to the Mowich Entrance to Mount Rainier. Stay on 165 for 0.6 mile past the entrance to the big Paul Peak Picnic Area and trailhead, 3,700 feet above sea level. You'll find an unmanned station at the parking area where you can pay the park entrance fee if you don't have an annual pass.

Continue past the fee station for 5 miles to Mowich Lake. The Tolmie Peak trailhead, 4,950 feet above sea level, is located at the west end of the lake on the left, just as the road flattens above the lake. You can park alongside the north side of the road, or if you continue to the larger parking area at the east end of the lake, add about 0.6 mile round-trip to the hike. GPS trailhead coordinates: N46°55.970′; W121°51.820′

THE TRAIL

Your feet will insist this trail is longer than it really is, the result of a 0.5-mile climb up to Eunice Lake that is more root and mud than trail. Though it is often recommended as a good hike for families with small

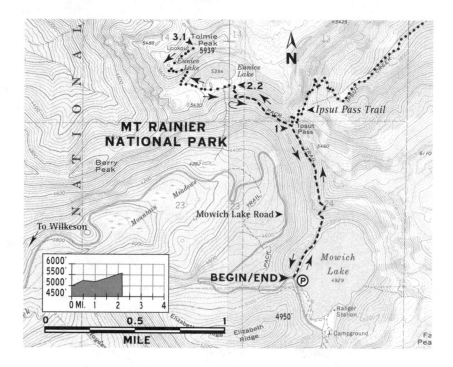

children, your kids might have more fun if you took them to a big tar pit and threw them in.

The meadows around Eunice Lake are a kaleidoscope of wildflowers, and the lake is a spectacular mirror for Mount Rainier. The hike begins with a walk along the west shoreline of Mowich Lake, with peekaboo views of Rainier and across the lake. The trail climbs in 0.2 mile to a low pass, then switches back and traverses through forest to the Ipsut Pass Trail junction, at 1.0 mile. Stay left at the junction (or for a good view of the Carbon River and Ipsut Creek valleys, you can follow the short trail to Ipsut Pass).

Back on the Tolmie Peak Trail, traverse underneath cliffs on a gentle descent for about 0.8 mile to a wide, wet gully where the trail switchbacks up to the meadows around Eunice Lake. Here the path widens and gets soggy, as hikers have attempted to circumnavigate slippery mud and roots, in some places carving little more than a wide dirt or mud road up the hillside.

This portion of the trail is short, however, and is easily forgotten once you reach the meadows around Eunice Lake, 2.2 miles from the trailhead. The lake is a good spot to picnic and turn around if you've brought the youngsters.

37. Berkeley Park

RATING	🚶 🚶 🚶
DISTANCE	7.8 miles round-trip
HIKING TIME	4 hours, 30 minutes
ELEVATION GAIN	1,600 feet
HIGH POINT	6,773 feet
EFFORT	Moderate Workout
BEST SEASON	Summer
PERMITS/CONTACT	Entrance fee/White River Wilderness Information Center, (360) 663-2273; www.nps.gov/mora
MAPS	USGS Sunrise; Green Trails Mount Rainier East
NOTES	Good family hike

THE HIKE

This walk to Berkeley Park takes you first up, then down, through alpine tundra to a wide meadow filled with just about every wildflower on Mount Rainier.

GETTING THERE

Follow White River Road 14 miles from the White River Entrance Station to Sunrise. The trailhead begins on the north side of the parking lot at the paved access to the Sourdough Ridge Trail, 6,385 feet above sea level. GPS trailhead coordinates: N46°54.877′; W121°38.540′

THE TRAIL

Sunrise gets mighty crowded in the late summer, but the meadows of Berkeley Park might not be visited as frequently because day hikers have so many trails from which to choose. Since the walk to Berkeley involves a steady, 800-foot climb on the way home, fewer hikers might go there.

Regardless, there's plenty of view- and wildflower-watching to share with anyone you encounter. Begin by climbing from the trailhead to a junction with the Sourdough Ridge Trail, at 0.1 mile. Keep left at the junction and climb briefly in another 0.1 mile to a junction with the Huckleberry Creek Trail. Stay left here and continue along the Sourdough Ridge toward Frozen Lake, 1.4 miles from the trailhead.

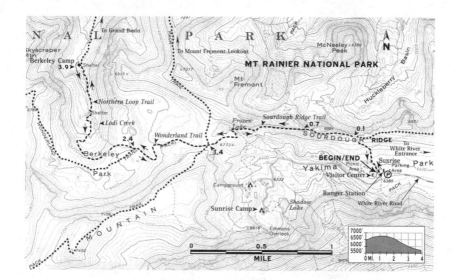

Just before getting a view of Frozen Lake—the Sunrise reservoir and high point of this hike—you'll strike a junction with trails leading every which way. Follow the Wonderland Trail as it heads west from the junction past Frozen Lake, on your right, and begins to descend gently under the cliffs of Burroughs Mountain. Crumbled parts of the mountain decorate the hillside on your left as you descend, and you'll hear pikas squeaking *knee* from the rocks beside the trail.

Continue to descend into a wide, flat meadow at 2.4 miles to a junction with the Northern Loop Trail. Turn right on the Northern Loop Trail and follow it as it descends more steeply into Berkeley Park, the valley formed by Lodi Creek. Above the flower-filled valley is Mount Fremont on the right and Skyscraper Mountain on the left.

The trail winds through the valley for about a mile before entering the subalpine forest and, at 3.9 miles, passing Berkeley Camp. This is the turnaround point for day hikers.

GOING FARTHER

Strong hikers who don't mind climbing 1,500 vertical feet back to the trailhead should consider continuing past Berkeley Camp for another 3 miles to Grand Park, a mile-long meadow flat as a pancake griddle with a splendid view of Mount Rainier on the return trip. The trail first climbs, then descends past the camp, leveling off and striking the Lake Eleanor Trail junction 6.9 miles from the trailhead. Follow the Lake Eleanor Trail to the right into Grand Park.

38. Paradise Trails

RATING	🥾 🥾 🥾 🥾 🥾
DISTANCE	4- to 5-mile loops
HIKING TIME	3–4 hours
ELEVATION GAIN	1,000–1,400 feet
HIGH POINT	6,400–6,800 feet
EFFORT	Moderate Workout–Knee-Punishing
BEST SEASON	Summer, fall
PERMITS/CONTACT	Entrance fee required/Longmire Wilderness Information Center, (360) 569-4453; www.nps.gov/mora
MAPS	USGS Mount Rainier West; Green Trails Paradise
NOTES	Dogs prohibited; expect crowds

THE HIKE

These are two of the very best day hikes to be found in the Paradise area of Mount Rainier National Park. Midsummer wildflowers are spectacular, the view of the state's highest mountain inspires awe, and you can rub elbows with Real Mountain Climbers.

GETTING THERE

From Interstate 5 in Tacoma, take the Highway 7 exit 133 south to Elbe and Highway 706. Follow Highway 706 east through Ashford to the Nisqually Entrance Station of Mount Rainier National Park, where the entry fee will be collected, and continue past Longmire to Paradise. Park in the big lot just west of Paradise Lodge, 5,400 feet above sea level. GPS trailhead coordinates: N46°47.162′; W121°44.099′

To bypass the urban areas of Tacoma, Parkland, and Spanaway, continue north on I-5 in Tacoma and take Highway 512, exit 127, south for 0.2 mile to the Steele Street exit. Turn left on Steele Street and follow it to Spanaway Loop Road. Follow Spanaway Loop Road back to Highway 7 on the southern outskirts of Spanaway.

THE TRAIL

Paradise is one of the most popular outdoor recreation destinations in the state, so there is virtually no time when you will have the trail or

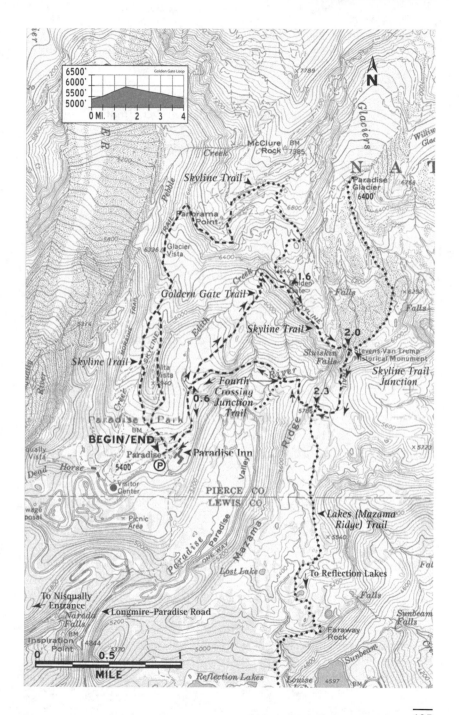

the view all to yourself. That is of little consequence, because there's plenty of view and trail for everyone. A number of trails radiate from the big parking area, and almost all begin at the stone steps just west of the restrooms.

You can combine a number of trails for loop hikes; if you're looking for a really strenuous workout, follow the climbers' route 5 miles and 5,000 vertical feet up to 10,000-foot-high Camp Muir, the high camp where the Real Mountain Climbers congregate. This hike usually takes me five hours up and about three hours down; put that in perspective by knowing that in 2008, some hardbody climbed to the summit of Rainier from Paradise and returned in just over two hours.

Two easier but nonetheless spectacular hikes in Paradise are the 4-mile hike to Golden Gate and the 5-mile climb to Panorama Point, which Real Mountain Climbers call Pan Point. Whenever I climb up to Camp Muir (in five hours), I call it Panting Point.

Anyway, for the Golden Gate loop, follow the paved Skyline Trail northeast from the parking area as it skirts above the remodeled Paradise Lodge, rounds a forested ridge, and climbs through an alpine meadow that is filled with every imaginable wildflower. You'll climb from a bench at 0.6 mile to a bridge across Myrtle Falls, which tumble down a deep canyon to the Paradise Creek valley to the east. Cross the bridge to a junction with the Golden Gate Trail and turn right.

The Golden Gate Trail climbs through the Edith Creek Basin, strewn with huge boulders, decorated with green moss, and blanketed by wildflowers that give way to the purple and orange of huckleberry and partridge foot in the fall. You'll climb toward the headwall of the valley for 0.7 mile, then switchback to a notch at the top of the basin. This is Golden Gate, with spectacular views to the south of the Tatoosh Range, the high point of your hike.

Just beyond, at 1.6 miles, you'll strike a junction with the Skyline Trail. Turn right here and descend, steeply at first, into a basin to cross a tributary of Paradise Creek, then follow the ridge past Sluiskin Falls to a junction with the Mazama Ridge Trail. Turn right and traverse the upper Paradise Valley to close the loop at Myrtle Falls. Stay left and drop back to the parking area.

For the more strenuous 5-mile loop, take the Skyline Trail to the northwest or the Alta Vista Trail to the north. Both climb into meadows, with the Alta Vista Trail climbing over the top of the sharp 5,900-foot peak to the north, west of the Edith Creek Basin. The trails rejoin on the north side of Alta Vista. They continue as the Skyline Trail past Glacier Vista, which—by no strange coincidence—offers a great view down onto the blue crevasses of the Nisqually Glacier. Turn right at **1.6** miles, climb the trail around a ledge past Panorama Point, 6,700 feet above sea level, and contour around the upper Edith Creek Basin, then descend to the junction with the Golden Gate Trail, **3.4** miles from the trailhead.

Turn right at the junction and follow the Golden Gate Trail as it drops steeply, first in switchbacks, through Edith Creek Basin to Myrtle Falls, at **4.4** miles. Keep right at the junction with the Skyline Trail and drop to the parking area.

GOING FARTHER

If you don't plan on joining the Real Mountain Climbers at Camp Muir, you can make a longer loop hike of about 6 miles by combining the two loops and following the Skyline Trail. For a tougher workout, follow the trail that leads from Sluiskin Falls on the Skyline Trail loop for a mile up to the melting Paradise Glacier and Paradise Ice Caves. Combined with the Skyline loop, this would be a hike of 8 miles.

39. Pinnacle Saddle

RATING	🚶 🚶 🚶
DISTANCE	3.0 miles round-trip
HIKING TIME	3 hours
ELEVATION GAIN	1,200 feet
HIGH POINT	5,840 feet
EFFORT	Prepare to Perspire
BEST SEASON	Fall
PERMITS/CONTACT	Entrance fee required/Longmire Wilderness Information Center, (360) 569-4453; www.nps.gov/mora
MAPS	USGS Mount Rainier West; Green Trails Paradise
NOTES	Dogs prohibited

THE HIKE

This climb to a great vista of Mount Rainier to the north and Mount Adams to the south may not be quite as crowded as the hikes around Paradise, yet it yields fine wildflower meadows and a great picnic spot.

GETTING THERE

From Interstate 5 in Tacoma, take the Highway 7 exit 133 south to Elbe and Highway 706. Follow Highway 706 east through Ashford to the Nisqually Entrance Station of Mount Rainier National Park, where the entry fee will be collected, and continue past Longmire to Paradise. Drive past the Paradise parking lot to the one-way Stevens Canyon Road connector at the east end of the lot and drive through Paradise Valley to the Stevens Canyon Road. Turn left and follow it to the Reflection Lakes parking areas and trailhead, 4,850 feet above sea level. GPS trailhead coordinates: N46°46.097´; W121°43.885´

To bypass the urban areas of Tacoma, Parkland, and Spanaway, continue north on I-5 in Tacoma and take Highway 512, exit 127, south for 0.2 mile to the Steele Street exit. Turn left on Steele Street and follow it to Spanaway Loop Road. Follow Spanaway Loop Road back to Highway 7 on the southern outskirts of Spanaway.

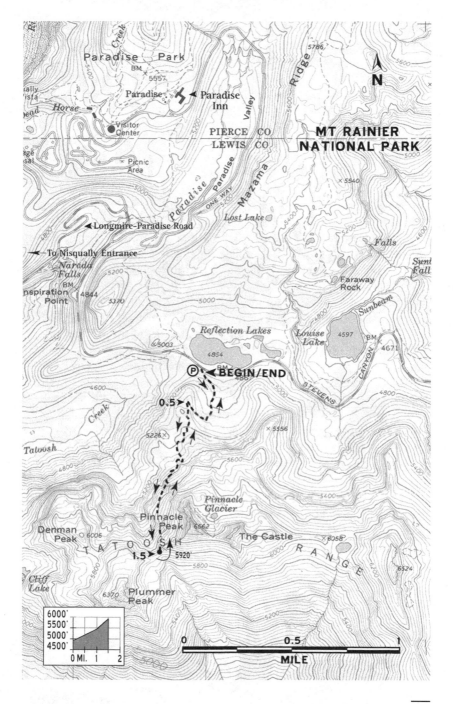

THE TRAIL

This hike begins at a trailhead on the south side of the Stevens Canyon Road, near the western end of the largest Reflection Lake. It climbs north in alpine forest and slopes covered by white heather and avalanche lilies. At 0.5 mile, the trail makes a broad switchback and begins to climb more steeply, following a rugged ridge in steps to a wide bowl between Pinnacle Peak on the right and Plummer Peak to the left. You'll climb past rock gardens tended by those tiny farmers, pikas, which squeak *knee!* from their rocky perches and in the fall can be seen gathering grass for the coming winter. These cousins of the rabbit don't hibernate; instead, they collect grasses for drying and storing as winter food.

The trail traverses these rock gardens, which often hold steep snowfields through much of the summer, perhaps discouraging casual hikers. Though wilderness pedestrians in the autumn won't be rewarded with spectacular wildflower displays, they won't suffer from a lack of color—fall is exceptional around Mount Rainier. The climb ends at the flat saddle between Plummer and Pinnacle peaks, two of several 6,000-plus-foot mountains in the Tatoosh Range. Other mountains in the range include Unicorn, the far mountain to the southeast, and Castle, which—by no strange coincidence—looks something like a castle, to the left of Unicorn.

The saddle is the end of the maintained trail; route- and rock-climbing skills are necessary to follow the rough way trail up the rocky wall to the summit of Pinnacle Peak. Take it from a Real Mountain Climber (retired), the view isn't any better up there. Look north for a splendid photo op of Rainier and 11,000-foot Little Tahoma to the right; look south across the Cowlitz River valley to Mount Adams.

GOING FARTHER

The best way to get more exercise on this hike is to return to the parking area and walk east on the road to the eastern end of the Reflection Lakes; there, take the path that contours above Louise Lake and joins the Mazama Ridge Trail at 0.2 mile. Stay left and climb through alpine forest for 1 mile to an alpine tarn and a 5,210-foot-high overlook named Faraway Rock, even though it is only 1 mile from the trailhead.

40. Spray Park

RATING	🚶 🚶 🚶
DISTANCE	7.0 miles round-trip
HIKING TIME	4 hours, 30 minutes
ELEVATION GAIN	1,800 feet
HIGH POINT	6,400 feet
EFFORT	Prepare to Perspire
BEST SEASON	Summer
PERMITS/CONTACT	Self-issue entry fee required/Carbon River Ranger Station, (360) 829-9639; www.nps.gov/mora
MAPS	USGS Mount Rainier West, Green Trails Mount Rainier West
NOTES	Dogs prohibited

THE HIKE

The hike to Spray Park is one of the best wilderness walks in Mount Rainier National Park: you'll climb from deep forest to alpine meadows and close-up views of the north face of The Mountain.

GETTING THERE

From Interstate 5 north in Tacoma, take the Puyallup River Road (Highway 167) at exit 135, and follow it through Puyallup, crossing the Puyallup River, to Highway 410. Stay right on Highway 410 and drive past Bonney Lake to Buckley. Turn south on Highway 165 at Buckley and drive through Wilkeson and Carbonado, crossing the high Carbon River Bridge. Just beyond, turn right on Mowich Lake Road and follow it 12 miles to the Mount Rainier National Park boundary, where you'll be asked to issue yourself a park entrance fee. Continue on the road for 5 bumpy miles to Mowich Lake. The trailhead, 4,800 feet above sea level, is located on the north side of the road near the tent campsites. GPS trailhead coordinates: N46°55.962′; W121°51.817′

THE TRAIL

Popular with wildflower-gazers and summertime skiers and boarders, this classic hike might be slightly less crowded than the trails around

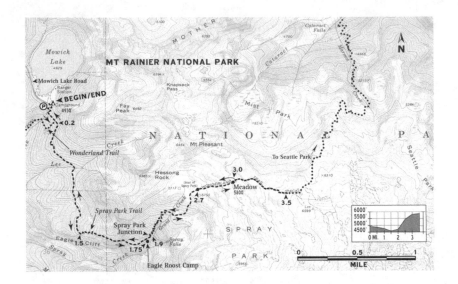

Paradise or Sunrise. The rough gravel Highway 165 to Mowich Lake and the lack of "civilized" facilities discourage some folks, while others appreciate the primitive surroundings and the beauty of a subalpine lake that can be reached by automobile.

Your hike begins with a steep switchback descent to cross Crater Creek, the Mowich Lake outlet, then winds down through the deep forest to a junction with the Wonderland Trail, at about 0.2 mile. Stay left as the trail begins a gentle climb along a forested hillside and passes the Eagle overlook campsites on the left at about 1.5 miles. In another 0.2 mile, you'll find a junction with a side trail leading to Spray Falls. It's a 0.5-mile round-trip to a view of the falls; I usually visit them on my return from Spray Park.

The serious climbing begins at this junction. Turn left and head upward in short switchbacks that might yield good views down to Spray Falls. The forest grows thinner, and at about 2.7 miles, you'll cross Grant Creek and enter the alpine country. Look to the left to 6,385-foot Hessong Rock and to the south at the north face of Mount Rainier. The trail climbs in benches around a tarn and across meadows, eventually reaching a rocky spine and often year-round snowfield that leads south to Observation and Echo rocks and the Flett Glacier. This snowfield is about 3.5 miles from the trailhead, a good picnic spot and turnaround point.

41. Glacier View

RATING	🚶 🚶 🚶 🚶
DISTANCE	5.8 miles round-trip
HIKING TIME	3 hours, 30 minutes
ELEVATION GAIN	1,000 feet
HIGH POINT	5,450 feet
EFFORT	Moderate Workout
BEST SEASON	Summer
PERMITS/CONTACT	Northwest Forest Pass required; free Wilderness Use Permit at trailhead/ Packwood Ranger District, (360) 497-1100; www.fs.usda.gov/giffordpinchot
MAPS	USGS Mount Wow; Green Trails Mount Rainier West
NOTES	Leashed dogs welcome

THE HIKE

Walk along a forested ridge with views of Mount Rainier to the east and Mount St. Helens to the southwest, to an airy site of a fire lookout with an unbeatable view of the west face of Tahoma.

GETTING THERE

Follow Highway 706 east from Ashford for 3.1 miles to Forest Road 59, on the left. You'll see a Mount Tahoma Trail Association access sign near the junction. Turn left on FR 59 and follow it 9 miles up and over a pass with a spectacular view of Rainier, to the gated road closure and trailhead, 4,750 feet above sea level. GPS trailhead coordinates: N46°46.405'; W121°56.674'

THE TRAIL

This hike begins in the shade of an old forest, where you'll climb 100 feet in less than 0.1 mile to a trail junction on the ridge crest. Turn left here, on Trail 267, and follow it as it climbs into the sunshine of a logged area on the west.

At 0.5 mile, you'll find an opening in the forest that frames Rainier between silver snags and likely wonder whether the view can get any

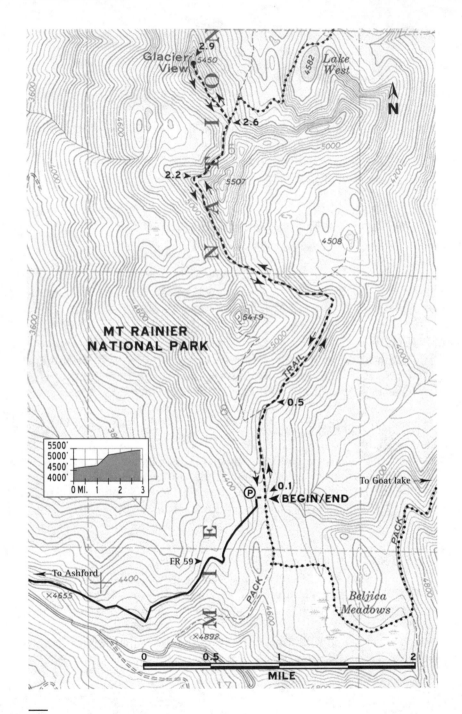

better at Glacier View, your destination. It doesn't, but you drove all this way for some exercise, right?

Continue climbing a gentle grade as the trail traverses to the east around a 5,600-foot peak and angles back to a forested saddle, traversing under a second 5,500-foot peak. Look southwest through openings in the trees for a view of Mount St. Helens.

The trail alternately traverses steep meadows, hillside forest, and under cliffs. At 2.2 miles, you'll cross a ridge and descend to a saddle and trail junction at 2.6 miles. Turn left here and climb the steepest section of the trail for 0.3 mile to the old lookout site.

A flat campsite to the right of the trail, just short of the open rock summit, might be the best picnic spot. The features best seen from here include the Sunset Amphitheater, Tahoma and Puyallup glaciers, and Success Cleaver. The trail ends on the summit rock, unless you brought your hang glider.

GOING FARTHER

On a hot summer day, the cold waters of Lake West might make a refreshing stop. Return 0.3 mile to the trail junction and turn left. The trail drops steeply for 0.1 mile to a junction with the Lake Helen Trail. Keep right and continue the steep 600-foot descent to the lake, another 0.7 mile.

42. Comet Falls

RATING	🚶 🚶
DISTANCE	3.8 miles round-trip
HIKING TIME	3 hours
ELEVATION GAIN	1,000 feet
HIGH POINT	4,600 feet
EFFORT	Prepare to Perspire
BEST SEASON	Summer, fall
PERMITS/CONTACT	Entrance fee required/Longmire Wilderness Information Center, (360) 569-4453; www.nps.gov/mora
MAPS	USGS Mount Rainier West, Green Trails Mount Rainier West
NOTES	Dogs prohibited

THE HIKE

This is a steady climb to a view of one of the prettiest waterfalls in Mount Rainier National Park.

GETTING THERE

From Interstate 5 in Tacoma, take the Highway 7 exit 133 south to Elbe and Highway 706. Follow Highway 706 east through Ashford to the Nisqually Entrance Station of Mount Rainier National Park, where the entry fee will be collected, and continue 10.7 miles, passing Longmire to the trailhead on the left side of the road, 3,600 feet above sea level. GPS trailhead coordinates: N46°46.742'; W121°46.938'

To bypass the urban areas of Tacoma, Parkland, and Spanaway, continue north on I-5 in Tacoma and take Highway 512, exit 127, south for 0.2 mile to the Steele Street exit. Turn left on Steele Street and follow it to Spanaway Loop Road. Follow Spanaway Loop Road back to Highway 7 on the southern outskirts of Spanaway.

THE TRAIL

You'll start up a steep, rock-lined trail into the forest beside Christine Falls, which plummet under the Longmire-to-Paradise Road. The trail flattens and turns to cross a bridge just above the falls at 0.3 mile, giving

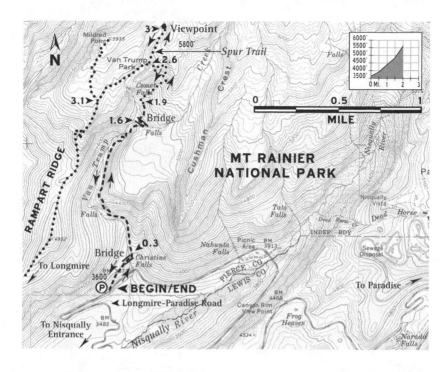

you a view to the tumbling water, then turns again and begins a long climb above Van Trump Creek. The watercourse was named for P. B. Van Trump, the dude who made the first successful climb of Mount Rainier with Hazard Stevens in 1870.

The route continues to climb at a steady pace and after about 1.0 mile begins switching back to climb a ridge below Cushman Crest. At 1.5 miles, you'll turn up a valley and cross a bridge with views of a cascade to the northeast; then you'll cross a low ridge, arriving at a great view of 320-foot-high Comet Falls, which—as you might guess—resemble the tail of a comet. This viewpoint is 1.9 miles from the trailhead.

GOING FARTHER

From the first falls viewpoint, the trail climbs the steep slope beside the falls, switching back a couple of times and gaining another 300 feet in less than 0.5 mile, then circles through lower Van Trump Park and climbs another mile in meadows. The trail turns to the west and crosses Van Trump Creek to join a trail that climbs about 0.5 mile to Mildred Point, about 1.5 miles one-way beyond the falls viewpoint.

Mount Adams and Takhlakh Lake (#44).

MOUNT ADAMS

If you like alpine hiking under skies that are more likely to be blue than those you'll find farther west, I'd recommend the north and south slopes of 12,276-foot Klickitat, also known as Mount Adams. This snow giant basks in the sunshine on the east side of the Cascades and its trails are relatively quiet, in contrast to the throngs of hikers that visit Mount Rainier and Mount St. Helens. It's probably the easiest big mountain in the state to climb, but the trails around the peak are what make it popular with hikers and equestrians in the summer and hunters and berry pickers in the fall. Check out the following pathways, the best easy hikes Mount Adams has to offer.

Marsh marigold along the Bird Creek Meadows trail (#43).

MOUNT ADAMS

43. Bird Creek Meadows

RATING	🚶 🚶 🚶
DISTANCE	7.0 miles round-trip
HIKING TIME	4 hours
ELEVATION GAIN	950 feet
HIGH POINT	6,300 feet
EFFORT	Prepare to Perspire
BEST SEASON	Summer, fall
PERMITS/CONTACT	Northwest Forest Pass required/Mount Adams Ranger District, (509) 395-3400; www.fs.usda.gov/giffordpinchot
MAPS	USGS Mount Adams West; Green Trails Mount Adams West
NOTES	Leashed dogs welcome; good family walk

THE HIKE
The climb to Bird Creek Meadows yields beautiful views, summer snow-fields for cooling play, and alpine wildflowers until late summer.

GETTING THERE
From Trout Lake, drive north on Forest Road 23 for 1.3 miles to the Y junction with FR 80. Turn right on FR 80 and drive 4.3 miles to a junction with FR 8040. Stay right on FR 8040 for 5.2 miles to Morrison Creek, bear right, and follow FR 8040-500 for 2.8 miles to the Cold Springs trailhead, 5,600 feet above sea level. GPS trailhead coordinates: N46°08.150′; W121°29.673′

THE TRAIL
Climb in sunny pine forest up the southern slopes of 12,276-foot Mount Adams, a rock-pocked volcano. The first 1.2 miles of this trail is the beginning of the South Climb route, so expect to share the path with Real Mountain Climbers. The steepest part of this climb is the first mile, which was once a road leading to the old Timberline Campground, used by pack trains that headed all the way to the summit of the mountain.

You'll climb through forest that grows increasingly sparse to a junction with the Round the Mountain Trail No. 9, which—as you might guess—

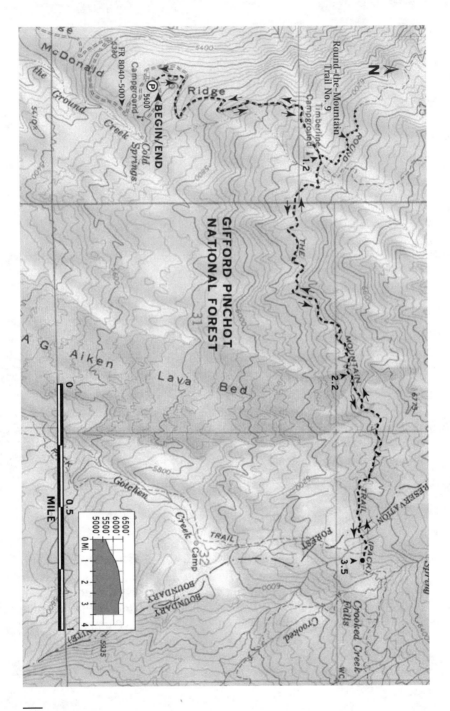

goes round the mountain. At least, that is what I guessed, and as usual, I was wrong. The trail actually only goes partway, and once you reach the Yakama Nation's section of the mountain, you'd best have permission to hike cross-country. The trail junction might make a good turnaround spot for families with young children.

Anyway, hang a right on the (not-so-) Round the Mountain Trail and walk through alpine meadows, volcanic sand, rock gardens, and sparse pine woods. Look up at Mount Adams and south across the White Salmon River valley to the Columbia Gorge and Wy'East—Mount Hood—beyond. The trail crosses a number of snowfields that could be present far into July, but the route is easy to follow. At about 2.2 miles, cross the upper tip of the Aiken Lava Bed, a crumpled basalt river of rock that flows down the mountain to the south. The trail descends briefly, climbs back through a sparse pine forest, and crosses the marked boundary with the Yakama Reservation. The junction with the Gotchen Creek Trail, 3.5 miles from the trailhead, is your turn-around spot.

GOING FARTHER

You can descend the Gotchen Creek Trail for 1 mile and about 300 vertical feet to a campsite along the creek, making a round-trip hike of 9 miles.

44. Takhlakh Lake Loop

RATING	🚶 🚶 🚶 🚶
DISTANCE	3.0 miles round-trip
HIKING TIME	2 hours
ELEVATION GAIN	100 feet
HIGH POINT	4,460 feet
EFFORT	Stroll in the Park
BEST SEASON	Summer, early fall
PERMITS/CONTACT	Northwest Forest Pass required/Mount Adams Ranger District, (509) 395-3400; www.fs.usda.gov/giffordpinchot
MAPS	USGS Mount Adams West; Green Trails Blue Lake
NOTES	Leashed dogs welcome; great family hike

THE HIKE

Surely one of the best photo ops for catching Mount Adams reflected in a clear mountain lake, the hike around Takhlakh is a great walk in the evening or early morning.

GETTING THERE

Turn south on Forest Road 25 off US Highway 12 in Randle and in 1 mile, turn left onto FR 23. Drive 22 miles on paved road and about 10 miles on gravel road to FR 2329. Turn left on paved FR 2329 and drive 1 mile to the Takhlakh Lake Campground, which has parking in the day-use area, 4,460 feet above sea level. GPS trailhead coordinates: N46°16.593'; W121°35.950'

THE TRAIL

The Takhlakh Lake Campground makes an ideal starting point for this easy walk, as well as a base camp for other hikes in the high country around Mount Adams. The RV spots are in the woods, for the most part, but the walk-in tent sites on the north side of the lake yield some of the finest mountain views to be found anywhere. Snow lingers on the north side of Adams, so plan to camp here after mid-June—and call ahead to make certain the campground is open.

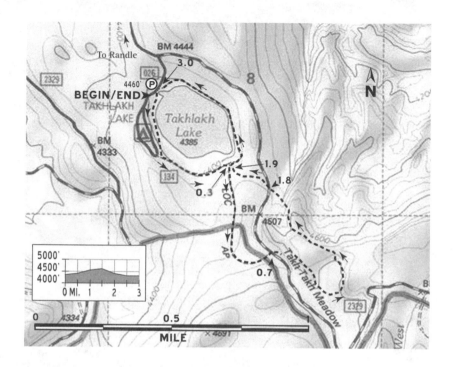

Begin this walk on the west side of the lake and walk along the shore to the east. The trail passes six or seven RV sites but is distant enough that you needn't worry about invading someone's privacy. Walk east around the lake along the shore and through evergreen forest to a trail junction at the southeast end of the lake, 0.3 mile from the trailhead. Turn right here, and climb through huckleberry bushes forever. If you'd like purple hands and faces, plan to visit around the third week in August. Stay right at a trail junction in 0.1 mile, which is your return trail to the lake.

At 0.7 mile, you'll turn to the east again and cross Forest Road 2329 to a find a big basalt rib of black rock sticking out of the meadow like the fin of a giant shark. It's a great place for scrambling and exploring, but the rock gets egg-frying hot in summer. The route meanders through Takh Takh Meadow to the north and at 1.8 miles, recrosses FR 2329 and descends to the junction with the lake trail, 1.9 miles from the trailhead. Turn right and follow the lakeshore to the north for another mile. The northeast shore of the lake unveils awesome views of the north face of Mount Adams. You'll be looking right into the bowl carved by the Adams Glacier and perhaps an ancient explosive eruption like the one at Mount St. Helens in 1980.

45. West Fork Trail

RATING	🚶 🚶 🚶
DISTANCE	5.0 miles, round-trip
HIKING TIME	4 hours
ELEVATION GAIN	1,300 feet
HIGH POINT	6,000 feet
EFFORT	Moderate Workout
BEST SEASON	Summer
PERMITS/CONTACT	Northwest Forest Pass required; Gifford Pinchot National Forest, (509) 395-3400; www.fs.usda.gov/giffordpinchot
MAPS	USGS Green Mountain, Mount Adams West; Green Trails Blue Lake, Mount Adams West
NOTES	Equestrians and leashed dogs welcome; good family hike

THE HIKE

Take this moderate climb to an eye-popping view of the Adams Glacier, so close you can hear rockfall and the grinding of ice tumbling down the north face of the state's second-highest volcano into a frozen river.

GETTING THERE

Turn south on Forest Road 25 off US Highway 12 in Randle and in 1 mile, turn left onto FR 23. Drive 22 miles on paved road and about 10 miles on gravel road to FR 2329. Turn left on paved FR 2329 and follow it past Takhlakh Lake Campground for 3.5 miles to the West Fork trailhead on the right, 4,700 feet above sea level. GPS trailhead coordinates: N46°16.156′; W121°34.715′

THE TRAIL

This makes an excellent hike for wilderness pedestrians camped at Takhlakh Lake Campground or any of the other Forest Service campgrounds nearby. It's a moderate climb through open pine forest and meadowland shining with wildflowers in the summer; there are incredible views of Mount Adams on the way up and Mount Rainier on the way down.

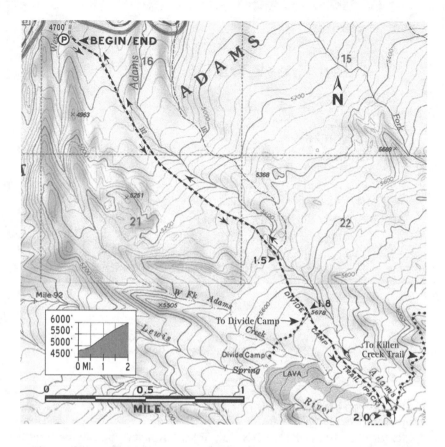

The trail is typical of routes on the lower slopes of Northwest volcanoes, beginning with a gradual grade and increasing in steepness as you head for higher ground. This trail climbs to the southwest, ascending directly toward the mighty cracks and crevasses of the Adams Glacier. The path stays on a round ridge just above the crashing West Fork of Adams Creek, which in the summer is usually gray with glacial flour from the massive icefall's frigid mouth. You'll begin to climb more steeply at about 1.5 miles, and at 1.8 miles, you'll find a fork in the trail. To the right is Divide Camp; you'll stay left and continue climbing another 0.2 mile to your turnaround spot at a junction with the Pacific Crest Trail.

Return the way you came, but visit Divide Camp, 0.5 mile from its junction with the West Fork tail, on the way down.

46. Killen Creek Trail

RATING	🚶 🚶 🚶 🚶 🚶
DISTANCE	6.2 miles round-trip
HIKING TIME	4 hours
ELEVATION GAIN	1,520 feet
HIGH POINT	6,100 feet
EFFORT	Moderate Workout
BEST SEASON	Summer, fall
PERMITS/CONTACT	Northwest Forest Pass required/Gifford Pinchot National Forest, (509) 395-3400; www.fs.usda.gov/giffordpinchot
MAPS	USGS Mount Adams West; Green Trails Mount Adams
NOTES	Equestrians and leashed dogs welcome

THE HIKE
For scenery, wildflowers, berry-picking, wildlife-watching, or just plain working up a sweat, this might be one of the best easy day hikes in the Washington Cascades.

GETTING THERE
Turn south on Forest Road 25 off US Highway 12 in Randle and in 1 mile, turn left onto FR 23. Drive 22 miles on paved road and about 10 miles on gravel road to FR 2329. Turn left on paved FR 2329 and follow it past Takhlakh Lake Campground, where it turns to gravel, for 6 miles to the Killen Creek trailhead on the right, 4,580 feet above sea level. GPS trailhead coordinates: N46°17.308´; W121°33.151´

THE TRAIL
Popular with equestrians and hikers alike, the Killen Creek Trail to Adams Creek Meadows serves up lush alpine greenery set apart by summer snowfields. You'll climb toward the ice-wrinkled face of the mountain Native Americans called Klickitat on the way up and return with the mountain they called Tahoma filling the northern horizon. Deer and elk graze in the meadows and head to snowfields to cool off and keep the bugs at bay.

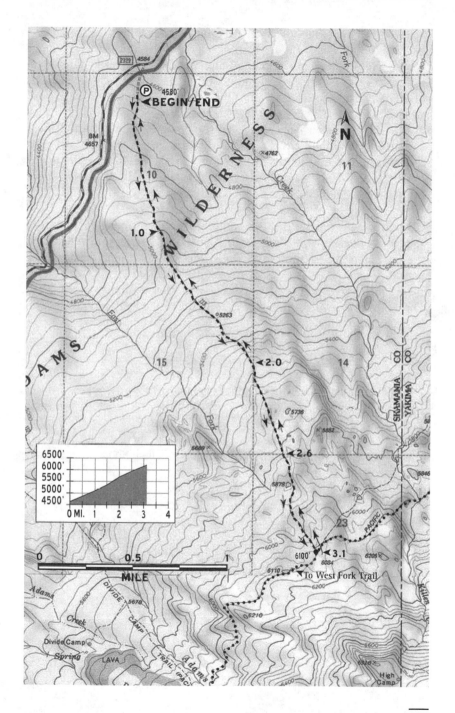

Begin climbing through open evergreen forest along the broad crest of a ridge that divides Killen Creek, to your left, and the East Fork of Adams Creek. The climb is gradual and even, a common feature on the lower slopes of Northwest volcanoes, and aims directly at the north face of Mount Adams and the icefall of the Adams Glacier. At 1.0 mile, you'll climb past a flat bench, 5,000 feet above sea level, and the forest thickens to shade you on hot days as you approach 2.0 miles. You'll angle toward the south and, 2.6 miles from the trailhead, cross the East Fork of Adams Creek into the splendid Adams Creek Meadows, decorated by heather, paintbrush, and lupine, as well as yellow monkey flower, shooting stars, and marsh marigold along the creek.

The trail meanders upward, perhaps a bit steeper, and for the next 0.5 mile, you'll wander through some of the finest alpine country to be found anywhere in the state. At 3.1 miles, 6,100 feet above sea level, the trail joins the Pacific Crest Trail, which passes Mount Adams on its way to Canada. This is your turnaround point: a great spot to ogle the mountain above, the meadow scenery, and Mount Rainier to the north. The East Fork of Adams Creek, 0.5 mile down the trail, might make the best spot for a picnic.

GOING FARTHER

Parties with two cars can combine this hike with the West Fork Trail (hike #45 in this guide) for a key-exchange hike of about 7 miles. Another option would be to follow a way trail south from the junction with the Pacific Crest Trail. This trail, which runs more steeply up the mountain, leads to a backpackers' and Real Mountain Climbers' campsite, 1 mile and another 800 feet higher on the mountain. This high camp is named—not without reason—High Camp.

47. Indian Racetrack

RATING	🚶 🚶
DISTANCE	7.0 miles round-trip
HIKING TIME	4 hours, 30 minutes
ELEVATION GAIN	840 feet
HIGH POINT	4,250 feet
EFFORT	Moderate Workout
BEST SEASON	Summer, fall
PERMITS/CONTACT	Northwest Forest Pass and free Wilderness Use Permit required; Gifford Pinchot National Forest, (509) 427-5171; www.fs.usda.gov/giffordpinchot
MAPS	USGS Gifford Peak; Green Trails Wind River
NOTES	Leashed dogs welcome; good family hike

THE HIKE

Crowds of hikers visit beautiful Race Track Meadows, named for the rough troughs, still visible today, carved by Native American riders and their horses over centuries. A shorter hike to the meadow is possible, provided you have a high-clearance vehicle and (sometimes necessary) four-wheel drive.

GETTING THERE

From exit 27 on Interstate 205 in Vancouver, follow Highway 14 for 43 miles east to the Wind River Road, turn left, and drive past Carson for about 12 miles to the Panther Creek Road (Forest Road 65). Turn right and follow FR 65 for 11.3 miles to a junction with FR 60. Turn right on FR 60 and drive 2.2 miles to the Crest Horse Camp on the right. The trailhead is across the road, 3,450 feet above sea level. GPS trailhead coordinates: N45°58.816′; W121°45.593′

THE TRAIL

Several trails lead to this late-summer berry patch, alpine meadow, and lake on the edge of Indian Heaven Wilderness. The shortest route begins near the summit of the Red Mountain Lookout, 1.0 mile south of the meadows—but the 4.0-mile road leading to the trailhead is narrow, steep,

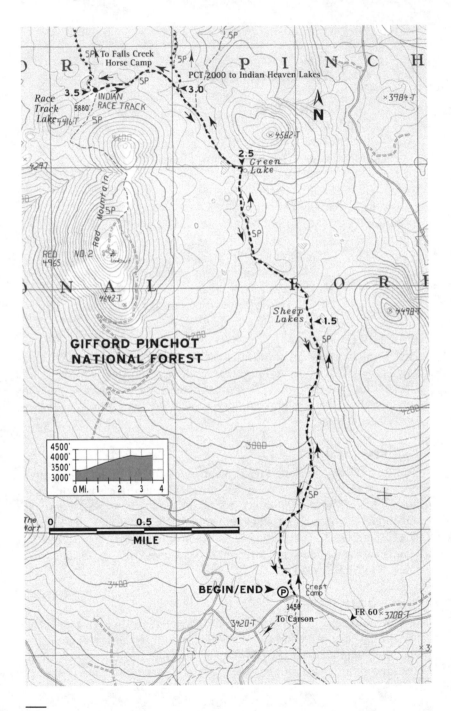

rutted, and slippery when wet. Besides, you'll face a 700-foot climb to get back to your car.

So take the kinder, gentler route along the Pacific Crest Trail north from the Crest trailhead. Unless you absolutely must eat all those huckleberries, I'd suggest you wait until the first frost of fall to take this hike, as Indian Heaven Wilderness is notorious for its bug population.

Begin by following the Pacific Crest Trail as it climbs steadily along seasonal creeks that drain Sheep and Green lakes. The path is popular with equestrians—not surprisingly, since the trailhead is a horse camp—and climbs gently through pine forest for 1.5 miles to Sheep Lakes, which might be a good turnaround spot for families with young children. From Sheep Lakes, the route begins to climb more steeply for another 0.7 mile to the Indian Heaven Wilderness, where you'll issue yourself a free Wilderness Use Permit. Beyond, the trail levels off at Green Lake, 2.5 miles from the trailhead, and meanders to a junction with the Race Track Trail 171A at 3.0 miles.

Leave the Pacific Crest Trail here and turn left to walk 0.5 mile into the wide, flat meadow and tarn, your turnaround point at 3.5 miles. Native Americans hunted and picked berries at this camp for centuries, and entertained themselves racing their horses here.

GOING FARTHER

The best way to extend your hike from here—assuming you've overdosed on glucosamine recently—would be to return to the junction with the Pacific Crest Trail and turn north for a steeper climb to switchbacks under Berry Mountain, about 1 mile north of the trail junction. You can continue north on the Pacific Crest Trail for another 3 miles to Sebago, Blue, and Tombstone lakes, or until you come down from your glucosamine high.

Mount St. Helens from Norway Pass.

MOUNT ST. HELENS

The trails around the Mount St. Helens National Monument are unique in the Lower 48. The routes pass through land and by lakes that did not exist until May 18, 1980. You can watch a video of the blast and hear stories about what it was like, but absolutely nothing compares to walking through the dust that was once a mountain, or through the shattered forest.

I was rushing to Mount Rainier for a springtime ski on that mighty day, and St. Helens blew her top about the time I arrived at the Tacoma Narrows. I thought I was watching a thunderstorm and stupidly drove on. It was not until I was near Ashford, where I ran into the ash cloud and watched hot clumps of mountain rain upon my car, that I realized St. Helens had blown. It was just as well I didn't get to Rainier—friends told me that the ash really put a damper on their skiing.

One of the critters you're likely to spot along the Coldwater Lake Trail (#48).

MOUNT ST. HELENS

48. Coldwater Lake Trail

RATING	🚶 🚶 🚶
DISTANCE	6.0 miles round-trip
HIKING TIME	3 hours, 30 minutes
ELEVATION GAIN	200 feet
HIGH POINT	2,800 feet
EFFORT	Easy Walk
BEST SEASON	Late spring, early summer
PERMITS/CONTACT	Northwest Forest Pass required/Mount St. Helens Volcanic Monument, (360) 247-3900; www.fs.usda.gov/mountsthelens
MAPS	USGS Elk Rock, Spirit Lake West (trail not shown); Green Trails Spirit Lake
NOTES	Dogs prohibited

THE HIKE

This is a good walk to witness the destruction—and rebirth—caused by the 1980 eruption of Mount St. Helens, including the lake created by the blast. Elk herds are frequently sighted in open areas off the trail.

GETTING THERE

Take the Castle Rock exit 49 off Interstate 5 and follow Highway 504 east for 45.2 miles, passing the Coldwater Visitor Center, to the Coldwater Lake boat launch and trailhead, 2,540 feet above sea level. GPS trailhead coordinates: N46°17.490'; W122°16.027'

THE TRAIL

This is an easy walk, with only occasional short climbs at the beginning and around stream crossings and gullies. In the spring, expect to see elk grazing in open areas above the trail and across the lake. Begin by climbing above the lake's high-water mark and walking above the lakeshore. You'll cross a couple of streams that may be dry in summer, and at 0.7 mile, you'll arrive at a junction with the Elk Bench Trail. Stay right and continue another 0.3 mile to a spur trail leading down to the lakeshore. This is one of only two areas along Coldwater where public access to the shore is permitted. Signs on the shore mark the area.

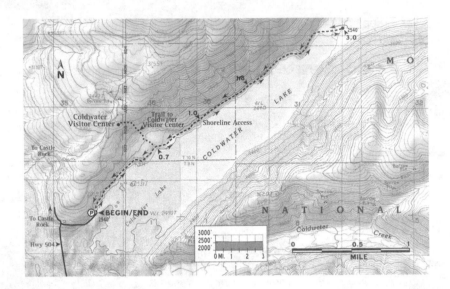

Beyond, the trail passes by stands of cottonwood and through infant alder woods. You'll cross several more creeks and dry gullies, and 1.8 miles from the trailhead, you'll get a photo op of a waterfall plunging over rocks above. Continue another 1.2 miles to the end of the lake for views up the Coldwater Canyon and across the lake to Coldwater Ridge.

GOING FARTHER
You can continue another 0.8 mile to the second public access point to the lake, where you'll find a junction with a trail leading steeply up Coldwater Ridge, or continue up Coldwater Creek Trail for as many miles as your body allows. This distance, for some reason, is always a good deal shorter than I imagine.

49. Windy Ridge

RATING	🚶 🚶 🚶 🚶 🚶
DISTANCE	4.0 miles round-trip
HIKING TIME	2 hours, 30 minutes
ELEVATION GAIN	200 feet
HIGH POINT	4,200 feet
EFFORT	Easy Walk
BEST SEASON	Summer, fall
PERMITS/CONTACT	Northwest Forest Pass required/Mount St. Helens Volcanic Monument, (360) 247-3900; www.fs.usda.gov/mountsthelens
MAPS	USGS Mount St. Helens, Spirit Lake West; Green Trails Mount St. Helens
NOTES	Dogs prohibited; good family hike

THE HIKE

Here's the easiest hike from which to view the devastation caused by the May 18, 1980, eruption that ripped the top off Mount St. Helens.

GETTING THERE

From US Highway 12 in Randle, turn south on Forest Road 25 and follow it to the junction with FR 99, just beyond Iron Creek Falls. Turn right and drive to the end of the road at the Windy Ridge trailhead, 4,000 feet above sea level. GPS trailhead coordinates: N46°14.997′; W122°9.169′

THE TRAIL

You can't beat the Windy Ridge Trail if you're looking for an easy hike toward the Mount St. Helens crater. Be forewarned: Windy Ridge did not get its name because of the gentle breezes that occasionally float past. Sunglasses (and often, dirt-bike goggles) will protect you from the blowing ash and volcanic sand that sometimes become airborne.

The route to the south follows an old logging road that was blown to Oblivion, a small town in Iowa, on May 18, 1980. Feel free to check my research on that point. This road winds gently down the ridge past an impressive array of trees blown down by the eruption, which stripped them of their bark and blew their limbs to Smithereens, a village just west of Oblivion.

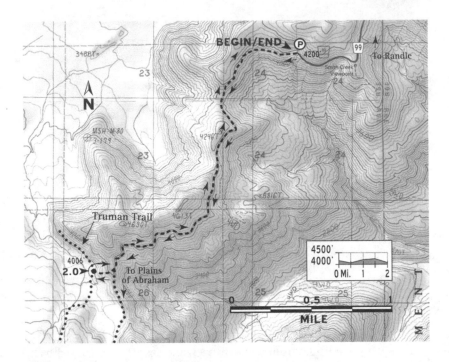

At **0.5** miles, round an unnamed peak on the ridge to the south and continue along the crest of the ridge. After **1.7** miles, begin a steeper descent towards the Plains of Abraham. You'll be facing south into the crater for the entire 2.0 miles to your turnaround point, a junction with the trail to the Plains of Abraham. Return the way you came.

GOING FARTHER

You can make a loop trip of 8 miles and add another 500 vertical feet to your hike by following the trail left at the junction to the Plains of Abraham, then following the Loowit Trail north over Windy Pass and rejoining the Windy Ridge Trail just beyond a junction with the Truman Trail.

50. Norway Pass

RATING	𝅺 𝅺 𝅺 𝅺 𝅺
DISTANCE	4.2 miles out and back
HIKING TIME	3 hours
ELEVATION GAIN	850 feet
HIGH POINT	4,555 feet
EFFORT	Prepare to Perspire
BEST SEASON	Summer, fall
PERMITS/CONTACT	Northwest Forest Pass required/Mount St. Helens National Historic Monument, (360) 449-7800, www.fs.usda.gov/mountsthelens
MAPS	USGS Spirit Lake West, Spirit Lake East; Green Trails Spirit Lake 332
NOTES	Dogs and bikes prohibited; good family walk

THE HIKE

Start early for solitude on this climb to an unbeatable view of Mount St. Helens. If hiking in the late summer, you may never reach Norway Pass if you stop to pick huckleberries.

GETTING THERE

Take US Highway 12 from I-5 to Randle and turn south on Forest Road 25, turning right on Forest Road 99 after passing Iron Creek Falls. Follow FR 99 to its junction with Forest Road 26 and turn right. Follow FR 26 for about 1 mile to the parking area and trailhead on the left, 3,710 feet above sea level. GPS trailhead coordinates: N46°18.267′; W122°4.914′

THE TRAIL

A reader took me to task for describing this trail as an "easy walk" in an earlier guide, and she was correct. I blame an old analog altimeter; my wife, B. B. Hardbody, insists it was operator error.

Anyways, Norway Pass is no easy walk, but rather a steady climb that shouldn't be missed by anyone who is capable of climbing a moderately steep path that gives little quarter for 2 miles. You'll drop a bit to cross a creek that may be dry in the summer, then begin climbing

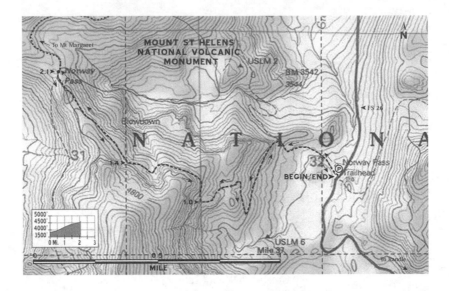

over a hillock before turning south and starting up a brushy ridge, 0.2 miles from the trailhead.

Here the trail makes a broad switchback and begins a long ascending traverse to the south where you'll get views to the trailhead and Meta Lake below. After a short 0.5 mile, switch back and round a small hill to a junction with the Independence Ridge Trail. Switch back to the right and continue climbing along the ridge, which in late summer is densely populated by huckleberries and the people who pick them. If you like huckleberries, expect to get purple hands and perhaps never reach Norway Pass.

The trail continues to climb, and you may notice that unlike many mountain trails, this one might be a bit smoother. The reason is that much of the former Mount St. Helens is under your feet and many rocks and roots are covered. You can look ahead to the broad and barren slopes of Mount Margaret, where the 1980 eruption leveled the forest.

At 2.1 miles, you'll reach Norway Pass and a grand view of Mount St. Helens, hidden until now by the ridge you've been climbing. The best views are up the trail to your left, on the Independence Pass Trail.

GOING FARTHER

You can make a loop trip of about 8.0 miles by hiking south on the Independence Pass Trail 227 to its junction with the Independence Ridge Trail 227A. Follow it back to the junction with the Norway Pass

Trail and turn right to the trailhead. The Independence Ridge Trail was rough and not recently maintained in the fall of 2014.

Another more popular alternative is to climb another steep one-way mile to the right to Mount Margaret, where the view of Mount St. Helens is even better than it is from Norway Pass.

Lichen decorates a weathered stump along the Hurricane Hill trail (#59), with Mount Angeles in the background.

OLYMPIC AND KITSAP PENINSULAS

The mountains and rivers of the Olympic Peninsula—and those little lumps of green in the Kitsap foothills—offer the chance to escape to Real Wilderness, making a perfect getaway from the hustle and rush of the crowded side of Puget Sound. If I could just adopt these mountains and move them to Spokane, I'd die with a grin the size of Grand Coulee Dam on my face. The rivers run pure, and the meadows grow wildflowers of every shape and color. Herds of Roosevelt elk tromp the high country in the summer and feast on lowland vegetation in the winter. We can thank Olympic National Park and Forest for most of what is wild and wonderful in the Olympics—the park stands a conservative guard over the interior of the mountains and the coast, while the forest buffers the park with its wilderness areas. The price for such beauty and wild country, some argue, is the more-than-occasional precipitation that keeps this land green. Promise you won't tell anyone if you hike one of the following trails on a bluebird day.

Clouds hide the Skokomish River above Spike Camp (#52).

OLYMPIC PENINSULA

51. Lower Skokomish River

RATING	🚶 🚶
DISTANCE	6.2 miles round-trip
HIKING TIME	3 hours, 30 minutes
ELEVATION GAIN	350 feet
HIGH POINT	850 feet
EFFORT	Moderate Workout
BEST SEASON	Spring; open year-round
PERMITS/CONTACT	Parking pass required/Hoodsport Information Station, (360) 877-2021; www.fs.usda.gov/olympic
MAPS	USGS Mount Tebo; Green Trails Mount Tebo
NOTES	Leashed dogs OK; bikes allowed

THE HIKE
Don't let the steep beginning of this walk put you off. The trail levels off shortly, and you'll enjoy an excellent springtime outing, with a trail decorated by trillium and other harbingers of spring.

GETTING THERE
From the intersection of Highways 101 and 106 at Potlatch, follow 101 south to the Skokomish Valley Road and turn west. Follow the Skokomish Valley Road for 5 miles to a Y intersection and turn right onto Forest Road 23. Drive 9 miles to FR 2353 and turn right downhill to the Skokomish River Bridge. Cross the bridge and turn left. The Lower Skokomish Trail No. 873 begins on the left, about 0.1 mile upstream from the bridge, 580 feet above sea level. GPS trailhead coordinates: N47°25.110'; W123°19.755'

THE TRAIL
This hike begins with a joint-cracking, tough climb in steep switchbacks guaranteed to get your ticker ticking and set you huffing like a blowfish out of water. At least, that's how I felt when I took this hike. You'll gain around 150 feet before the path levels a bit, **0.4** mile from the trailhead, at a junction with a path leading to the LeBar Horse Camp. Stay left and climb more gently to a second junction with the No. 120 Trail access in

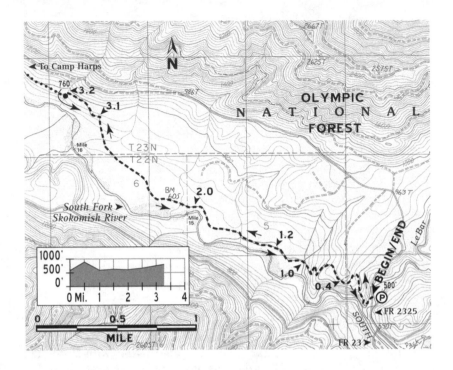

another 0.1 mile. Stay left and at **0.6** mile, you'll reach the crest of a ridge overlooking the South Fork of the Skokomish River.

Here you'll begin to drop in switchbacks through a splendid old forest painted in the spring by hundreds of trillium blossoms. Just after crossing a tumbling creek at **1.0** mile, the trail descends to the river flats. A riverside camp at **1.2** miles makes a great picnic and turnaround spot for families with young children. You'll walk the river flats beyond, under bigleaf maples and alders decorated with mosses, dwarfed by giant cedar and fir trees. Several bridges across small creeks were being repaired and replaced as of spring 2008.

At **2.0** miles, you'll find the site of the homestead settled by Rufus LeBar in the 1890s. This is another good picnic area for those seeking a shorter hike. To continue, follow the trail as it winds through the forest, never far from the rush of the river. You'll climb a gentle hill and descend around a wide flat marked by a rocky wash before climbing a short hill above the river, **3.1** miles from the trailhead. This is a good point to turn around. If you'd like a sandy picnic bench by the river, take the trail back to the rocky wash and follow the wash down to the river.

52. Spike Camp

RATING	🚶 🚶
DISTANCE	7.2 miles round-trip
HIKING TIME	4 hours
ELEVATION GAIN	625 feet
HIGH POINT	1,500 feet
EFFORT	Moderate Workout
BEST SEASON	Early spring; open year-round
PERMITS/CONTACT	None/Hoodsport Information Station, (360) 877-2021; www.nps.gov/olym
MAPS	USGS Mount Steel; Custom Correct Mount Skokomish–Lake Cushman; Green Trails Mount Steel
NOTES	Dogs prohibited; good family hike

THE HIKE

This is a good walk along an abandoned road to a forested campsite that four decades ago was the trailhead for the Flapjack Lakes Trail.

GETTING THERE

From US Highway 101 in Hoodsport, turn west on Lake Cushman Road and follow it 9 miles to Forest Road 24. Turn left on FR 24 and follow it 6 miles around Lake Cushman to the Staircase Ranger Station. Turn right just before the ranger station to the trailhead parking lot at 825 feet above sea level. GPS trailhead coordinates: N47°30.946′; W123°19.798′

THE TRAIL

The path up the North Fork of the Skokomish River was one of the first in the Olympic Mountains to be blazed by white explorers, back in 1890. This hike follows an old roadbed that was closed in the early 1970s, on the opposite side of the river from that pioneer trail.

Begin by climbing to a promontory about 100 feet above the river, then dropping gently in 0.5 mile to a footlog crossing Slate Creek. You'll be in the midst of an ancient forest where some trees were saplings before Columbus arrived on our shores. At 1.0 mile, the trail branches. The left fork drops to the river where a bridge crosses to the Four Stream Trail on the opposite bank.

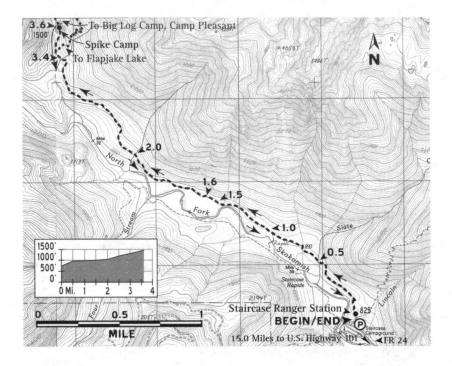

Stay right at the junction and continue upstream to Slide Camp, at **1.5** miles. Here the river flows languidly past parklike river bottom land where elk can sometimes be seen in the early spring. This is a good turnaround spot for families with young children. At **1.6** miles, the trail crosses the 200-yard-wide 1986 mudslide that gave the camp below its name. And in another 0.1 mile, you'll enter a 2-mile stretch of trail that traverses the burned forest of the Beaver Fire. Infant trees are reclaiming the land from the 1985 fire, believed to have been started by a camper on the opposite side of the river. It is thought that the mudslide occurred because no vegetation was left to hold the land in check.

At about **2.0** miles, the route begins to climb more steeply past a spring-fed creek. The Mount Lincoln Way Trail junction, at **2.5** miles, is barely discernible through the fire debris above. Continue to climb, crossing a creek and campsite at **3.4** miles to a junction with the Flapjack Lakes Trail at **3.5** miles. Stay left here and continue another 0.1 mile to Spike Camp, where you'll find an outhouse and another campsite complete with a bear wire, the turnaround point for most day hikers.

GOING FARTHER

If you'd like a longer hike, two options are possible: you can continue up the North Fork Trail past Spike Camp for another 2 miles to Big Log Camp or another 3 miles to Camp Pleasant. Or you can climb up to Flapjack Lakes, a steep 3.5 miles from the trail junction—making a round-trip hike to the lakes of 14.2 miles and about 3,000 vertical feet.

53. Dosewallips Road

RATING	🚶 🚶 🚶 🚶
DISTANCE	10.6 miles round-trip
HIKING TIME	4 hours, 30 minutes
ELEVATION GAIN	115 feet
HIGH POINT	695 feet
EFFORT	Moderate Workout
BEST SEASON	Spring; open year-round
PERMITS/CONTACT	None/Quilcene Ranger Station, (360) 765-2200
MAPS	USGS The Brothers, Tyler Peak; Custom Correct Buckhorn Wilderness; Green Trails The Brothers, Tyler Peak
NOTES	Bicyclists and leashed dogs welcome to park boundary; great family walk

THE HIKE

This is a prime walk along a dirt road washed away by the Dosewallips River rushing alongside, past a riverfront walk-in campground, and through a magnificent old forest to crashing Dosewallips Falls.

GETTING THERE

From Brinnon on US Highway 101, take Dosewallips River Road to its end at a washout 9.7 miles from the highway. Park at the side of the road or look for parking spots on the river side of the road, just east of the washout, 600 feet above sea level. GPS trailhead coordinates: N47°44.332′; W120°04.376′

THE TRAIL

This walk may soon be recycled into a forest and river road, because Olympic National Forest officials propose to build a bypass around the washout, providing access to the old Elkhorn auto campground and the Dosewallips Campground in Olympic National Park. But for now, the old roadbed makes a fine walk.

Begin by climbing the steep but short trail that starts on the right, about 100 feet east of the spot where the road was washed away by the river. When the river is low, scramble down the bank and walk along the river's edge, then climb back up and follow a foot-worn pathway to

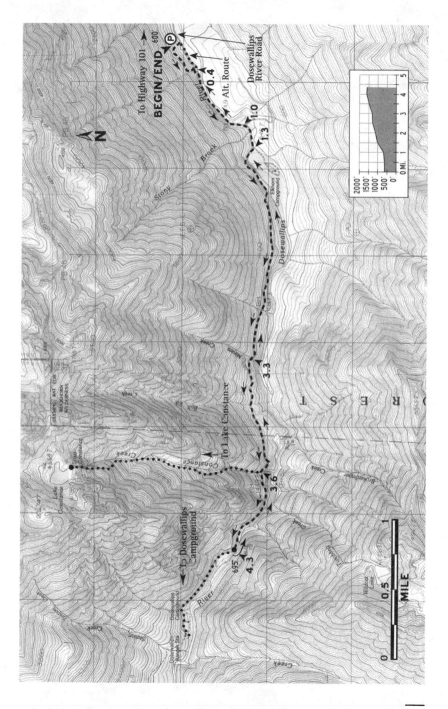

the road. The upper trail climbs in a few switchbacks to a plateau above the river, winds through the forest, and then drops back to the road as steeply as it climbed. Both routes rejoin the road from opposite sides near a Forest Service trail register, 0.4 mile from the trailhead.

Stroll along the nearly flat road, first through moss-covered trees, then beside the tumbling Dosewallips River. Elk and deer often cruise the road, though much of the time the best elk-watching is along the Dosewallips Road, just west of Brinnon. The hike gains about 100 feet in the first mile, passing a road junction at 1.0 mile and arriving at a junction with the Elkhorn Campground entrance road at 1.3 miles. Families with young children and those with *really* creaky knees might choose to stop at the campground, which offers riverside picnic tables and big sitting rocks for foot-freezing in the Dosewallips, which is ice and snow about 16 miles upstream.

Stay right at the junction to continue the hike and begin climbing more steeply through the forest to splash across a creek at 3.0 miles; 0.3 mile beyond, cross an excellent bridge over dry Miner's Creek, which—no surprise—is named for the abandoned mine near the river below the road. Beyond, you'll find a gate at the boundary of Olympic National Park, 3.6 miles from the trailhead. The road crosses crashing Constance Creek at 3.9 miles, crests a hill at the high point of the hike another 0.1 mile farther, then descends to the turnaround point underneath cliffs of pillow lava, with Dosewallips Falls cascading over huge boulders, at 4.3 miles. About four decades ago, two men who should have known better attempted to ride down the falls on inner tubes. The largest part of their remains, found several years later, was a piece of jawbone.

GOING FARTHER

It's another mile from the turnaround point to the end of the road at Dosewallips Campground in Olympic National Park. Here you'll find picnic tables and riverside campsites and several closed buildings, including a restroom with running water. Strong hikers may wish to continue another 1.2 miles one-way to Dose Forks—a fine picnic spot beside the river.

Hikers wishing to put their knees and most other parts of their bodies to the supreme test can turn right at the junction with the Lake Constance Trail, 3.9 miles from the Dosewallips trailhead, and climb the steepest trail in the Olympic Mountains to Lake Constance. The path snakes straight up the mountainside, gaining more than 3,200 vertical feet in 2 miles.

54. Mount Townsend

RATING	🚶 🚶 🚶 🚶
DISTANCE	8 miles round-trip
HIKING TIME	5 hours
ELEVATION GAIN	2,880 feet
HIGH POINT	6,280 feet
EFFORT	Knee-Punishing
BEST SEASON	Summer, fall
PERMITS/CONTACT	Northwest Forest Pass required/Quilcene Ranger Station, (360) 765-2200; www.fs.usda.gov/olympic
MAPS	USGS Tyler Peak; Custom Correct Buckhorn Wilderness; Green Trails Tyler Peak
NOTES	Leashed dogs welcome

THE HIKE

This is one of the most strenuous hikes in this guide, but it's well worth the effort if you're in good condition and in the mood for views north to our Canadian neighbors, with Olympic Mountain peaks and river valleys everywhere.

GETTING THERE

From Quilcene, follow US Highway 101 south 1.4 miles to Penny Creek Road. Turn right and follow Penny Creek Road to its junction with the Big Quilcene River Road; turn left and follow it 3 miles to Forest Road 27. Follow FR 27 for 14.8 miles, passing a sign at 14.3 miles directing traffic left to the Lower Mount Townsend trailhead. Instead, continue right on FR 27 to FR 190 and turn left on FR 190, following it 0.7 mile to the Upper Mount Townsend Trail No. 839, at 3,400 feet above sea level. GPS trailhead coordinates: N47°51.385'; W123°02.153'

THE TRAIL

One of the 27 switchbacks on this trail—the longest of three leading to the summit of Mount Townsend—is likely to make you want to gobble nonsteroidal anti-inflammatory drugs. The first half dozen of these switchbacks help you climb the first 0.4 mile through a nice forest of

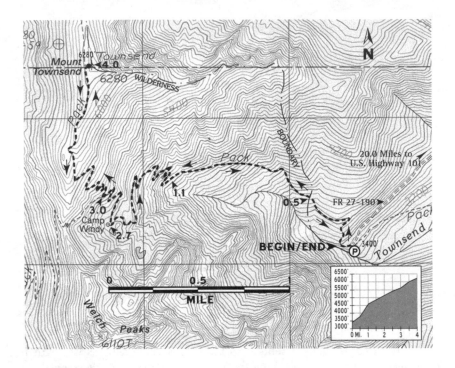

rhododendrons that usually bloom long before the snow melts from the trail at Camp Windy. Past the switchbacks, the trail enters the Buckhorn Wilderness at **0.5** mile.

From here, begin a climbing traverse through the forest, arriving at a steep subalpine meadow and open avalanche chutes at **1.1** miles. If you have lots of courage, from here you can glance up—more than 1,000 vertical feet—and view your destination. The trail climbs above a waterfall on the major tributary to Townsend Creek, then begins the remaining 18 switchbacks to the summit. On crowded summer days, you'll be able to hear hikers above and below moaning about the grade or the blisters on their barking dogs—or maybe real barking dogs.

Assuming you are still breathing **2.7** miles up the trail, you'll find a pleasant flat spot at Camp Windy where you can feign a heart attack to get a rest before continuing. Just south of the trail, you'll find a small tarn for filtering water. Sidle out onto a big flat rock to take in the north views of Mount Baker and the north Cascades.

Continue climbing and at **3.0** miles, you'll find the junction with the Silver Lakes Trail. Stay right and keep climbing toward the trail, at the **4.0**-mile mark, that heads to the right to the summit. A big rock overlooking the north side of the mountain, 0.4 mile farther, offers another perch; while you catch your breath, point yourself toward Mount Rainier and rotate counterclockwise to see the Cascades, Glacier Peak, Mount Baker, and the mountains of Vancouver Island. Olympic peaks include The Needles and Graywolf Range in front, The Brothers toward the west, and Mount Constance to the south. Just imagine: you're only 27 switchbacks from your tube of Bengay.

GOING FARTHER

It is difficult to imagine anyone but a marathon hiker wanting to go any farther—but wilderness pedestrians with a masochistic streak might try the hike from the lower trailhead, which would add 1.8 round-trip miles and 300 vertical feet to the hike.

55. Marmot Pass

RATING	🚶 🚶 🚶 🚶
DISTANCE	10.4 miles round-trip
HIKING TIME	7 hours
ELEVATION GAIN	3,500 feet
HIGH POINT	6,000 feet
EFFORT	Knee-Punishing
BEST SEASON	Summer, fall
PERMITS/CONTACT	Northwest Forest Pass required/Quilcene Ranger Station, (360) 765-2200; www.fs.usda.gov/olympic
MAPS	USGS Tyler Peak; Custom Correct Buckhorn Wilderness; Green Trails Tyler Peak
NOTES	Leashed dogs welcome

THE HIKE

Try this long, strenuous climb of almost three-quarters of a vertical mile to alpine meadows and one of the most scenic views of the northern Olympics, made better still by the greater chance for dry weather afforded by its rain-shadow location. Hikers placing two cars at separate trailheads have a one-way option.

GETTING THERE

From Quilcene, follow US Highway 101 south 1.4 miles to Penny Creek Road. Turn right and follow Penny Creek Road to its junction with the Big Quilcene River Road; follow it 3 miles to Forest Road 27. Follow FR 27 for 6.1 miles to FR 2750; follow FR 2750 for 4.5 miles to the Upper Big Quilcene Trail No. 833, 2,500 feet above sea level. GPS trailhead coordinates: N47º49.667´; W123º02.434´

THE TRAIL

The hike to Marmot Pass is the champagne walk of the northeastern Olympics. It starts with a shaded forest walk and ends high above timberline, where you will keep company with the cute little furballs for whom the pass is named, and where the view will melt your mind.

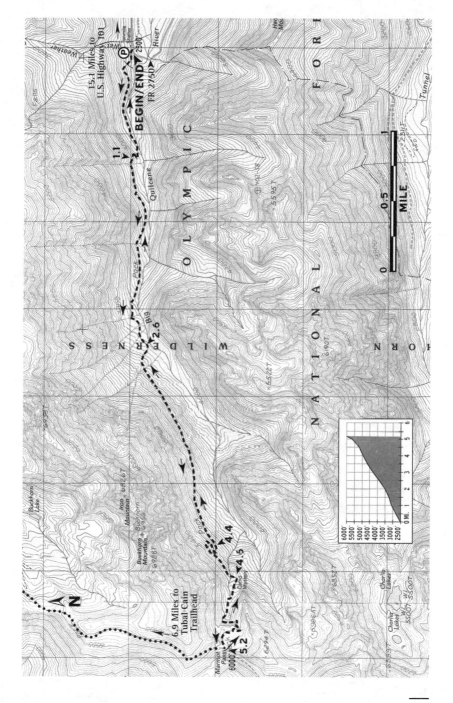

The trail, located on the fringes of the dry section of the park, known as the "rain shadow," begins with a gentle climb through a rhododendron grove that is spectacular in midspring, which is a bit too early if you plan to reach Marmot Pass without wading through snow in the high country. After climbing above the river for 1.1 miles, the path switches back away from the river and climbs steeply to another switchback, then traverses through a big forest back to the river.

It crosses one major creek before climbing gently toward Shelter Rock, at 2.6 miles. This is the trail's final brush with the Quilcene, which is reduced to a chattering creek.

Beyond Shelter Rock you'll begin climbing steeply, first alongside a little creek that dives through the meadow beside the trail. The path eventually crosses the creek and begins a climbing traverse of the slopes of Buckhorn and Iron mountains.

If you're hiking this section in early summer, expect to cross the snow-fields of at least two avalanche paths—the springtime goal of backcountry snow riders. At 4.4 miles, the trail switches back twice—expansive views to the northeast include the Cascade Mountains and Puget Sound basin—then climbs along a creek to Camp Mystery at 4.6 miles.

The camp, an excellent picnic spot, is located in a windbreak of alpine trees. Beyond, the trail follows the creek before climbing into a wide, wildflower-filled bowl just below the pass. Here's another spot sheltered from the frequent winds you may encounter at Marmot Pass, another 0.3 mile up the trail.

Continue to the pass for stunning views of the highest peaks of the northeastern Olympics, including Mount Deception and The Needles.

GOING FARTHER

Create a 14.3-mile one-way option for two-car parties by following the Tubal Cain Trail No. 840 right at the pass and first climbing, then descending 7.3 miles to the trailhead.

56. Camp Handy

RATING	🚶 🚶 🚶 🚶
DISTANCE	6.6 miles round-trip
HIKING TIME	3 hours, 30 minutes
ELEVATION GAIN	600 feet
HIGH POINT	3,100 feet
EFFORT	Moderate Workout
BEST SEASON	Spring, fall
PERMITS/CONTACT	Parking pass required; Quilcene Ranger Station, (360) 765-2200; www.fs.usda.gov/olympic
MAPS	USGS Tyler Peak; Custom Correct Buckhorn Wilderness; Green Trails Tyler Peak
NOTES	Leashed dogs OK; good family hike

THE HIKE

This is a wildlife-watcher's walk to a sunny subalpine meadow beside a clear creek, a great picnic spot for the whole family. A shelter stands ready in the unlikely event rainfall tries to spoil the fun.

GETTING THERE

From US Highway 101 just south of Sequim Bay State Park, turn left on Louella Road and follow it for 0.9 mile to Palo Alto Road. Turn left on Palo Alto Road and follow it for 4.6 miles, where it becomes Forest Road 28. Follow FR 28 another 1.1 miles to FR 2880. Turn right on FR 2880, cross the Dungeness River to FR 2870, turn left, and follow FR 2870 for 2.7 miles to FR 2860. Turn right and follow FR 2860 for 6 miles to the Upper Dungeness Trail No. 833, 2,500 feet above sea level. GPS trailhead coordinates: N47°52.675′; W123°08.217′

THE TRAIL

This hike is one of my personal favorites in the Olympic Mountains. It starts at an elevation that allows an easy climb to subalpine country, yet stays low enough to avoid the chance of extreme weather in the high country. And it is located in the dry part of the Olympic Mountains, where rainfall is just slightly greater than the annual average for Spokane.

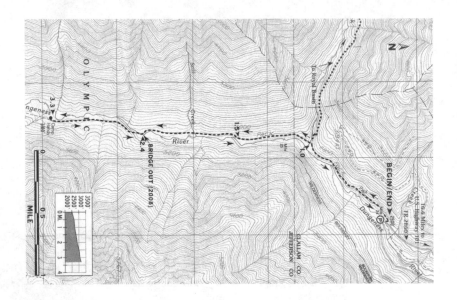

Begin by climbing from the parking lot in a short switchback and contouring along the hillside back to river level. You'll climb gently along the river for 1.0 mile to a junction with the Royal Basin Trail. Turn left here and cross Royal Creek at the Buckhorn Wilderness boundary.

The trail continues to climb gently along the river, passing a mineral lick at **1.5** miles where game trails radiate into the forest. The trail steepens briefly, then drops back to cross the river.

The path gets slightly steeper across the river as it climbs past a rounded forest ridge. At about **3.0** miles, it becomes gentle again and contours toward the scenic meadows of Camp Handy, **3.3** miles from the trailhead.

The shelter is located off the trail to the right, overlooking the meadows. Hikers seeking a more solitary setting will find a way trail leading upstream to larger meadows on the creek.

I've seen bears in the meadows along the creek almost every time I've visited Camp Handy. It's a great spot for wildlife-watching; families with small children should know that it's also the site of one of the very rare cougar attacks recorded in the Olympics during the past 15 years.

57. Dungeness Spit

RATING	🚶 🚶 🚶
DISTANCE	7.0 miles round-trip
HIKING TIME	3 hours
ELEVATION GAIN	110 feet
HIGH POINT	120 feet
EFFORT	Easy Walk
BEST SEASON	Winter; open year-round
PERMITS/CONTACT	Trail fee required/Dungeness National Wildlife Refuge, (360) 457-8451; www.dungeness.com/refuge
MAPS	USGS Dungeness; Wildlife Refuge map at trailhead
NOTES	Dogs prohibited; good family walk

THE HIKE

Walk through the forest for 0.5 mile to reach a sandy beach that stretches along the Strait of Juan de Fuca's sunny side for 3 miles.

GETTING THERE

Drive west on US Highway 101 from Sequim to Kitchen-Dick Road, turn right, and follow it to the 90-degree corner at Lotzgesell Road; turn left at the entrance to Dungeness National Wildlife Refuge. Follow the road past the Dungeness Recreation Area to a parking lot at the trailhead, 120 feet above sea level. GPS trailhead coordinates: N48°08.480'; W123°11.393'

THE TRAIL

Save this walk for the winter, when storms sweep the Strait of Juan de Fuca and the crowds of summer don't exist. Carry rain and wind gear, but expect more sunshine here than at any other place on the Olympic Peninsula.

After paying a modest fee at the trailhead, hike the well-graveled, wide path for 0.5 mile to a wooden observation deck overlooking the spit. This portion of the trail is navigable by folks in wheelchairs, although many may require assistance if the gravel is soft.

The trail drops steeply here for 0.1 mile to the spit, where it disappears. For the long walk, turn right and walk up the spit. The south side is closed, unless

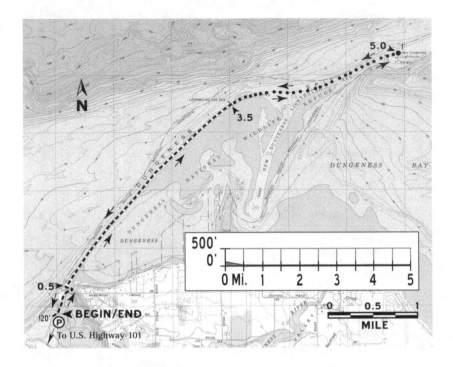

you happen to be a shorebird or other wild creature, for which the inner Dungeness Bay is reserved; that's why they call it a wildlife refuge.

Never mind—there's plenty of room to walk along the northern, or Strait, side of the spit. You'll find the easiest going closest to the water, which may also be the wettest walking. Here is one path where high waterproof boots might be more appropriate than hiking boots.

Look seaward for signs of marine mammals, including orcas and seals, and for interesting human-doings: watch pilots practice landings and takeoffs on one of the Navy's supercarriers or see a Trident submarine slip silently past like a giant dolphin.

Hikers can also climb to the high middle ground of the spit, where several observation decks have been built to allow bird-watchers the chance to spot migrating and native waterfowl on the inland bay. Besides wildlife-watching, the view to the northern barrier of the Olympic Mountains, dazzling white in winter, is almost startling. On clear days, Mount Baker floats like a big ice-cream sundae to the northeast.

Beach hikers often stop to picnic on driftwood perches about 3.5 miles down the spit, where it bends inward and affords a view along the sweep of sand from end to end.

58. Maiden Peak

RATING	🚶 🚶 🚶 🚶
DISTANCE	6.2 miles round-trip
HIKING TIME	3 hours, 30 minutes
ELEVATION GAIN	1,200 feet
HIGH POINT	5,620 feet
EFFORT	Prepare to Perspire
BEST SEASON	Summer, fall
PERMITS/CONTACT	None/Olympic National Park Wilderness Information Center, (360) 565-3100; Olympic National Park Visitor Center, (360) 565-3130; www.nps.gov/olym
MAPS	USGS Mount Angeles; Custom Correct Graywolf-Dungeness; Green Trails Mount Angeles
NOTES	Dogs prohibited; narrow, steep road

THE HIKE

Walk above the timberline—and on some days, above the clouds—on this spectacular trek through alpine meadowland to a rocky vista that serves as a picnic spot and car-key trading point for a one-way option.

GETTING THERE

From US Highway 101 at the Deer Park Cinemas on the eastern outskirts of Port Angeles, take the Deer Park interchange and follow the Deer Park Road 17.2 miles to Deer Park. Take the road signed "Deer Park Ranger Station" to the right at Deer Park. Motorists who have never driven outside Kansas or Iowa should not attempt the last 8 miles of this steep, winding one-lane dirt road without first gobbling copious amounts of tranquilizers. The trailhead, 5,200 feet above sea level, is located below the ranger station. GPS trailhead coordinates: N47°56.983′; W123°15.875′

THE TRAIL

Carry water on this hike, and don't expect the spring across the road from the trailhead—the only water available—to be running in late fall. Another caution: If you hike this trail in August, you will be accompanied by your

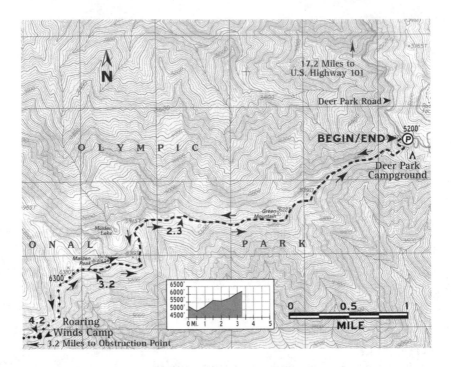

very own squadron of deerflies, which will buzz you if you keep moving but seldom settle for a bite.

The trail drops almost 400 feet in the first mile, following an old road-bed that was originally planned to connect with Obstruction Point Road, 7.4 miles distant. The route was never completed, leaving the incredible scenery for lucky wilderness pedestrians.

After crossing a wide, flower-filled bench, the trail begins to climb gradually to a meadow with views north to the Strait of Juan de Fuca and south to the sky-scratching peaks of The Needles and Graywolf Range. This is Grassy Meadow, 2.3 miles from the trailhead, a fine picnic spot for those seeking a shorter family hike.

To continue, follow the trail up a long, wide ridge as it climbs under-neath 6,434-foot Maiden Peak. The view of the rocky peaks to the east is fantastic, from Mount Walkinshaw on the north to Mount Deception on the south. Leave the trail and scramble up through sloping meadow and scree to the top of Maiden Peak, at 3.1 miles. You can pretty much see everything from here: the mountains of Vancouver Island and perhaps even the Coast Range of Canada on a clear day, most of the Olympic peaks, and the blue sweep of the Strait of Juan de Fuca below.

59. Hurricane Hill

RATING	🚶 🚶 🚶 🚶 🚶
DISTANCE	3.2 miles round-trip
HIKING TIME	3 hours, 30 minutes
ELEVATION GAIN	1,700 feet
HIGH POINT	5,757 feet
EFFORT	Moderate Workout
BEST SEASON	Summer, fall
PERMITS/CONTACT	Entrance fee required/Olympic National Park Wilderness Information Center, (360) 565-3100; Olympic National Park Visitor Center, (360) 565-3130; www.nps.gov/olym
MAPS	USGS Mount Angeles, Hurricane Hill; Custom Correct Hurricane Ridge; Green Trails Mount Angeles, Mount Olympus
NOTES	Dogs prohibited; good family hike

THE HIKE

Climb for 1.6 miles along a paved nature walk to the site where an aircraft-spotter's cabin once stood for one of the finest views of the interior Olympic Mountains.

GETTING THERE

From US Highway 101 in Port Angeles, turn left on Race Street and follow it past the Olympic National Park Visitor Center to Hurricane Ridge Road. Turn right and follow Hurricane Ridge Road for 5.7 miles to Heart O' the Hills, where you'll pay a fee to enter the park. Continue up Hurricane Ridge Road 11.8 miles to the Hurricane Ridge Visitor Center. Follow the road through the parking area 2.5 miles down a steep, curving road past a picnic area—the last chance to stock up on water—and up to a parking loop at the trailhead, 5,075 feet above sea level. GPS trailhead coordinates: N47°58.595'; W123°31.068'

THE TRAIL

The hike to Hurricane Hill is on a paved nature trail almost the entire distance and offers stunning views of Mount Olympus, the highest peak of

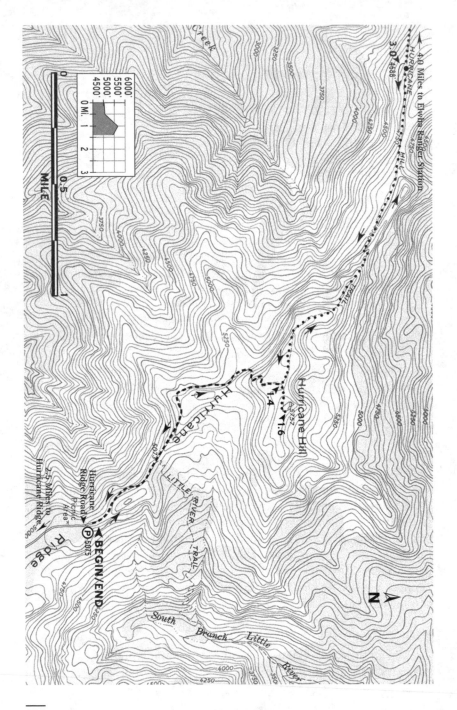

the Olympics at 7,965 feet, and Mount Carrie, the 6,995-footer that is so close across the Elwha River valley you might hear its glacier grumble.

The path first drops to a little knoll where you can look north across the Strait of Juan de Fuca to Vancouver Island, then climbs underneath a 5,250-foot peak to a saddle and junction with the Little River Trail. Stay left here and begin a long sidehill climb across steep, open slopes with awesome views to the interior Olympics. You'll round a forested ridge and emerge on a saddle below Hurricane Hill, the grassy-sloped mountain above.

The trail begins climbing in switchbacks here, and the pavement ends at the second switchback. Continue climbing to a trail junction at 1.4 miles, and follow the trail to the right through a wide meadow to the rocky summit of Hurricane Hill, 5,757 feet above sea level.

The view from here is enough to overload the senses of most hedonists. Mountains scratch clouds; rivers carve notches in the deep green forest. Look north to salt water and Canada, northeast to Mount Baker and the north Cascades.

An aircraft-spotter's cabin was once lashed to the summit rock by cables whose anchors may still be visible. Herb Crisler—the Disney cinematographer who filmed *The Olympic Elk*—spent a winter here with his wife, Lois.

GOING FARTHER

For a longer hike, walk back to the trail junction and turn right, following the trail as it crosses a green, flat meadow to gain the crest of an increasingly narrow, rocky ridge. You'll walk the crest, switching back once to pass on the south under steep rocky peaks, 2.4 miles from the trailhead. Continue past a flat saddle to a point where the trail begins to angle down the grassy knoll in front of you, at 3 miles.

This is a good turnaround point for most hikers because the trail switches back steeply down the meadow to enter the forest, dropping like a dead goose 4,400 feet and 3 miles to the Elwha Ranger Station.

60. Elwha Loop

RATING	🚶 🚶 🚶
DISTANCE	6.6 miles round-trip
HIKING TIME	3.5 hours
ELEVATION GAIN	250 feet
HIGH POINT	1,150 feet
EFFORT	Moderate Workout
BEST SEASON	Spring; open year-round
PERMITS/CONTACT	Olympic National Park entrance fee/Olympic National Park Wilderness Information Center, (360) 565-3100; Olympic National Park Visitor Center, (360) 565-3130; www.nps.gov/olym
MAPS	USGS Hurricane Hill; Custom Correct Elwha Valley; Green Trails Mount Olympus
NOTES	Dogs prohibited; good family hike

THE HIKE

This is a pleasant walk along one of the mightiest rivers in the Olympics, where you may see Roosevelt elk, the animals for which the river was named. You'll pass a couple of historic buildings and hike country first seen by white people little more than a century ago.

GETTING THERE

Follow US Highway 101 west 8.7 miles past Port Angeles to the Elwha River. If you wish to bypass the downtown section of Port Angeles, turn left on Race Street and follow it to Lauridsen Boulevard. Turn right on Lauridsen and follow it to its junction with 101 at the west end of town. Just before crossing the Elwha River, turn left and follow Olympic Hot Springs Road about 4 miles to Whiskey Bend Road, stopping to pay a fee at the entrance to Olympic National Park. Turn left on Whiskey Bend Road, just beyond the Elwha Ranger Station. Follow this single-lane, winding gravel road 5 miles to the trailhead, 1,100 feet above sea level. GPS trailhead coordinates: N47°58.055'; W123°34.941'

Note: In early 2015, a slide closed the Whiskey Bend Road and hikers may have to add 4 miles to their walk if repairs haven't yet been made. Call the numbers above for current road conditions.

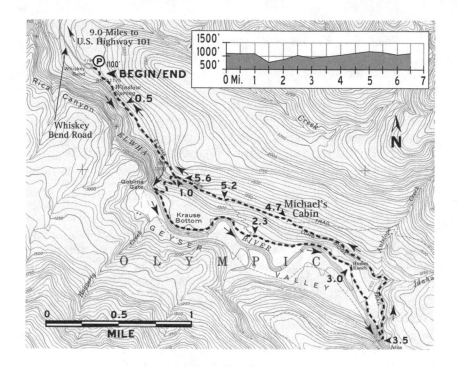

THE TRAIL

The Elwha River now runs free, thanks to the removal of two dams built nearly a century ago. You'll see the remains of one of those dams as you drive to the trailhead, and note the color of the river, which changes from cement to blue as you arrive at the trailhead.

This hike follows the route blazed by the first white explorers up the Elwha River valley, the Press Expedition in 1899–90. Begin by traversing for 1.0 mile above the river, which can be heard below.

At **0.5** mile, you'll see a sign directing you to an overlook and a short, steep trail leading down. Unless you're hiking early in the morning, I'd suggest you save this short side trip for the way home in the evening, as you will have a better chance of seeing elk on the river flats below.

Continue left for another 0.5 mile to a junction with the Rica Canyon Trail at the edge of an old forest-fire scar. Turn right and plunge steeply down to green flats in the forest above the river. A trail junction here offers a very short, steep side trip to the right to Goblin Gates, where the Elwha River narrows and smashes against cliffs in a steep, rocky canyon.

After a look and a chance to catch your breath, follow the trail to the left toward Krause Bottom, a flat, wide stretch of river flats where, at **2.3** miles from the trailhead, you'll strike another trail descending from the main Elwha Trail above. Keep right here and continue along the flats to a wide, grassy field marking the pastureland of the Humes Ranch.

The old building is located at the south end of the field, where Grant and Will Humes homesteaded and Herb Crisler, the last mountain man of the Olympics, later lived. The trail drops to a wide campsite and then winds through woods to a good lunch spot above the river. A new trail negotiates a big washout and joins the Dodger Point Trail at **3.5** miles.

If you wish, take a short side trip to the right down the Dodger Point Trail to the suspension bridge across the Elwha River. Then return to the trail junction and follow it as it climbs gently for a little more than 1.0 mile to a junction with the Lillian River Trail, at **4.7** miles.

This is the site of another historic building, Michael's Cabin. Keep left at the junction and follow the trail as it climbs again through the old burned area to a junction with the Krause Bottom Trail at **5.2** miles. Stay right here and climb more steeply in 0.4 mile to the Rica Canyon Trail junction to close the loop. The trailhead is 1.0 mile to the right.

GOING FARTHER

Those looking for more exercise and river scenery can turn right at Michael's Cabin to follow the main Elwha Trail another 2.9 miles to the Lillian River crossing. Return the way you came for a long hike of 12.4 miles.

61. Spruce Railroad Trail

RATING	🧍 🧍 🧍
DISTANCE	6.2 miles round-trip
HIKING TIME	3 hours
ELEVATION GAIN	60 feet
HIGH POINT	660 feet
EFFORT	Easy Walk
BEST SEASON	Fall; open year-round
PERMITS/CONTACT	None required/Olympic National Park Wilderness Information Center, (360) 565-3100; Olympic National Park Visitor Center, (360) 565-3130; www.nps.gov/olym
MAPS	USGS Lake Crescent; Custom Correct Lake Crescent–Happy Lake Ridge
NOTES	Bicyclists welcome; great family walk

THE HIKE

This is a gentle trail along a historic abandoned railroad grade on the shores of Lake Crescent. Hikers with autos parked at either end of the trail can make it a one-way walk with a picnic and key swap.

GETTING THERE

Take US Highway 101 for 17 miles west of Port Angeles to East Beach Road. Turn right and follow it past the Log Cabin Resort, cross the Lyre River bridge, and turn left to the trailhead, 640 feet above sea level. For the western trailhead, stay on 101 to the west end of Lake Crescent and turn right on Fairholme–North Shore Road. Follow it about 5 miles to the trailhead, 660 feet above sea level. GPS trailhead coordinates, east end: N48°05.593'; W123°48.122'

THE TRAIL

The Spruce Railroad Trail is a local favorite, and just about any time the weather is good, you'll find folks of all ages, shapes, and sizes riding bikes, jogging, or walking along the old roadbed. With the recent addition of part of the Olympic Discovery Trail near the eastern trailhead, cyclists and hikers have another 5 miles of relatively easy walking and pedaling.

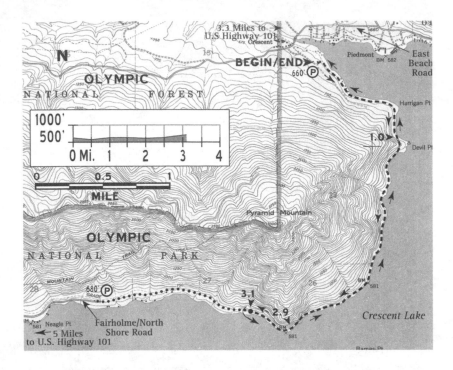

I've both hiked and pedaled this trail several times; the last time I rode my bike (the Great Emasculator) on the trail, the bike pretty much rode me the last few hundred feet. It was on a section of turnpike—a rock-filled path between two logs—and I somehow got going a bit faster than the bike, pitching over the handlebars. It was not a pretty sight, though B. B. Hardbody said she was entertained.

From the east trailhead, the trail climbs gently to gain the old railroad route, used to haul huge Sitka spruce from the Olympic Peninsula. The wood, lightweight yet strong, was perfect for World War I and early World War II aircraft. The route is level for about 1.0 mile to the blocked entrance to the first of two tunnels blasted through the side of Pyramid Mountain, which hunkers over gin-clear Lake Crescent. The trail drops to the lakeside to round Harrigan Point and crosses a metal footbridge over an inlet. A sign was once located here, warning hikers of poison ivy growing nearby.

The trail winds around Devil's Point and follows the lakeshore to the entrance of the second tunnel, 2.9 miles from the eastern trailhead. Like the first tunnel, this one is filled with debris, and walking through it is extremely dangerous. Prudent pedestrians are advised to climb the trails on either end of the tunnel for safer views. Just beyond is a good picnic spot and turnaround point, at **3.1** miles.

Hikers with autos at either end can walk the entire 4.1 miles, meeting halfway for a key exchange.

GOING FARTHER

Consider two options for a longer walk: first, the Fairholme–North Shore Road doesn't get much traffic and would make a quiet 5-mile one-way hike to the western trailhead. Second, pick up the western end of the Adventure Route of the Olympic Discovery Trail, just off the Lyre River Road, thereby adding as many as 5 miles one-way to your hike.

62. Rialto Beach

RATING	🚶 🚶 🚶
DISTANCE	5.2 miles round-trip
HIKING TIME	2.5 hours
ELEVATION GAIN	80 feet
HIGH POINT	80 feet
EFFORT	Easy Walk
BEST SEASON	Winter, spring; open year-round
PERMITS/CONTACT	Entry fee required/Olympic National Park Wilderness Information Center, (360) 565-3100; Olympic National Park Visitor Center, (360) 565-3130; www.nps.gov/olym
NOTES	Leashed dogs OK; great family outing

THE HIKE

This beach walk follows smooth sand all the way to a big rocky headland that can be passed at low tide by walking through a natural tunnel carved by the surf.

GETTING THERE

From US Highway 101 on the northern outskirts of Forks, turn west on La Push–Mora Road (Highway 110) and follow the signs to Mora Campground and Rialto Beach, turning right at Three Rivers. Drive past the campground to Rialto Beach. The trailhead is about 20 feet above sea level. GPS trailhead coordinates: N47°55.261'; W124°38.324'

THE TRAIL

This walk begins on a plastic plank path, which gives wheelchair hikers a chance to look out at the Pacific Ocean. After 0.2 mile, you'll cross to a sandy beach on a cobblestone apron furnished by the Pacific.

Once on the beach, head to the right, aiming for the big rock that marks the northern end of the bay. At 1.1 miles, you'll cross Ellen Creek; leashed dogs are not allowed beyond this point.

Hole in the Wall, that big rock to the north with the hole in it, is another 1.4 miles past Ellen Creek on sandy beach. If the tide is high, look for a trail climbing steeply to the right. The trail climbs up and over

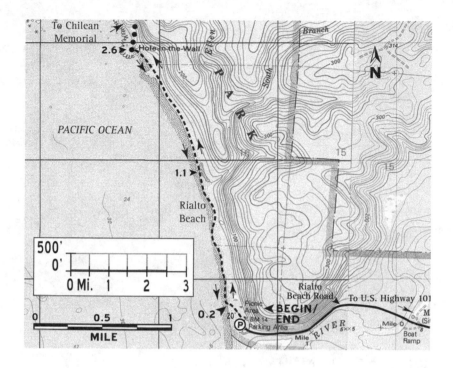

the rock to drop to the beach again; if the tide is out, you can avoid this climb by walking through the Hole in the Wall.

GOING FARTHER

The beach trail follows the wild Pacific coastline north for more than 16 miles to Cape Alava. Day hikers seeking a longer walk from Rialto Beach might make the Chilean Memorial, 1.2 miles beyond Hole in the Wall, their goal.

The Mora Campground in Olympic National Park makes a good car-camping base to explore other beach walks in the area.

Mountain bikers sometimes stage races along the Port Gamble Trails (#63).

KITSAP PENINSULA

63. Port Gamble Trails

RATING	🧍
DISTANCE	3.6–4.8 miles round-trip
HIKING TIME	2–3 hours
ELEVATION GAIN	200–300 feet
HIGH POINT	480 feet
EFFORT	Easy Walk
BEST SEASON	Fall; open year-round
PERMITS/CONTACT	None/Kitsap Peninsula Visitor and Convention Bureau, (800) 337-0580; www.visitkitsap.com
MAPS	USGS Port Gamble; trail map available at Kitsap VCB office, Port Gamble
NOTES	Bicyclists, equestrians, and leashed dogs welcome

THE HIKE

This is a pleasant getaway from the Big City Across Puget Sound, a walk through shaded forests with occasional hilltop views of Puget Sound and Whidbey Island.

GETTING THERE

From the Kingston Ferry Terminal, follow State Route 104 for 8 miles to Port Gamble. The parking most convenient to the trailhead is south of the log-scaling area, north of 104 across from the espresso stand. Cross 104 to the south and look for the trail—a gravel road heading south into the forest—west of several houses along the highway, 60 feet above sea level. GPS trailhead coordinates: N47°51.270′; W122°35.575′

THE TRAIL

Olympic Resource Management, the firm overseeing 4,300 acres around the historic Port Gamble townsite, has opened the extensive logging road system to nonmotorized traffic, and hikers, equestrians, and mountain bikers will find a variety of trails to follow. Several of the trails could form the seed for the North Kitsap String of Pearls, a plan to link a number of Kitsap Peninsula communities with nonmotorized trails.

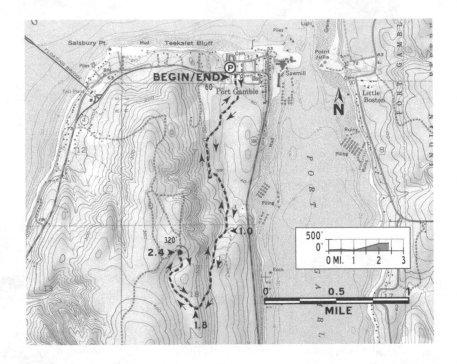

The main trail meanders south past the townsite's water reservoir through a mixed forest of alder, maple, and evergreens and climbs gently to the south for 1.0 mile to a junction with an access trail to State Route 104 on the left. Stay right and climb at a slightly steeper grade to an opening in the forest that yields views of Puget Sound to the east and Whidbey Island to the north. The trail climbs to a second junction at the crest of a low hill, 1.8 miles from the trailhead. This is a good turnaround point for families with small children.

To continue, follow the trail to the right as it makes a broad turn to the north and climbs a hill to a junction with another trail on the left, at about 2.4 miles. This is a good turnaround spot.

GOING FARTHER

You can combine the main trail with a series of connectors, including some short, steep, and often muddy sections that for some reason attract mountain bikers looking to add dirt stripes to the backs of their jerseys. The connectors can add an additional 3 miles or more to your walk and give you a full autumn day of hiking.

64. Green Mountain Trail

RATING	🏃
DISTANCE	9.5 miles round-trip
HIKING TIME	5 hours, 30 minutes
ELEVATION GAIN	1,200 feet
HIGH POINT	1,640 feet
EFFORT	Prepare to Perspire
BEST SEASON	Fall, early spring; open year-round
PERMITS/CONTACT	Discover Pass required/Washington State Department of Natural Resources, (800) 527-3305; www.dnr.wa.gov
MAPS	USGS Point Misery; DNR Green Mountain State Forest Map
NOTES	Bicyclists, equestrians, and leashed dogs welcome; ATVs permitted on some trails

THE HIKE

Green Mountain State Forest is the west Puget Sound version of Tiger Mountain—except it lacks the crowds, especially on weekdays. A network of trails circles the mountain, allowing loop hikes up to 12 to 15 miles round-trip. This hike is one of the best out-and-back trails (for a shorter version, see hike #65 in this guide).

GETTING THERE

From State Route 3 north of Bremerton, take the Newberry Hill Road (Silverdale) exit. Turn left, west, onto Newberry Hill Road and follow it uphill for 3.1 miles to the Seabeck Highway. Turn left onto the Seabeck Highway and follow it 2 miles to Holly Road. Turn right on Holly Road and follow it 1.8 miles to the Wildcat trailhead, 460 feet above sea level. GPS trailhead coordinates: N47°35.965′; W122°47.452′

THE HIKE

You'll climb about 1,200 feet in 4.2 miles to the summit of Green Mountain, but the view from the summit is worth the climb. The hike begins with a brief detour around a recently logged section of the Green Mountain State Forest. After crossing logging roads several times, the trail enters an older section of the forest, where big wild rhododendrons splotch the green with pink around mid-May and winter wrens chirp long greetings from the understory. In recent years, a small herd of elk has taken up residence here and around nearby Gold Mountain, which is a Bremerton city watershed and closed to the public. Black bears, deer, cougars, and bobcats also inhabit these woods.

The first mile of the trail climbs gently, but at **1.2** miles the path turns to serious uphill. Here I once traded places with my mountain bike, the Great Emasculator, and it rode me for a few feet while I slid along facedown in the mud. After about 1.0 mile of steady climbing, the trail crosses a road to the Green Mountain Campground, used primarily by the Olympic chapter of the Backcountry Horsemen, who stage regular volunteer work parties to maintain the trails and campground on Green Mountain. Walk through the campground on the upper road to find the continuation of the Wildcat Trail.

Beyond the campground, the trail climbs steeply before traversing around another clear-cut. Here views open to the east, with the Seattle skyline and the big hammerhead crane of Bremerton's Puget Sound Naval Shipyard prominently featured.

Climb into forest again, crossing another old logging road at **3.7** miles. You can follow the road as it climbs and joins the main Green Mountain Road, GM-1. The road climbs to the Vista parking area, but you can cross the road and look right for the continuation of the trail. At **3.9** miles, you'll join the Vista Trail; turn left and follow it to the Green Mountain Vista parking area, walk past the outhouse to the Vista Trail, and climb the final 0.2 mile to the summit. Return the way you came.

GOING FARTHER

For a longer route on the descent, you can follow the Vista and Gold Creek trails down to the junction with the Beaver Pond Trail, then follow the Beaver Pond Trail for 3.1 miles to the Green Mountain Campground. Return to the trailhead via the Wildcat Trail from the campground.

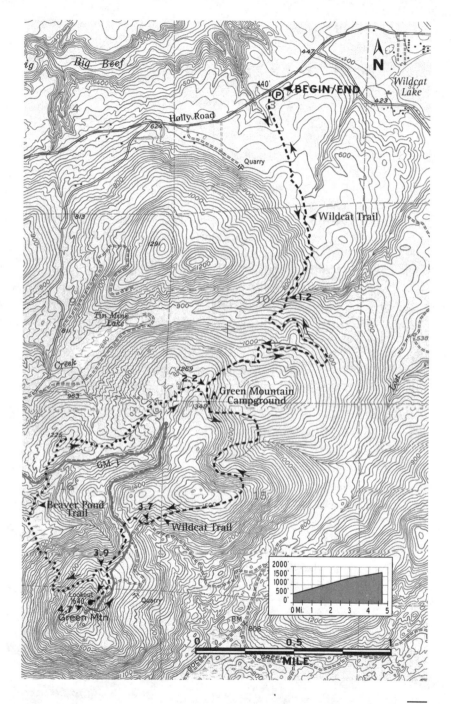

65. Gold Creek Trail

RATING   🚶 🚶
DISTANCE   5.0 miles round-trip
HIKING TIME   3 hours
ELEVATION GAIN   1,000 feet
HIGH POINT   1,640 feet
EFFORT   Moderate Workout
BEST SEASON   Spring, fall; open year-round
PERMITS/CONTACT   Discover Pass required/Washington State Department of Natural Resources, (800) 527-3305; www.dnr.wa.gov
MAPS   USGS Green Mountain; DNR Green Mountain State Forest Map
NOTES   Bicyclists and leashed dogs welcome

THE HIKE

This is a forested climb to great views of Puget Sound and the Cascades, Hood Canal country, and the Olympic Mountains, at the summit of Green Mountain. You won't find crowds of hikers tromping this path as you might on similar hikes on the eastern side of Puget Sound.

GETTING THERE

From State Route 3 north of Bremerton, take the Newberry Hill Road (Silverdale) exit. Turn west onto Newberry Hill Road and follow it uphill 3.1 miles to Seabeck Highway. Turn left onto Seabeck Highway and follow it 2 miles to Holly Road. Turn right on Holly and follow it 4.1 miles to Lake Tahuya Road. Turn left on Lake Tahuya Road and follow it 1.2 miles to a Y junction with Gold Creek Road. Turn left at the Y onto Gold Creek Road and follow it around Tahuya Lake for 1.7 miles to the Gold Creek trailhead, 630 feet above sea level. GPS trailhead coordinates: N47°33.110′; W122°49.601′

THE TRAIL

This is a good weekday workout in suburban woods where you might spot deer or an occasional black bear. A bobcat crossed my path on

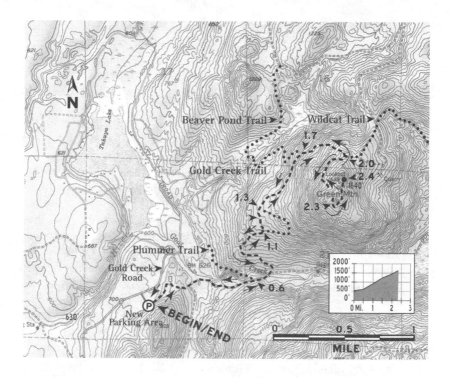

one recent hike here; count yourself lucky if you see one of the several mountain lions that wander these woods.

Spring is a fine time for this hike, when yellow skunk cabbage peeks from the forest edge and fawn lily winks along rocky outcrops above the trail. Rhododendrons turn the woods pink in mid-May.

Begin at the trailhead at the north end of the parking lot and meander through a clear-cut area, climbing a short hill onto an old road 0.25 mile from the parking area. Turn right and follow the old road as it climbs gently above chattering Gold Creek. At 0.6 mile, cross a metal bridge over the creek and turn left off the road on a trail that may be signed "Gold Creek Trail." Families with young children or those seeking a gentler walk can continue on the old road for another mile to a large beaver pond, where you might spot eagles, herons, or osprey—even one of those shy little guys who built the pond.

If you're heading up to the summit on the trail, you'll encounter a junction with the Plummer Trail about 100 feet from the bridge. Stay right here and continue climbing through the forest on moderate switchbacks. At 1.1 miles, choose the steeper Gold Creek Trail to the left or the gentler, longer trail to the right. The trails merge at **1.3** miles. After passing an old trail junction on the right, you'll cross under a utility line that climbs straight to the Green Mountain summit. If you're in the mood for a more strenuous workout, follow the rough way trail under the utility line. You'll know you're near the top when you pass the hulk of an old Volkswagen Beetle to the left of the trail.

The developed trail levels off a bit and at **1.7** miles, arrives at the Green Mountain and Vista trails. Keep right and continue climbing to a junction with the Wildcat Lake Trail at **2.0** miles. Stay right and eventually switchback and climb to the Vista parking lot just below the summit at **2.3** miles. This is as far as autos can go on the Green Mountain Road, which is open on summer weekends only.

Walk past the outhouse to find the Vista Trail and climb the final 0.25 mile to the Green Mountain summit, where you'll find concrete benches and picnic tables. You'll get a cliffside view of Bremerton, Puget Sound, Seattle, and the Cascades to the east; Mount Baker and Glacier Peak to the north; Mount Rainier to the south; and the Olympic Mountains to the west.

GOING FARTHER

A network of trails meanders through Green Mountain State Forest; for a longer loop hike, follow the Plummer Trail to the Beaver Pond Trail, and climb to the Gold Creek Trail. On the return, follow the Beaver Pond Trail to the Plummer Trail, turn right on the Aurora Trail, and descend to the Gold Creek Road. Cross Gold Creek on the road bridge, turn left, and follow the old road uphill to the junction with the Gold Creek Trail. Turn right, climb, and then descend to the trailhead.

Hikers check the view of the Puget Sound basin from the top of Green Mountain (#64).

A portion of the Ginkgo Petrified Forest Trail (#68) is paved. The old Vantage Highway stretches down to the Columbia River, right.

CENTRAL WASHINGTON

Interstate 84 to Yakima was still on the drawing board the first time I hiked on trails around the Yakima Canyon, walking the golden hills above the river and flailing the Yakima River to a froth with really bad fly casting. Today, after decades of practice, I can tell you without reservation that I am no better.

Central Washington trails vary in nature, from hill climbs to river walks, but they all share the fine weather that visits this country as often as the Westsiders who come to enjoy it. Most of the hikes are best taken in the spring, when the sun doesn't bake your backside and the wildflowers turn the canyons yellow. Frosty autumn mornings make a nice time for hiking the following trails, too.

Equestrians ride down the Ancient Lakes trail (#72).

CENTRAL WASHINGTON

66. Umtanum Canyon

RATING	🚶 🚶 🚶 🚶
DISTANCE	6.0 miles round-trip
HIKING TIME	4 hours
ELEVATION GAIN	350 feet
HIGH POINT	1,650 feet
EFFORT	Moderate Workout
BEST SEASON	Spring; open most of the year
PERMITS/CONTACT	Daily fee required May–September/Bureau of Land Management, (509) 536-1200, www.blm.gov/or
MAPS	USGS Umtanum Creek; Washington State Department of Natural Resources Yakima Canyon map
NOTES	Bicyclists and leashed dogs welcome; great family walk; very hot in summer

THE HIKE

It's tough to find a nicer springtime walk on the dry side of the mountains, especially if you'd like to see abundant wildlife and wildflowers popping up all over.

GETTING THERE

The trailhead is located off the scenic Yakima Canyon Road (State Route 821), about 12 miles south of Ellensburg. Follow Interstate 90 to the Ellensburg exit 109, turn south onto Yakima Canyon Road (watch the speed trap!), and follow it for 11 miles to the trailhead at the Umtanum Recreation Area, which includes a Bureau of Land Management campground. The trailhead is 1,300 feet above sea level. GPS trailhead coordinates: N46º51.316′; W120º28.976′

THE TRAIL

Whenever I hike with my wife, B. B. Hardbody, in Eastern Washington, I warn her to be on the lookout for snakes. I'm always on the lookout for snakes, so you can imagine my surprise when I stepped on one the last time I hiked this trail. I imagine the snake was a bit surprised, too. I was ogling the black basalt hillside above the canyon, trying to spot bighorn sheep, and felt the earth move beneath my feet. I've never been

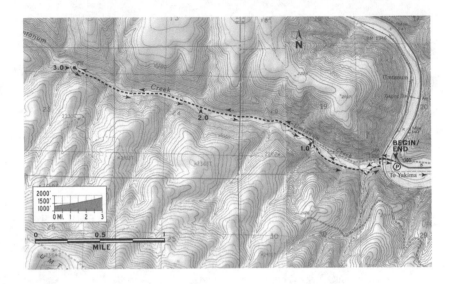

great at high-jumping, but Hardbody says I cleared at least 3 feet at that moment. I didn't stop to find out what kind of snake it was, and the snake didn't stop to find out what kind of fool would wander along its favorite sunning spot without looking where he was stepping.

Begin your walk by crossing the Yakima River on the suspension bridge at the north end of the trailhead parking lot. In the springtime the river is full, and you are likely to see fly anglers floating or wading the river after trophy rainbow trout. The trail crosses underneath a railroad trestle over Umtanum Creek and begins a gentle climb above the creek. The creek, cloaked in greening cottonwood, sings to you to the north. You'll continue to climb, ever gently, above the creek for about 1.0 mile through sage flats and ancient orchards carpeted with wildflowers.

Cross the creek at about 1.0 miles to a steeper but short climb over a ridge etched with basalt. If you're hiking in the spring or summer, here's where you'll most likely see snakes, most commonly rattlesnakes and bull snakes.

The trail eventually drops close to the creek and crosses it again to a shaded creekside campsite. It turns upstream once again and meanders through cottonwood clumps and open meadows for about 1.0 mile. Eventually, the canyon narrows, and the trail climbs up and over two ridges of broken basalt—easy crossings thanks to the work of trail volunteers. This is a good turnaround point, about 3.0 miles from the trailhead. Beyond, the trail narrows and begins climbing more steeply.

67. Manastash Ridge

RATING   🏃
DISTANCE   4.0 miles round-trip
HIKING TIME   3 hours
ELEVATION GAIN   1,700 feet
HIGH POINT   3,560 feet
EFFORT   Knee-Punishing
BEST SEASON   Spring
PERMITS/CONTACT   Discover Pass required/Washington Department of Fish and Wildlife, (509) 662-0490, www.wdfw.wa.gov
MAPS   USGS Badger Gap
NOTES   Leashed dogs welcome; very hot in summer

THE HIKE

This is a good hike for wildflowers and bird-watching in the spring, with wide views of the farms and flatlands below.

GETTING THERE

From Thorp exit 101 on Interstate 90, turn right on South Thorp Road and drive 2 miles to Cove Road; turn right. Follow Cove Road for 6.2 miles, crossing Manastash Road and parking at the trailhead at the parking area on the right, 1,877 feet above sea level. GPS trailhead coordinates: N46º58.120'; W120º38.737'

THE TRAIL

Begin by following an old double-track path across an irrigation canal toward the steep gully directly to the south. You'll climb along the western sidehill of the gully for about 0.3 mile to a trail junction. Both pathways rejoin in about 1.0 mile; I'd suggest staying left. This is a steep climb, gaining most of the elevation in the next mile as it follows the crest of the ridge to the south.

Your reward for all that sweat as you climb is expanding views of the Kittitas Valley and the central Cascade Mountains, with Mount Stuart the most prominent peak. Keep a lookout on the ground, too: expect to see snakes, including rattlers, on this hike. As you gain elevation, the variety and sheer number of wildflowers grow, with lupine, balsamroot,

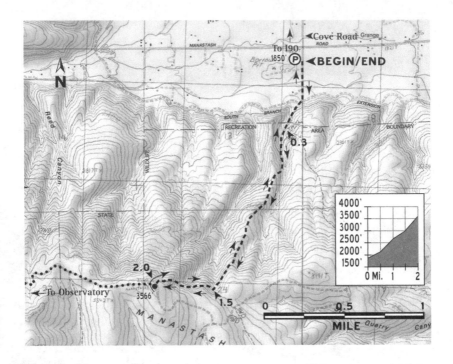

bitterroot, and phlox among the primary types. At **1.5** miles, you'll turn to the west and climb in rare broad switchbacks to a flat bench area and viewpoint at the Ray Westberg Memorial, your turnaround spot **2.0** miles from the trailhead. Westberg was a well-liked Ellensburg wrestling coach who died at the age of **47** in 1997.

GOING FARTHER

The trail continues through the L. T. Murray State Wildlife Recreation Area for another 3 miles to the University of Washington Manastash Ridge Observatory.

68. Ginkgo Petrified Forest Trails

RATING	🚶 🚶 🚶
DISTANCE	3 miles round-trip
HIKING TIME	2 hours
ELEVATION GAIN	200 feet
HIGH POINT	2,600 feet
EFFORT	Easy Walk
BEST SEASON	Spring; open year-round
PERMITS/CONTACT	Discover Pass required/Ginkgo Petrified Forest State Park, (509) 856-2700; www.parks.wa.gov
MAPS	USGS Ginkgo
NOTES	Leashed dogs welcome; very hot in summer

THE HIKE

Sunny spring days and wildflower-draped slopes make this a great hike for Westsiders who want to get out from underneath that wet, gray funk and see what the bright side of the state has been enjoying all year long.

GETTING THERE

Follow Interstate 90 to the Vantage exit 136 and turn north on Huntzinger Road. Drive past Vantage for 2.3 miles on old Vantage Highway to the Ginkgo Petrified Forest Interpretive Center and parking area on the right, 1,063 feet above sea level. GPS trailhead coordinates: N46°56.861′; W120°02.184′

THE TRAIL

When I reflect on this sunny little loop trail that passes through one of the largest petrified forests in the world, I'm reminded of Mark Twain's put on of the Egyptian guide in *Innocents Abroad*. So—if you'd like—as you pass one of those mineralized trees in the cage beside the trail, ask your hiking partner:

"Um, do you think that tree is dead?"

The basalt columns and cliffs surrounding the Columbia River here tell a story of mighty lava flows that turned spruce, fir, elm, and walnut trees to stone. It's a fine walk that begins with a 0.25-mile paved loop past several examples of mineralized trees.

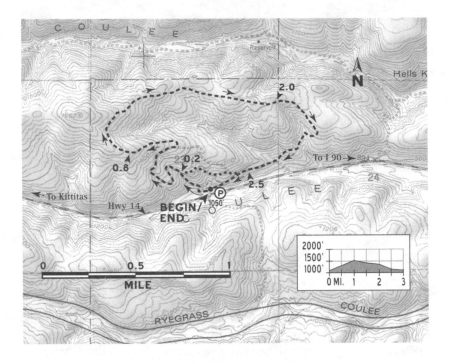

You'll climb a short hill to the northwest and leave the paved trail at a junction about **0.2** mile from the parking area. Climb the hillside to the left in broad switchbacks, then head west up a gully, circling to the north at **0.8** mile. The trail traverses the hillside and contours east along slopes that show off wildflowers foreign to Westside hikers, such as grass widows and prairie star flowers.

Trailside signs along the way explain how the trees were turned to stone and point out various land and geologic features. The sunny south-facing slopes provide a good early source of food for wildlife and birds. Look for raptors above, listen for the distinctive call of meadowlarks, and keep a lookout in late spring and summer for snakes sunning themselves on the trail. Don't hassle the ones that rattle their tails at you. At **2.0** miles, the route swings back to the east along a steep hillside, rounds a dry gully at **2.5** miles, and drops back to the parking area.

69. John Wayne Trail West

RATING	🚶 🚶
DISTANCE	7.0 miles round-trip
HIKING TIME	4 hours
ELEVATION GAIN	400 feet
HIGH POINT	2,400 feet
EFFORT	Moderate Workout
BEST SEASON	Spring
PERMITS/CONTACT	Self-issue free Army permit/Iron Horse State Park, (360) 902-8844
MAPS	USGS Doris
NOTES	Bicyclists, equestrians, and leashed dogs welcome; very hot in summer

THE HIKE

This long walk in desert country is a fine springtime outing for wildflowers and wildlife-watching, with the prospect of a tunnel hike for those who wish to go farther.

GETTING THERE

From the Kittitas exit 115 off Interstate 90, drive north to Kittitas and turn right on First Avenue. Drive 2.6 miles to Prater Road, turn right, and drive 0.3 mile, crossing I 90; turn left on Boylston Road. Follow Boylston for 3.5 miles, passing underneath the old railroad trestle over I-90. Turn right just under the trestle and, in 250 feet, take the first left to the trailhead parking area, 2,000 feet above sea level. GPS trailhead coordinates: N46°57.258′; W120°17.860′

THE TRAIL

This portion of the John Wayne Pioneer Trail, the old railroad route of the Chicago, Milwaukee, St. Paul, and Pacific Railroad, travels across the US Army's Yakima Training Center. Don't worry: you're safe from GIs training on you as long as you stay within the 200-foot-wide corridor that is your pathway. Begin by walking a wide double track to the east up to the old railroad grade and a self-issuing permit box, about

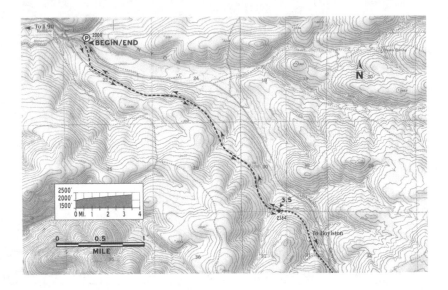

150 yards from the parking area. Carry your permit with you and drop it off in the box at the end of your hike.

The trail climbs ever-so-gently through a sage garden that flashes wildflowers of every color in the springtime. If you hail from the wet side of the mountains, tote a wildflower book that shows the plants of the desert: you won't recognize much of the greenery that grows here. The wide, well-graded trail is popular in the spring with mountain bikers. As it climbs, it leaves the noise of Interstate 90 behind and, in 1.0 mile, dips behind a low hill to follow the southern hillside above Johnson Canyon.

If you can take your eyes off the wildflowers, check the surrounding countryside and big sky for wildlife. Badgers tunnel in nearby hillsides, coyotes trot through the sage hills, and meadowlarks sing familiar tunes, while hawks and vultures float on thermals above. The trail continues along a swale below the Boylston Mountains to the south, which reach to just over 3,000 feet. At 3.5 miles, you'll round a broad curve to the south and reach your turnaround point.

GOING FARTHER
The old railroad stop of Boylston is another mile southeast on the trail, which would make a round-trip hike of 9 miles. If you're willing to go that far, you should plan on hiking another mile through the Boylston Tunnel, which will cool you off on a hot day. The tunnel is 1,970 feet

long and curves slightly, so it gets dark in there. Make certain everyone totes a headlamp with extra batteries. If you turn around at the east end of the tunnel, your hike would be 9.8 miles round-trip, with an elevation gain of 500 feet.

70. John Wayne Trail East

RATING	🚶 🚶 🚶
DISTANCE	8.0 miles
HIKING TIME	5 hours
ELEVATION GAIN	1,450 feet
HIGH POINT	2,450 feet
EFFORT	Moderate Workout
BEST SEASON	Spring; open year-round
PERMITS/CONTACT	Free self-issue Army permit/Iron Horse State Park, (360) 902-8844
MAPS	USGS Beverly
NOTES	Bicyclists, leashed dogs, and equestrians welcome; hot in summer

THE HIKE

Climb the eastern slope of the hills above Vantage along an old railroad grade through fields of wildflowers in the spring and sage gardens throughout the year.

GETTING THERE

From Interstate 90 at Vantage, take the Huntzinger Road exit 136 and drive south on Huntzinger Road for 7.1 miles. Turn right at the road signed "John Wayne Trail 2.5 miles." At certain times in the fall hunting season, this road may be gated; in that event, you can either walk up the road—which is just about as nice as the hike—or try the western end of this trail (hike #69 in this guide). If the road is open, drive 2.5 miles to the trailhead, 1,000 feet above sea level. GPS trailhead coordinates: N46°52.120'; W119°59.978'

THE TRAIL

I prefer this hike to the west-slope John Wayne Trail for a couple of reasons: you'll get morning light at your back, good for wildflower photography and perhaps seeing more wildlife, and it's usually cooler and less windy in the morning in the dry hills above the Columbia River. Begin by issuing yourself a free permit at the trailhead kiosk, which you'll carry with you and deposit on your return. The trail—an old railroad grade—

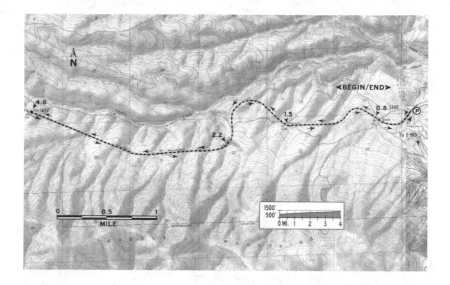

crosses the Army's Yakima Training Center for 17 miles. Your path is a 200-foot-wide swath along the rail route, and if you stray from this path, you will have to answer to Staff Sergeant Dilrod Grub, my old drill sergeant, or at least someone as tough and mean as he was.

Begin by climbing a short hill at the trailhead that is the steepest part of the hike. Once on the railroad grade, you'll find a splendid wildflower display likely dominated by yellow balsamroot. White and pink phlox spreads out across the desert floor, and other wildflowers cling to cracks in the basalt banks beside the trail. Look for raptors above, who in turn are looking for rabbits and reptiles below.

The trail climbs at a barely noticeable grade for **0.8** mile to the abandoned railroad siding of Doris, where a couple of collapsed buildings decorate the ground and Chicago, Milwaukee, St. Paul, and Pacific Railroad relics can be found lying around. The route past Doris continues to climb due west for **0.8** mile before making a broad swing to the north to gain elevation toward the Johnson Creek basin, curving back to the west 2.2 miles from the trailhead. You'll continue climbing above Johnson Creek for another 1.8 miles, crossing a number of dry gullies where your chances of spotting wildlife increase. At **4.0** miles, you'll find Rye, another abandoned railroad siding. This is your cue to sit down, drink liquids, and eat cold fried chicken or Tofurky, and head back down the hill.

71. Cowiche Canyon Trail

RATING	🚶 🚶 🚶
DISTANCE	6.4 miles round-trip
HIKING TIME	4 hours
ELEVATION GAIN	200 feet
HIGH POINT	1,500 feet
EFFORT	Easy Walk
BEST SEASON	Spring; open year-round
PERMITS/CONTACT	None/Cowiche Canyon Conservancy, (509) 248-5065, www.cowichecanyon.org
MAPS	USGS Naches, Wiley City; www.cowichecanyon.org
NOTES	Bicyclists and leashed dogs welcome; good family hike; hot in summer

THE HIKE

Walk through a wild canyon filled with spring wildflowers, birds, and wildlife, just minutes away from urban Yakima.

GETTING THERE

From US Highway 12 in Fruitvale, take the Fruitvale Boulevard–North 40th Avenue exit and take 40th Avenue south for 1.5 miles to Summit-view Avenue. Turn right and follow Summitview for 4.1 miles, bearing right onto Summitview–Cowiche Road and ignoring Summitview Extension. Follow Summitview–Cowiche up and over a hill for 2.9 miles to Weikel Road and turn right to the trailhead, 1,300 feet above sea level. GPS trailhead coordinates: N46°37.882′; W120°39.938′

THE TRAIL

You have the volunteers of the Cowiche Canyon Conservancy to thank for this splendid walk through a basalt-rimmed canyon chock-full of wildflowers in the spring and wildlife pretty much year-round. In winters with heavy snow, you can enjoy a nice cross-country ski in the canyon. This is another gentle climb that follows an abandoned Burlington Northern railroad grade.

In spring, the canyon floor is yellow with balsamroot, a bright contrast against the dark basalt cliffs of the canyon. Raptors soar above, and you

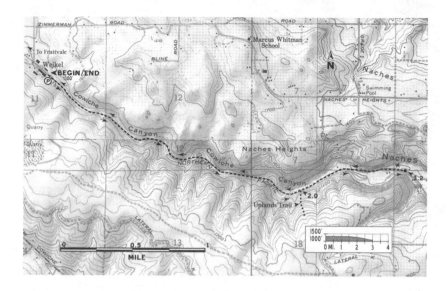

can mark their nesting and roosting spots along the cliffs by the white streaks on the rock formations. Bluebirds and swallows also call the canyon home, as do badgers, rabbits, and reptiles, including rattlesnakes. The trail leaves the parking area to the southeast, passing a house on the left before entering the canyon and leaving civilization behind.

The railroad engineers used every inch of the canyon to negotiate the grade, crossing Cowiche Creek from side to side. As a result, you'll cross nine bridges along the way, roughly 0.3 mile apart. Just beyond the eighth bridge, about 2.0 miles, you'll find a junction with the Uplands Trail. Stay to the left here and continue along the canyon for another mile, crossing a final bridge to the East Entrance trailhead, 3.2 miles from your parking area.

GOING FARTHER

The Cowiche Canyon Conservancy serves up a number of great trails for hikers and mountain bikers, but the easiest extension for your hike is to return to the junction with the Uplands Trail and turn left, climbing a steep 400 vertical feet in 1.2 miles to the Scenic Drive trailhead, returning the way you came. That would make a round-trip total of 8.8 miles and 600 vertical feet. Want more? Explore the Ridgeline Trail, which crosses the Uplands Trail about 0.2 mile north of the Scenic trailhead.

72. Ancient Lake(s)

RATING   🚶 🚶 🚶
DISTANCE   5.0 miles round-trip
HIKING TIME   3 hours, 30 minutes
ELEVATION GAIN   180 feet
HIGH POINT   120 feet
EFFORT   Moderate Workout
BEST SEASON   Spring; open year-round
PERMITS/CONTACT   Discover Pass required/Washington Department of Fish and Wildlife, (509) 662-0490; www.wdfw.wa.gov
MAPS   USGS Babcock Ridge
NOTES   Leashed dogs welcome; hot in summer

THE HIKE

The Potholes area of central Washington serves up some surprises, including this walk to a lake and waterfall in surroundings you'd least expect.

GETTING THERE

From Interstate 90, take the George exit 149 and drive north on State Route 281 for 5.6 miles to White Trail Road; turn left and follow it 7.8 miles to Road 9-NW. Turn left and drive 5.9 miles on Road 9-NW, passing Crescent Bar on the right, to the road's end on Babcock Bench, 1,013 feet above sea level. GPS trailhead coordinates: N47°09.611´; W119°58.846´

THE TRAIL

I discovered that a coulee, such as the Potholes Coulee here, really isn't very cool in the summer. It gets so hot here that the game birds roast themselves every August. Feel free to check my research on that point if you don't believe me.

Begin this hike by following an old double-track road that climbs into the coulee, winding under cliffs to the east. You'll pass an old archaeological dig about 0.25 mile from the trailhead, then find a junction after another 0.4 mile. Turn left on the single-track trail as it climbs into the coulee. You'll find a kaleidoscope of wildflowers in the spring and just about every species of game bird. In fact, if you're looking for a lung-busting

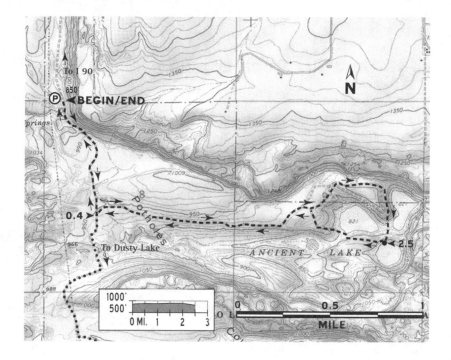

workout, find yourself a chukar and try to keep up with it as it runs through the sage.

You'll climb moderate slopes to the east for about 1.0 mile before turning to the northeast and arriving at a trail junction at 2.0 miles. The route above the Ancient Lake basin loops left around the first lake, with a view of a second lake to the east, where you'll get a look at a waterfall that drops into the lake. From there, circle to the south for a look at a third pothole lake, the "official" Ancient Lake—though it is likely the other two are just as old (geologically speaking). Beyond, the trail climbs back to the trail junction. Turn left to return to the trailhead.

GOING FARTHER

For a longer hike, drop back down to the junction with the double-track trail and turn left, following it to the south for 1 mile, then climb east into another coulee that holds Dusty Lake, returning as you came. The total round-trip distance to both lakes would be about 11 miles and a climb of about 400 vertical feet. Wilderness pedestrians looking for a gentler workout can skip the Ancient Lakes Trail and head directly to Dusty Lake, for a round-trip walk of 6 miles and a climb of about 200 vertical feet.

73. Umatilla Rock Loop

RATING	🚶 🚶
DISTANCE	3.0–5.0 miles round-trip
HIKING TIME	2–4 hours
ELEVATION GAIN	100 feet
HIGH POINT	1,300 feet
EFFORT	Moderate Workout
BEST SEASON	Spring; open year-round
PERMITS/CONTACT	Discover Pass required/Sun Lakes State Park, (360) 902-8844; www.parks.wa.gov
MAPS	USGS Coulee City
NOTES	Leashed dogs welcome

THE HIKE
Head for a desert walk around a massive basalt formation. It was once an island in the middle of a 3-mile-wide splash pool from an ancient waterfall 10 times larger than Niagara Falls.

GETTING THERE
From Interstate 90 west of George, take exit 151 to State Route 283 and turn north, driving through Ephrata and Soap Lake. Turn left on State Route 17 and drive 17 miles to the Sun Lakes State Park entrance on the right. Follow the park road for 1.3 miles and turn left at the Dry Falls Lake–Camp Delany Road. This road is gated in the winter; you can drive another mile to Camp Delany in the summer. Park at the signed trailhead, 1,200 feet above sea level; or if you can't drive to Camp Delany, park along the road. GPS trailhead coordinates: N47°35.459′; W119°22.049′

THE TRAIL
The official trailhead is located just below the southern end of Umatilla Rock near Camp Delany—but as noted above, you may not always be able to drive all the way to the trailhead. If so, your route is around that giant basalt formation jutting from the desert to the northeast. Follow the established trail among blooming wildflowers along bottomland that was once the pool below Dry Falls, which—curiously enough—have no water plunging over them today. Toward the end of the last Ice Age it

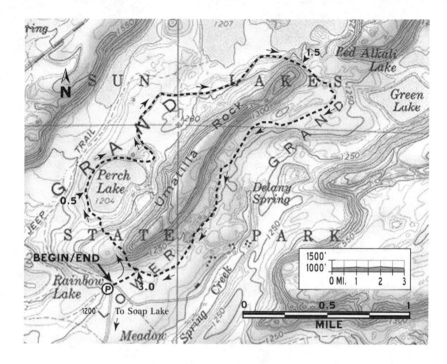

was a different story: the falls were 400 feet high and 3.5 miles wide, and Umatilla Rock was an island that split the runoff.

If you've parked near Camp Delany, head northwest around the southern end of Umatilla Rock and climb around the west side of Perch Lake, 0.5 mile from the parking area. Perch Lake—can you guess?—contains a population of perch. Round the lake and continue to the northeast to the southeastern shore of Dry Falls Lake. Turn to the east here, rounding the north end of Umatilla Rock, at 1.5 miles. Follow a trail that climbs to a low pass east of Umatilla Rock and turns to the south, descending into Monument Coulee. Head south along trails mainly engineered by the wildlife that calls this neck of the woods home, either closing the loop at Camp Delany or walking the road for another mile.

GOING FARTHER
Sun Lakes State Park serves up more than 15 miles of hiking trails and—not surprisingly—plenty of sunshine. The park is most popular with those who come to play on the water, however, so you might find yourself almost alone on some of the pathways that lead around lakes and geologic features.

74. Billy Clapp Lake Wildlife Area

RATING	🚶
DISTANCE	4.0 miles round-trip
HIKING TIME	2 hours, 30 minutes
ELEVATION GAIN	460 feet
HIGH POINT	1,400 feet
EFFORT	Easy Walk
BEST SEASON	Spring, summer
PERMITS/CONTACT	Discover Pass required/ Washington Department of Fish and Wildlife, (509) 662-0490; www.wdfw.wa.gov
MAPS	USGS Wilson Creek NW
NOTES	Leashed dogs welcome; good family hike; hot in summer

THE HIKE
Walk along a bluff overlooking an irrigation reservoir that is home to a variety of upland birds, waterfowl, and other wildlife.

GETTING THERE
From Interstate 90 at George, take exit 151 to State Route 283, turn north, and follow it through Ephrata to Soap Lake. Turn right on State Route 28 and drive east 10.3 miles. Turn left on the Pinto Dam–Billy Clapp Lake Road and drive 12.5 miles to the end of the road, just north of the earthen Pinto Dam. The trailhead is 1,200 feet above sea level. GPS trailhead coordinates: N47°27.178′; W119°15.184′

THE TRAIL
Pick up the trail at the northern end of the parking area and climb a hillside above the lake, then follow the shoreline of the lake to the north. The lake is more than 3.0 miles long, created by water tumbling out of Banks Lake at Summer Falls, which—by no odd coincidence—only flows during the summer. (OK, maybe they should have called it Spring and Summer Falls, because it does flow in the spring, too.)

At a viewpoint 0.2 mile from the trailhead, you'll look across the lake to basalt cliffs tumbling into the water. Turn and descend into a rocky canyon, following the trail up and down and traversing for 1.0 mile

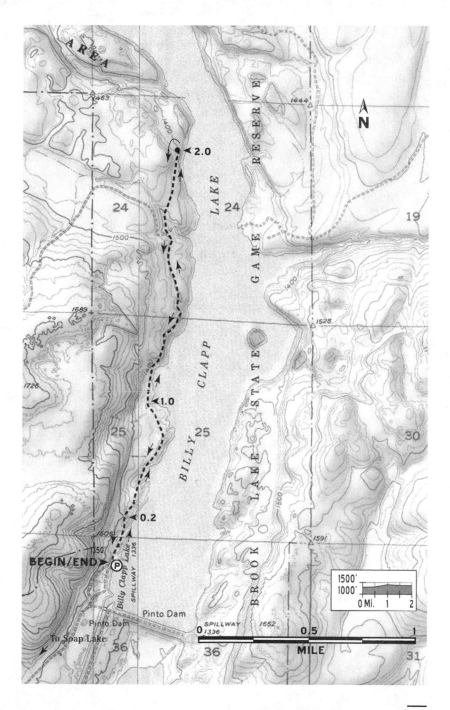

from the trailhead before descending to the lakeshore itself. This is a good turnaround spot for families with younger children.

From the lake, you'll climb about 400 feet in 1.0 mile along a bench above the lake. Basalt cliffs above house numerous coyote dens, and the sage plateau is covered with wildflowers in the spring. At 2.0 miles you'll reach a wide bend in the lake and a trail to the west, with a view to cliffs across the lake and north toward the Grand Coulee. This is a good spot for a picnic and turnaround.

GOING FARTHER
You can hike another 1.5 miles as the trail meanders inland to the west, then turns north again to reach a viewpoint above the lake before swinging west again and ending under power transmission lines at a viewpoint overlooking Summer Falls. The round-trip distance to this turnaround point is 7.0 miles, with an elevation gain of 540 feet.

75. Swakane Canyon Road

RATING	🚶 🚶 🚶
DISTANCE	5.0 miles round-trip
HIKING TIME	3 hours
ELEVATION GAIN	400 feet
HIGH POINT	1,750 feet
EFFORT	Moderate Workout
BEST SEASON	Spring
PERMITS/CONTACT	Discover Pass required/Washington Department of Fish and Wildlife, (509) 662-0490; www.wdfw.wa.gov
MAPS	USGS Wenatchee
NOTES	Leashed dogs welcome; good mountain biking; hot in summer

THE HIKE

This walk up a dirt road provides a rare chance to spot wildlife you won't see in too many places around the state: bighorn sheep on hillside cliffs and golden eagles soaring on the air currents.

GETTING THERE

From US Highway 97A in Wenatchee, drive north toward Entiat for 5.4 miles to the Swakane Canyon Road on the left. Turn left and follow the road as it climbs, steeply at first, for 2.9 rough gravel miles to a Y intersection. Take the right fork and park at the trailhead, 1,460 feet above sea level. GPS trailhead coordinates: N47°34.068′; W120°19.937′

THE TRAIL

Begin by hiking down to the Y intersection and turning right onto the little-used Swakane Canyon Road. This road meanders up the bottom lands of the Swakane Canyon and is a less painful alternative to the steeper Road 5215 above. Though open to traffic, the Swakane Canyon Road is never very crowded, even in the spring and fall, when game is abundant. On my first visit, I was passed by only one vehicle, a woman driving a truckload of Girl Scouts along the path she had taken as a Scout years before. She told me that the road continued all the way to Lake Chelan.

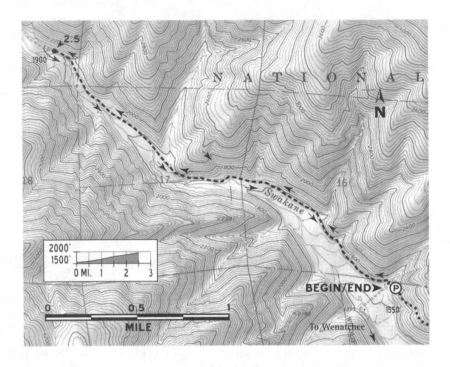

You needn't hike that far. Instead, follow the road as it climbs along the northern side of the canyon. Look for deer amid the cottonwoods on the canyon bottomlands and for bighorn sheep on the rocky hillsides above. Raptors, including golden and bald eagles, float on air currents, and the whole canyon practically glows with balsamroot in the spring. The road alternately climbs and drops toward the canyon bottom but never leaves the northern side, decorated with an increasing number of pine trees as you gain elevation. The road widens and flattens near a rocky outcrop, 2.5 miles from the beginning of your hike, a good turnaround spot.

GOING FARTHER

For a much steeper round-trip climb of about 6 miles and 1,500 vertical feet, hike the right fork at the Y parking area up Road 5215. The path is gated and closed to traffic, and switches back up the north side of the canyon to a stunning Columbia River overlook.

76. Potholes Dunes

RATING	🚶 🚶 🚶
DISTANCE	4.0 miles round-trip
HIKING TIME	2 hours, 30 minutes
ELEVATION GAIN	140 feet
HIGH POINT	1,130 feet
EFFORT	Easy Walk
BEST SEASON	Spring; open year-round
PERMITS/CONTACT	Discover Pass required/Washington Department of Fish and Wildlife, (509) 662-0490; www.wdfw.wa.gov
MAPS	USGS O'Sullivan Dam
NOTES	Leashed dogs welcome; good family walk; hot in summer

THE HIKE

This is one of the very best desert hikes in this guide. You'll stroll across sand dunes, see wildflowers of every color, and spot so many different kinds of waterfowl and wildlife they would fill an Audubon guide.

GETTING THERE

From Interstate 90, 8 miles west of Moses Lake, take exit 169 and turn south on Hiawatha Road. Cross the interstate and turn left on the frontage road. Drive 2.5 miles to the State Department of Fish and Wildlife access road, marked "Public Fishing." Turn right on this gravel road and drive 2.6 miles to a Y intersection. Stay right and drive another 1.1 mile to a second Y intersection and stay left, driving 1.2 miles to the end of the road and the trailhead, 1,100 feet above sea level. GPS trailhead coordinates: N47°03.062´; W119°23.202´

THE TRAIL

My introduction to the Potholes area was on opening day of fishing season, 1950. My best friend convinced his father to drive us from Spokane. We got up at 0-dark-30; I was surprised to hear how many birds were already awake. I am certain I haven't gotten out of bed that early since.

Once there, I wasn't eager to get out of the car because of all the tales I'd heard about rattlesnakes. The only other thing I remember about that early

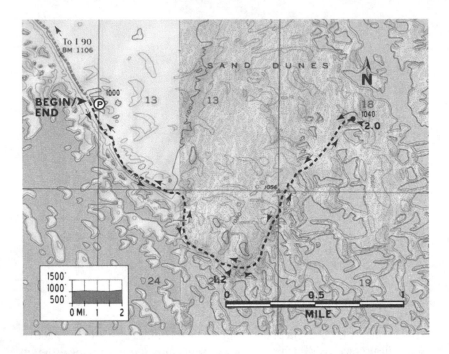

adventure was that anglers were catching stocked trout with corn, and my grandfather, who taught me all about angling, was a fly-fishing snob. I didn't see a single snake, rattle or otherwise, and I don't think I caught a single fish.

Corn-wielding anglers blazed the trail you'll be following, and today those anglers go after wily warm-water fish like crappie and bass. Begin by walking south over the rolling dunes and taking in the surprising views of all that water in the middle of a desert. In the spring, the ground is a symphony of wildflowers, with yellow carrying the main melody. Look to the sky for hawks and other raptors, and scan the dunes for coyotes and other critters. Walk about a mile across the undulating dunes and drop to water's edge at **1.2** miles. This might be a good turnaround spot for families with young children.

From here, your path turns to the east, alternately climbing and descending in 20-foot-high chunks as it curves through the dunes. The main Potholes Reservoir spreads south like a mottled arm pointing to the O'Sullivan Dam. Hike for 0.8 mile to the dunes overlooking Crab Creek, a good spot to pull up some sand, sit down, and enjoy a sunny picnic.

GOING FARTHER

Water covers about 20,000 acres of the Potholes Wildlife Area each spring, leaving you about 12,000 acres for walking. You can loop north and west for at least 1.5 miles from your turnaround spot along the dunes above Crab Creek, then wander to the west to pick up the path back to the trailhead.

The Beacon Rock trail (#79) is carved from solid rock.

COLUMBIA RIVER GORGE

M ost of the really good hiking trails in the Columbia Gorge are on the Oregon side of the river, with the exception of Dog and Hamilton mountains. I've included Dog Mountain here, but you'd be wise to try a few easier hikes first; Hamilton is a long hike and it would stretch the imagination to call it easy. The following hikes will give you a taste of Columbia Gorge hiking, which is all uphill on the way to your destination—no matter what it is—and downhill on the way home.

Don't worry. Humans are allowed on Dog Mountain (#80) too.

COLUMBIA RIVER GORGE

77. Hardy and Rodney Falls

RATING	🚶 🚶
DISTANCE	2.6 miles round-trip
HIKING TIME	2 hours
ELEVATION GAIN	640 feet
HIGH POINT	1,000 feet
EFFORT	Moderate Workout
BEST SEASON	Spring, fall
PERMITS/CONTACT	Discover Pass required/Beacon Rock State Park, (509) 427-8265; www.wdfw.wa.gov
MAPS	USGS Beacon Rock; Green Trails Bridal Veil
NOTES	Leashed dogs welcome; good family hike

THE HIKE

This is a pleasant walk through a shady forest, best taken in the spring when the falls are full of water.

GETTING THERE

From Interstate 205 in Vancouver, take exit 27 and follow Lewis and Clark Highway (State Route 14) for 27.5 miles to Beacon Rock State Park. Turn left on the campground road and follow it to the picnic area and trailhead, 360 feet above sea level.

Hikers coming from the east can drive 56 miles west on State Route 14 from the Maryhill junction with US Highway 97. GPS trailhead coordinates: N45°37.944'; W122°1.209'

THE TRAIL

Bring the dog. Bring the kids. Everyone should enjoy this climb along a forested hillside on an excellent trail to two of the nicest waterfalls on the Washington side of the Columbia Gorge. You'll hike past Little Beacon Rock on the left to a sunny patch out of the forest along power lines, courtesy of the Bonneville Dam. At 0.5 mile from the trailhead, you'll pass a trail junction by staying to the right, then climb to the north to round a ridge where you can hear the sound of Hardy Creek, shuffling off to the right. The water's rush gets louder as you approach the falls and cross a tributary creek.

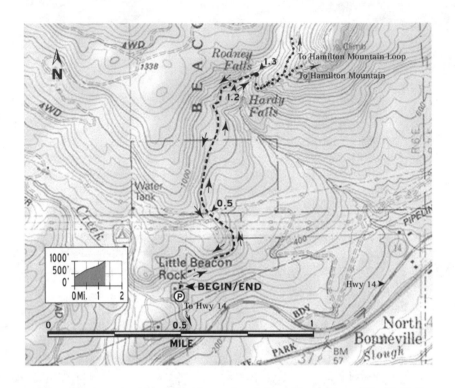

At **1.2** miles, a spur trail leads to the right with a view of Hardy Falls, the lower of the two cascades. Once you've taken in the view, head back to the main trail and continue climbing to a second spur to the left leading to the Pool of the Winds, between Hardy Falls and Rodney Falls. Back on the main trail, climb and drop to a bridge across Hardy Creek, your turnaround point at **1.3** miles.

GOING FARTHER

For a significantly tougher workout, consider a climb to the summit of Hamilton Mountain, a spectacular viewpoint above the falls—way above the falls. The trail climbs in steep switchbacks from the bridge for 0.3 mile to a trail junction: continue right and climb for 1.6 miles to the Hamilton Mountain summit. The total distance for this hike is 6.4 miles round-trip, with an elevation gain of 2,080 feet.

78. Klickitat Rail Trail

RATING	🚶 🚶 🚶
DISTANCE	7.0 miles round-trip
HIKING TIME	4 hours
ELEVATION GAIN	120 feet
HIGH POINT	260 feet
EFFORT	Easy Walk
BEST SEASON	Spring; open year-round
PERMITS/CONTACT	Discover Pass required/Klickitat Trail Conservancy, www.klickitat-trail.org
MAPS	USGS Stacker Butte
NOTES	Bicyclists and leashed dogs welcome; good family hike

THE HIKE

This old railroad route follows the Wild and Scenic Klickitat River as it winds through a canyon on its way to the Columbia River.

GETTING THERE

From Interstate 205 in Vancouver, follow Lewis and Clark Highway (State Route 14) at exit 27 for 70 miles to Lyle. From the Maryhill junction to the east, take SR 14 west for 28 miles to Lyle. From the State Route 142 junction in Lyle, turn north and drive 3 miles to a parking area at the Fisher Hill Road bridge at the Columbia River Gorge National Scenic Area sign. Cross the bridge and climb onto the trail on the right. Limited parking is available across the Fisher Hill bridge, along the road. The trailhead is 160 feet above sea level. GPS trailhead coordinates: N45°42.666'; W121°15.956'

THE TRAIL

The Klickitat Rail Trail is one of those gems known to local hikers and bikers that is not widely visited by wilderness pedestrians from the big urban centers. Yakima hikers visit this abandoned Spokane, Portland, and Seattle Railway spur in the spring, but it is seldom heavily used. You're just as likely to find anglers and tribal fishers along the Klickitat as other hikers.

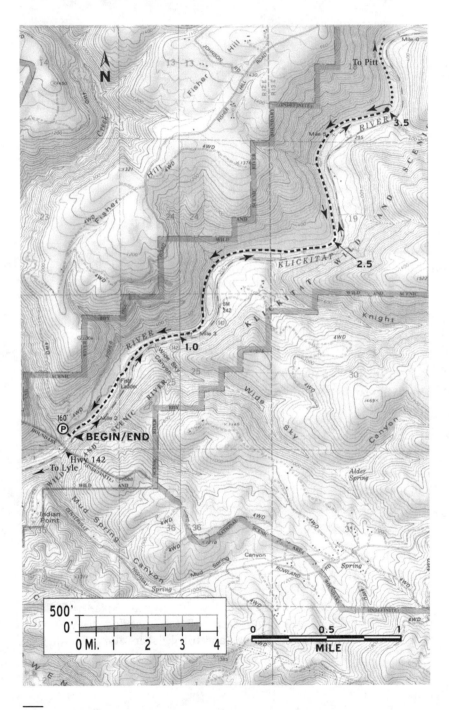

As you cross the Fisher Hill bridge, begin by looking down into the river canyon, where you'll likely see a fishing platform perched above the roil of the river. Tribal fishers net coho and chinook salmon here; it's one of only two Native American dip-net fisheries in the Columbia Basin. Once on the trail, you'll walk upstream past a number of privately owned river tracts, so make certain to stay on the trail. The path is covered with a rough rail ballast, so hikers with heavy boots will be thankful for stiff soles. The route continues upstream for 1.0 mile, where in season you'll find the site of a Yakama Nation fish trap, and the river gorge widens. Look for eagles and ospreys above and keep an eye out for the prolific poison oak that grows along the path.

Continue walking along the riverside as it winds farther north to wide flats and a good picnic turnaround point, 3.5 miles from the trailhead.

GOING FARTHER

The Klickitat Rail Trail continues upstream for another 5.5 miles one-way to the community of Pitt, where you'll find another access point to the trail. Hikers with two cars can arrange for a key-exchange hike, making a one-way trek of 9 miles.

Beyond, the trail climbs into the Swale Canyon, and you can hike or ride a bike or horse up to 31 miles one-way. Bike riders should be certain to pack extra tubes and patches; goat head thorns lurk everywhere.

79. Beacon Rock

RATING	🚶 🚶 🚶 🚶
DISTANCE	2.0 miles round-trip
HIKING TIME	1 hour, 30 minutes
ELEVATION GAIN	600 feet
HIGH POINT	848 feet
EFFORT	Moderate Workout
BEST SEASON	Summer, spring
PERMITS/CONTACT	Discover Pass required/Beacon Rock State Park, (509) 427-8265; www.parks.wa.gov
MAPS	USGS Beacon Rock; Green Trails Bridal Veil
NOTES	Leashed dogs welcome; good family walk

THE HIKE

Though not much of a hike, the climb to the top of Beacon Rock should rank high on your must-do list of trails in the state. Besides its mind-blowing view of the Columbia River Gorge, the trail is a real engineering masterpiece.

GETTING THERE

From Interstate 205 in Vancouver, take exit 27 and follow Lewis and Clark Highway (State Route 14) for 27.5 miles to Beacon Rock State Park and the wide parking area on the right, 248 feet above sea level. From the east, drive 56 miles west on SR 14 from the Maryhill junction with US Highway 97. GPS trailhead coordinates: N45°37.745'; W122°1.309'

THE TRAIL

The Lewis and Clark Expedition named Beacon Rock as the explorers boated down the Columbia on Halloween 1805. It probably wasn't half as scary for them as it was for me, a shameless acrophobe, when I saw Beacon Rock 200 years later. I got a callus on my right hand from clutching the safety rail as I climbed along the trail, wondering at all those idiots who could fall off the path at any minute. It is the acrophobe's curse that we think everyone is as frightened of sheer drops as we are, so we are afraid for you. Very afraid.

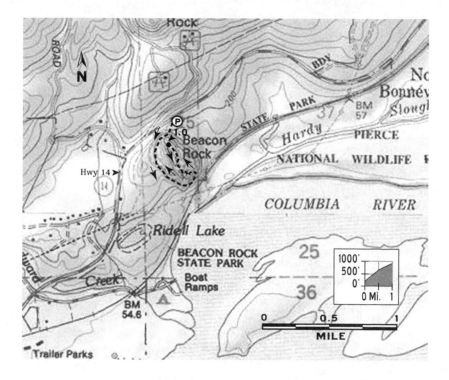

It makes little difference to us that a hiker would have to be blind, drunk, and able to step over a 3-foot-high railing without realizing it before falling to his or her death. The entire hike is along a trail wide enough—almost—to drive a Smart car. The trail climbs along the cliffs of Beacon Rock in switchbacks, sometimes crossing above itself on concrete ramps. Views open as you climb the west, south, and east sides of the monolith, and as you climb, the view gets grander.

The summit is a rocky perch that would comfortably seat a dozen hikers or more, but if you plan to move around a bit, I'd suggest taking this walk early in the morning or late in the afternoon.

GOING FARTHER

Scratch your itch for more exercise by taking the 2.6-mile hike to Hardy and Rodney Falls (hike #77 in this guide), which is just across the road from the Beacon Rock trailhead, or following that same trail for a 6.4-mile climb to Hamilton Mountain.

80. Dog Mountain

RATING	🚶 🚶 🚶 🚶
DISTANCE	8.0 miles round-trip
HIKING TIME	5 hours
ELEVATION GAIN	2,800 feet
HIGH POINT	2,948 feet
EFFORT	Knee-Punishing
BEST SEASON	Spring
PERMITS/CONTACT	Northwest Forest Pass required/Gifford Pinchot National Forest, (509) 395-3400; www.fs.usda.gov/giffordpinchot
MAPS	USGS Mount Defiance; Green Trails Hood River
NOTES	Leashed dogs welcome; hot in summer

THE HIKE
This steep climb leads to one of the finest wildflower hillsides in the Columbia Gorge and stunning views of the river below.

GETTING THERE
From Interstate 205 in Vancouver, take exit 27 and follow Lewis and Clark Highway (State Route 14) past Carson for 9 miles to the large parking area and trailhead on the left, 150 feet above sea level. GPS trailhead coordinates: N45°41.956´; W121°42.395´

THE HIKE
This is one of the toughest climbs in this guide, but crowds of hikers of all ages risk their knees and other joints in the spring to see the hillsides sprout colors that have yet to be named. Wildflowers cover almost every square inch of ground, the views can fry your eyeballs, and you'll certainly realize you've gotten some exercise when you get back to the trailhead.

Begin by climbing in switchbacks to a forested trail junction 0.5 mile from the trailhead. Both trails head to the summit, but stay right at the junction for a gentler grade to the summit. You'll climb for 2.3 miles to a spot on the broad shoulder of Dog Mountain where the trails rejoin. Continue climbing to the right for another mile and 500 vertical feet to the wide summit of the mountain.

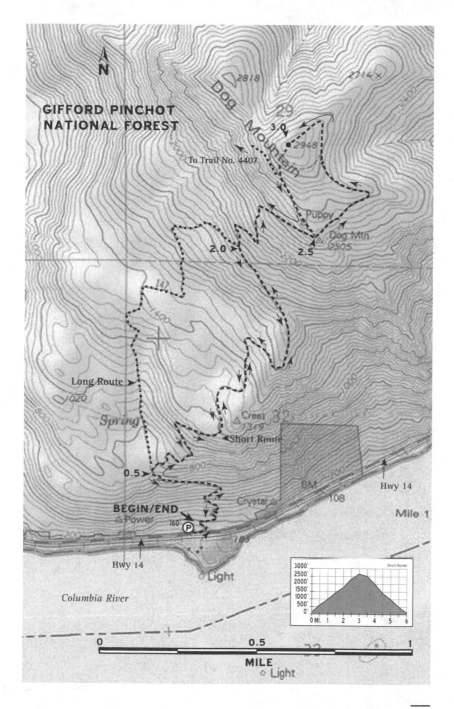

The Cheney trailhead of Columbia Plateau Trail North (#81) provides access to walks north, to Fish Lake, and south, to the Turnbull Wildlife Refuge.

SPOKANE AND NORTHEASTERN WASHINGTON

Since moving back to my hometown of Spokane in 2008, I've redis-covered why I fell in love with Mother Nature and began walking wild pathways in the first place. The mountains are splendid, and the Spokane River is a beautiful example of how a community can restore life to what was once essentially a storm drain. There are four distinct seasons, and each brings a new way to experience the great outdoors. I must surely have contracted a major case of rainbrain to have stayed away so long. Try the following hikes, and see for yourself.

Part of the Shedroof Mountain trail (#84) was an old forest service road.

SPOKANE AND NORTHEASTERN WASHINGTON

81. Columbia Plateau Trail North

RATING	🚶 🚶 🚶
DISTANCE	7.6 miles round-trip
HIKING TIME	4 hours
ELEVATION GAIN	80 feet
HIGH POINT	2,250 feet
EFFORT	Easy Walk
BEST SEASON	Spring; open year-round
PERMITS/CONTACT	Discover Pass required/Columbia Plateau Trail State Park, (509) 646-9218; www.parks.wa.gov
MAPS	USGS Cheney, kiosk map
NOTES	Bicyclists, equestrians, inline skaters, and leashed dogs welcome

THE HIKE

The desert blooms like a fireworks display in the spring, making this walk an early favorite.

GETTING THERE

Take exit 270 off Interstate 90, west of Spokane, and follow it to Cheney. Turn left on the Cheney-Spangle Road and drive 1 mile to the trailhead on the left, 2,324 feet above sea level. GPS trailhead coordinates: N47°28.771'; W117°33.644'

THE TRAIL

Let us pause a moment to thank the Spokane, Portland, and Seattle Railway for this excellent walk along a paved pathway frequented not just by pedestrians of all ages, shapes, and sizes, but by wildlife of equal variety. You're likely to see deer, elk, and even moose along sections of this path—the first paved portion of an abandoned roadbed that will eventually stretch 130 miles southwest.

Your hike leads north along the old roadbed, which saw its first trains heading out of Spokane more than a century ago. The route drops almost unnoticeably to the north, passing a landmark grain elevator in about 1.0 mile and crossing the old Union Pacific tracks about 1.2 miles from the trailhead. The trail continues through scabland that

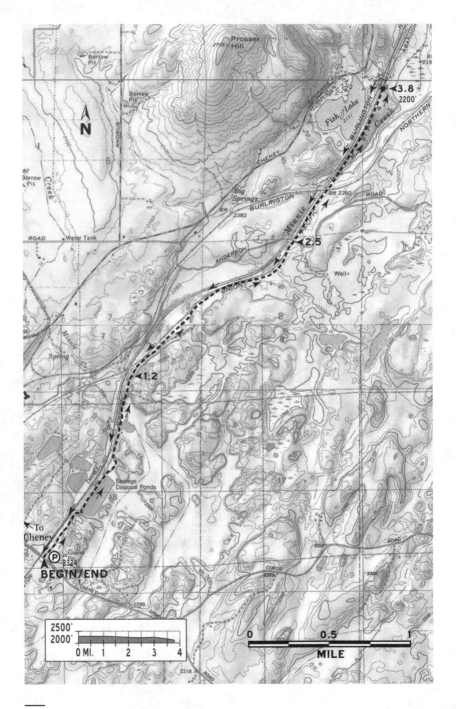

sprouts wildflowers of all shapes and sizes in the spring, through man-made canyons in the dark basalt rock. At 2.5 miles cross Anderson Road, and get your first view of Fish Lake in about another 0.5 mile. Walk above the lake on the southeast side to the county park at the north end of the lake, where you can enjoy a lakeside picnic at your turnaround point.

GOING FARTHER
Though the abandoned roadbed continues northeasterly through Marshall to Spokane, it hasn't been developed yet. A better alternative would be to combine this portion of the trail with the Columbia Plateau Trail South (hike #82 in this guide).

82. Columbia Plateau Trail South

RATING   🥾 🥾 🥾 🥾
DISTANCE   7.4 miles round-trip
HIKING TIME   4 hours, 30 minutes
ELEVATION GAIN   40 feet
HIGH POINT   2,330 feet
EFFORT   Easy Walk
BEST SEASON   Spring; open year-round
PERMITS/CONTACT   Discover Pass required/Columbia Plateau Trail State Park, (509) 646-9218; www.parks.wa.gov
MAPS   USGS Cheney, kiosk map
NOTES   Equestrians and leashed dogs welcome; great family walk

THE HIKE
Hey, you're going to hike through a national wildlife refuge. I'm guessing you know I'm not going to rave about the geologic features or the kaleidoscope of wildflowers you'll see in the springtime.

GETTING THERE
Take exit 270 off Interstate 90, west of Spokane, and follow it to Cheney. Turn left on the Cheney-Spangle Road and drive 1 mile to the trailhead on the left, 2,324 feet above sea level. GPS trailhead coordinates: N47°28.771′; W117°33.644′

THE TRAIL
Though the Columbia Plateau Trail will eventually stretch all the way to the Tri-Cities, the 4.0-mile stretch southwest from the Cheney trailhead is sure to be a favorite for decades to come. The reason? The Turnbull National Wildlife Refuge, which you'll enter less than 2.0 miles from the trailhead.

Start by walking the paved path to the trail, which passes under the Cheney-Spangle Road on its way south. The pavement ends at the underpass, though the gravel surface is smooth and well packed. Mountain bikers will barely notice the difference between the asphalt portion and the gravel. Do you disagree? Get yourself a gel seat.

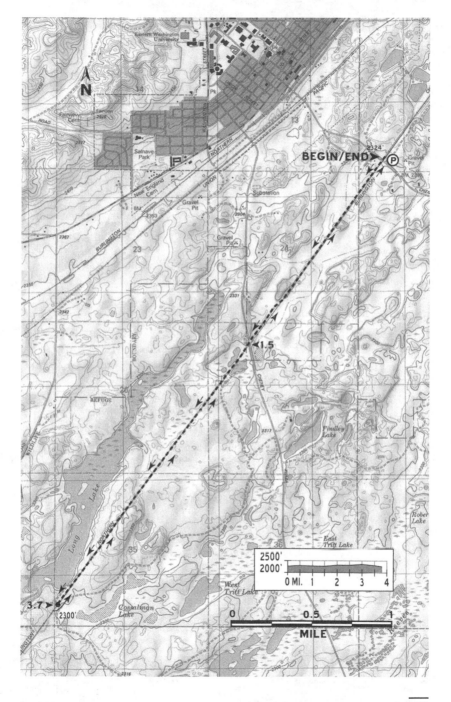

Walk south along the wide, flat trail, and in 1.5 miles, cross the Cheney-Plaza Road—the northern boundary of the Turnbull National Wildlife Refuge. Created in 1937, the 15,600-acre refuge is home to more than 100 bird species, as well as deer, elk, moose, badgers, coyotes, muskrats, and beavers. Elk herds can sometimes be seen in the autumn, often right along the trail. The trail passes along the western side of the refuge, and trail users are exempt from paying the entrance fee required from March through October at the refuge headquarters.

Just beyond the refuge boundary, you'll pass small ponds on the left and the north end of Long Lake on your right. This is one of the prime areas for wildlife-watching throughout the year. Springtime might be best for bird-watching, autumn for seeing elk and moose, and winter for cross-country skiers and snowshoe hikers. Continue above the shores of Long Lake for another mile to its southern end, 3.7 miles from the trailhead. Here's a good spot for a picnic and changing the memory card in your digital camera—you'll need it for the hike back to shoot all the photos you missed on your way here.

GOING FARTHER

You can walk another 1.7 miles along the trail to Ballinger and Campbell lakes, making a round-trip hike of 10.8 miles. Those wishing to punish their joints even more can add miles to the south or combine this hike with the trek north to Fish Lake.

83. Turnbull National Wildlife Refuge

RATING	🚶 🚶 🚶 🚶
DISTANCE	4.0 miles round-trip
HIKING TIME	3 hours
ELEVATION GAIN	100 feet
HIGH POINT	2,300 feet
EFFORT	Easy Walk
BEST SEASON	Spring, fall
PERMITS/CONTACT	Self-pay entrance fee/Turnbull National Wildlife Refuge, (509) 235-4723; www.fws.gov/turnbull
MAPS	USGS Cheney
NOTES	Leashed dogs welcome; great family walk

THE HIKE

The walk along the Bluebird Trail in the Turnbull National Wildlife Refuge is a great way to get to know the fauna of the inland Northwest. You have a chance to see everything from moose to mice, swans to swallows, elk to eagles.

GETTING THERE

From Interstate 90 in Spokane, drive west to the Tyler-Cheney exit 257 and follow State Route 904 south for 10.3 miles to Cheney and Cheney-Plaza Road. Turn left on Cheney-Plaza Road and follow it for 4.1 miles to the entrance to Turnbull National Wildlife Refuge. Turn left and drive to the self-pay entrance station, then continue to the refuge headquarters and trailhead parking, 2,300 feet above sea level. GPS trailhead coordinates: N4724.945'; W117°31.889'

THE TRAIL

My wife, B. B. Hardbody, and I drove the 5.5-mile auto-tour route around the Turnbull Refuge in the summer of 2008, expecting to see all manner of four-legged and winged creatures galloping and flying about. But by the end of the day, I would have paid a substantial sum of money just to spot a coyote, or even a rabbit. A skunk would have been acceptable.

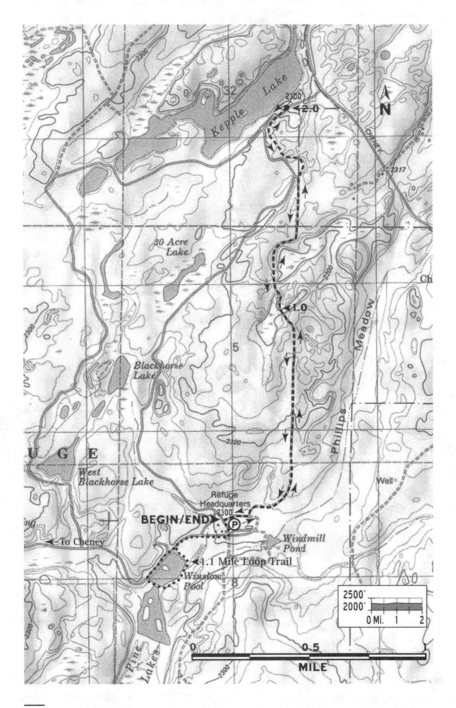

Alas, the only wildlife we saw that day was a couple parked at the Black-horse Lake overlook.

So take the advice of the experts at the refuge: plan your visit early in the morning or late in the evening. And instead of driving around, walk the Bluebird Trail to Kepple Lake, where you are much more likely to see ducks, geese, or even swans—more than two dozen species of quackers call Turnbull home.

The trail climbs gently east from the closed road northeast of the head-quarters building, then swings north and climbs into the low pine-dotted hills for 1.0 mile. Here is where you're most likely to see some of the larger critters that occupy the refuge, including deer, elk, or even moose. The trail heads due north for 0.8 mile, swings to the west and skirts a marsh, then parallels the auto-tour route to a parking area above Kepple Lake. Turn right and follow the closed road to pine forest views down to the lake, 2.0 miles from the trailhead.

GOING FARTHER

Trails lace the 2,200 acres of the 16,000-acre refuge that are open to the public; for a longer loop hike, follow the auto-tour road west from the Kepple Lake parking area to Blackhorse and West Blackhorse lakes for 2.0 miles, then hike the entrance road 0.8 mile back to the refuge headquarters.

84. Shedroof Mountain

RATING	🥾 🥾 🥾 🥾
DISTANCE	7.4 miles round-trip
HIKING TIME	5 hours, 30 minutes
ELEVATION GAIN	840 feet
HIGH POINT	6,764 feet
EFFORT	Prepare to Perspire
BEST SEASON	Late summer, fall
PERMITS/CONTACT	Northwest Forest Pass required/Colville National Forest, (509) 446-2691; www.fs.usda.gov/colville
MAPS	USGS Salmo Mountain
NOTES	Bicyclists, equestrians, and leashed dogs welcome; hot in summer

THE HIKE
This climb in the extreme northeastern corner of Washington gets highest marks for the gallons of huckleberries found here around mid-August and the top-of-the-world views of Idaho, Washington, and British Columbia.

GETTING THERE
From Spokane, drive about 120 miles north on Highways 2, 211, 20, and 31 to Metaline Falls. Follow State Route 31 north to Sullivan Lake Road 9345 and turn right. Follow Sullivan Lake Road for 4.9 miles to Forest Road 22 and turn left. Follow FR 22 for 6.2 miles to a three-way intersection. Bear left on FR 2220 to Salmo Mountain. Continue on FR 2220 for 13 miles to the trailhead. Stay right at the junction with FR 270 to Salmo Mountain. The trailhead is at the end of the road, 5,920 feet above sea level. GPS trailhead coordinates: N48°57.345′; W117°04.858′

THE TRAIL
It is worth taking this hike to the 19th-highest peak in Eastern Washington for the mountain's name alone. (For more mountain peaks, see James Johnson's excellent guide, *50 Hikes for Eastern Washington's Highest Mountains*.) You feel like you're sitting on a rooftop with acres of mountains and valleys below.

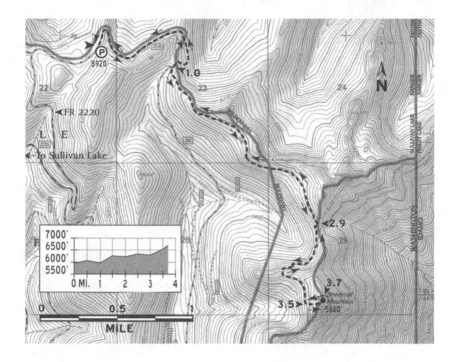

But if you don't take this walk for the name, take it for the several tons of huckleberries you can pick along the way. Since moving to the sunny side of the state, I have learned that wild huckleberries are probably the major reason anyone gets out-of-doors in this neck of the woods.

In fact, in August 2008, they inspired Rich Landers, the outdoor editor of Spokane's *Spokesman-Review*, to publish his and readers' huckleberry haiku. My favorite, from Jamie Redman of Spokane:

CASH CROP
Forty bucks a quart
My purple lips tell no lies
I ate a month's rent

But if you're not going to walk for huckleberries or the mountain's name, perhaps you'll take this hike for the scenery. Shedroof's summit once held a fire lookout, and you can see everything from Nome to Honolulu. Maybe not quite that far.

You'll find two trailheads at the parking area. Your trail, No. 535, follows an abandoned road that heads north on a closed road bordered by two- and three-man rocks before swinging in a wide switchback to the south. At 1.0 mile it turns into a single track. Walk another 0.1 mile to a junction with a spur trail and keep left, climbing through subalpine forest with peekaboo views to the south. The trail climbs gently and traverses the hillside for another mile, rounds a curve to the south, and enters a meadow with a view of Shedroof Mountain to the south.

At 2.9 miles, you'll arrive at a junction with Trail No. 512. Turn right here and begin the steep, switchbacking climb to the summit trail; at 3.5 miles, the path levels at a junction with a way trail leading to the old lookout. Take this trail as it climbs to the left and in another steep 0.2 mile emerges onto the broad summit. Views to the west include Gypsy Peak, which, at 7,309 feet, is the highest mountain in Eastern Washington. To the northeast is 7,572-foot Snowy Top Mountain in Idaho; to the north, a jumble of Selkirk range peaks lead to British Columbia.

GOING FARTHER

The Shedroof Divide Trail No. 512 stretches north and south of Shedroof Mountain, providing hikes of up to 32 miles along the crest of the divide. The trail is almost entirely in subalpine and alpine country, with huge vistas at every turn. One option for a longer hike—as if 7.4 miles weren't enough—would be to return to Trail No. 512 and turn south as it descends and climbs toward Thunder Mountain, about 4 miles distant. Walk until your hammies wilt and your knees quake.

85. Sullivan Lake Trail

RATING	🚶 🚶 🚶
DISTANCE	8.2 miles round-trip
HIKING TIME	5 hours
ELEVATION GAIN	100 feet
HIGH POINT	2,650 feet
EFFORT	Moderate Workout
BEST SEASON	Summer, fall
PERMITS/CONTACT	Northwest Forest Pass required/Colville National Forest, (509) 446-7500; www.fs.usda.gov/colville
MAPS	USGS Metaline Falls
NOTES	Bicyclists, equestrians, and leashed dogs welcome; good family hike

THE HIKE
Though you'll have company on this lakeshore hike in the summer, you can't beat the cooling waters of Sullivan Lake on a hot July day.

GETTING THERE
From Spokane, drive about 120 miles north on Highways 2, 211, 20, and 31 to Metaline Falls. Follow State Route 31 north to Sullivan Lake Road 9345 and turn right. Follow Sullivan Lake Road for 4.9 miles to Forest Road 22 and turn left. Drive 0.5 mile to FR 231 and drive 0.25 mile to the trailhead parking area on the left, 2,634 feet above sea level. GPS trailhead coordinates: N48°50.420'; W117°16.712'

THE TRAIL
Honored as a National Recreation Trail in 2008, the path along the east shore of Sullivan Lake makes a great summertime outing for the whole family. The National Forest Service campground at the north end of the lake serves up a rare opportunity: watch campers land their aircraft next to the campground and set their tents next to the planes. You can turn this hike into a 4.1-mile, one-way walk if you have two vehicles and meet for a key exchange. The southern trailhead is located at the Noisy Creek Campground at the south end of the lake.

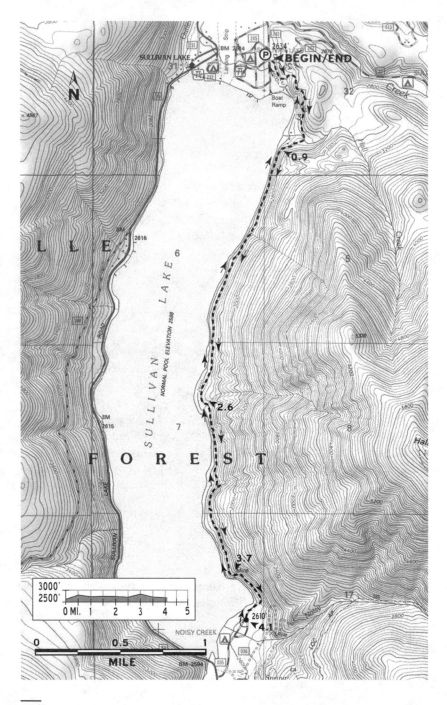

The hike begins with one of only two serious climbs on the entire trail, crossing Hall Creek, which may be dry in fall, and gaining about 80 feet in less than 0.25 mile to circle several buildings below. If it's still there, you'll welcome the bench overlooking the lake at the top of this climb. From here, the trail alternately drops and climbs in little chunks along the lakeshore, rounding several points with views up and down the lake. Hall Mountain is above, and Sand Creek Mountain rises across the lake. At about 2.6 miles, the trail passes a nice swimming hole where you may find a rope swing hanging from a big tree. Continue another mile to descend to Noisy Creek, which—by no strange coincidence—is not silent.

The Noisy Creek Campground, for those of you interested in Northwest lore, was the site of a close encounter with a Sasquatch several years ago.

GOING FARTHER

The Noisy Creek Trail, which starts at Noisy Creek Campground, climbs 2,900 feet and 5 miles one-way to the summit of Hall Mountain, where you are likely to see bighorn sheep. At the north end of the lake, the Sullivan Creek Road (Forest Road 2220) passes the campground and northern Sullivan Lake trailhead. It's not well traveled and makes a nice walk of several miles in the early morning and evening.

86. Columbia Mountain

RATING	🥾 🥾 🥾 🥾 🥾
DISTANCE	5.0 miles round-trip
HIKING TIME	4 hours, 30 minutes
ELEVATION GAIN	1,200 feet
HIGH POINT	6,782 feet
EFFORT	Prepare to Perspire
BEST SEASON	Summer, fall
PERMITS/CONTACT	Northwest Forest Pass required/Colville National Forest, (509) 684-7000; www.fs.usda.gov/colville
MAPS	USGS Sherman Peak
NOTES	Leashed dogs welcome

THE HIKE
Perhaps the most accessible peak in the scenic Kettle Range, Columbia Mountain makes a splendid climb through fragrant pine forests to the site of an old fire lookout.

GETTING THERE
From Spokane, follow US Highway 395 for 81 miles to Kettle Falls, cross the Columbia River, and take the North Cascades Highway (State Route 20) for 22 miles to the summit of Sherman Pass. Turn right and drive to the Kettle Crest trailhead, 5,575 feet above sea level. GPS trailhead coordinates: N48°36.516′; W118°28.607′

THE TRAIL
Sherman Pass has the distinction of being the highest mountain pass on a major Washington highway. It's also one of the most scenic, thanks to the fact that you can practically see the curvature of the earth from some vantage points, including the summit of 6,782-foot-high Columbia Mountain. This peak, just north of Sherman Pass, is Eastern Washington's 17th-highest peak. (For more peaks, check out James Johnson's *50 Hikes for Eastern Washington's Highest Mountains.*)

The Kettle Mountain Range holds some of the state's finest wilderness in its pine-perfumed arms (not to mention some awesome backcountry

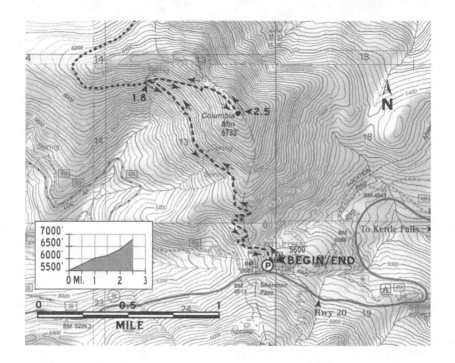

skiing), and you'll get an up-close look at it along this trail. Begin by following the Kettle Crest Trail No. 13, climbing in switchbacks along the south side of the mountain. After about 1.0 mile, the path heads to the northwest and climbs more gently, traversing under the summit of the peak. You'll continue to climb through open pine forest to a saddle 1.8 miles from the trailhead, at a junction with Columbia Mountain Trail No. 24. This trail junction is easily missed, because Trail No. 24 makes an abrupt U-turn to the right and climbs the open east slope of the mountain.

Climb the final 0.7 mile to the summit, where you'll find the remnants of an old fire lookout and cabin, and views in all directions. Look north to Wapaloosie Mountain and south to Sherman and Snow peaks.

GOING FARTHER

The Kettle Crest Trail No. 13 heads north and south from Sherman Pass for almost 60 miles along rolling mountains cresting more than 7,000 feet. For more views and climbs, return to the Crest Trail and continue north for about 1 mile to Jungle Hill, returning the way you came. Looking for more exercise? Continue north another 2.2 miles to Wapaloosie Mountain.

87. Painted Rocks

RATING	🚶 🚶 🚶 🚶
DISTANCE	4.0 miles round-trip
HIKING TIME	2 hours, 30 minutes
ELEVATION GAIN	120 feet
HIGH POINT	2,000 feet
EFFORT	Easy Walk
BEST SEASON	Spring
PERMITS/CONTACT	Discover Pass required/Riverside State Park, (509) 465-5064
MAPS	USGS Nine Mile Falls; Riverside State Park map
NOTES	Leashed dogs welcome; good family hike; hot in summer

THE HIKE

Follow the Little Spokane River downstream through elegant old pine forests past ancient Native American rock paintings where the riverside turns yellow with wild irises in the spring.

GETTING THERE

Take the Maple Street exit 280 off Interstate 90 in Spokane and drive north on Maple to Francis Avenue. Turn left on Francis and follow it to Indian Trail Road; turn right and follow Indian Trail Road to the Painted Rocks parking area and trailhead, 1,618 feet above sea level. GPS coordinates: N47°46.955′; W117°29.798′

THE TRAIL

The city of Spokane and the state of Washington are blessed with Riverside State Park, one of the finest state parks in the Northwest. It's a wildland of forests, rivers, basalt cliffs, lakes, and campgrounds within minutes of the center of the city—a day hiker's dream. The Little Spokane River Trail downstream from Painted Rocks is one of its premier showcases.

In the springtime, the banks of the river are lined with yellow irises, which attract a variety of birds, as well as people. The river is a popular canoe and kayak float in the summer and the trailhead is one of two put-ins or take-outs.

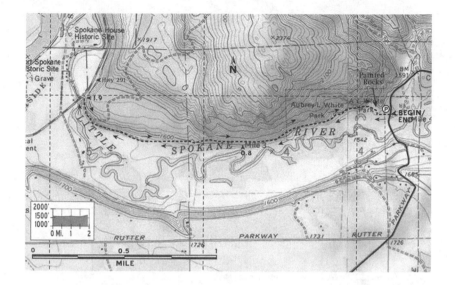

Walk a few hundred feet from the trailhead to view the Painted Rocks, pictographs left centuries ago by Native Americans, now protected from vandals by wire screens. Next, follow the trail underneath giant pines where the Little Spokane River slips quietly toward the Spokane River across a meadow 100 yards to the south. Massive basalt cliffs stretch into blue sky to the north.

The path strays close to the river before climbing a hill, then descends to a broad, glacier-polished granite slab where the trail becomes a sidewalk across the rock, about 0.8 miles from the trailhead. Back on the trail, you'll begin climbing a hill above the river, where the trail bypasses a heron nesting or roosting area.

Cross the gully and climb once again over a hill to a river viewpoint, then descend again to meadows above the Little Spokane. This portion of the trail follows an older, wider wagon road before climbing, 1.9 miles from the trailhead, to a downstream trailhead off Highway 291. This is your turnaround point.

GOING FARTHER
The excellent, exhausting 7-mile Knothead loop hike begins at the Painted Rocks trailhead and heads east, then north up a wide gully, crossing a pine ridge and dropping steeply down to the Highway 291 trailhead, where you can follow the Little Spokane upstream to the trailhead. Portions of this trail have recently been rerouted and vastly improved by volunteer crews from the Washington Trails Association.

88. Dishman Hills

RATING	🚶 🚶
DISTANCE	4.3 miles round-trip
HIKING TIME	2 hours, 30 minutes
ELEVATION GAIN	450 feet
HIGH POINT	2,426 feet
EFFORT	Moderate Workout
BEST SEASON	Spring, fall
PERMITS/CONTACT	None/Dishman Hills Conservancy, (509) 684-7474; www.dishmanhills.org
MAPS	USGS Spokane NE; trailhead map
NOTES	Hikers only; leashed dogs welcome; very hot in summer

THE HIKE
Walk within the sound of car salespeople being paged over loudspeakers into some of the finest urban wilds found around Spokane.

GETTING THERE
From Interstate 90 in Spokane, take the Broadway exit 286 and turn right on Broadway Ave. to Park Road. Turn right on Park and follow it to Appleway Blvd. Turn left on Appleway and look for a sign on the right for the Dishman Hills Natural Resource Conservation Area. Turn right on Sargent Road and drive 0.4 mile to Camp Caro and the trailhead, 2,070 feet above sea level. GPS trailhead coordinates: N47°39.188'; W117°17.355'

THE TRAIL
Long before the 518-acre Dishman Hills Natural Area was created in the late 1960s—perhaps before the discovery of the wheel—I hiked these very trails with a Spokane photographer named George Libby. He'd rent a city bus and fill it with kids who paid 75 cents to follow him around some of the wild pine woods near Spokane. He packed an old Army surplus canteen, an ax and machete, sacks of taffy he'd toss to his young followers, and a .22 rifle—everyone got a chance to shoot at a target he'd set up

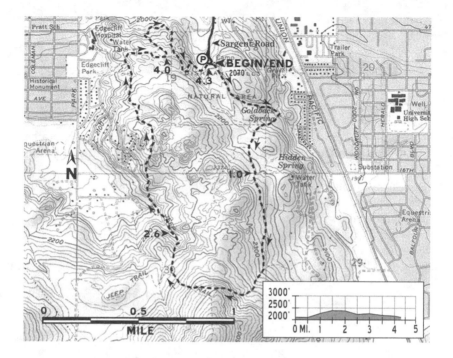

where it was safe. I earned my hiking money for the next weekend by carrying rich kids' packs for quarters.

Every Wednesday, George sent a postcard to his young hikers. "This Saturday," it read, "we'll explore the hills south of Dishman!" Or "This Saturday, we're heading to the Bowl and Pitcher and the wild canyon of Deep Creek." It was the best introduction to the great outdoors a youngster could get.

I'd suggest starting your hike on the Goldback Springs Trail, which joins the Tower Mountain Trail in 0.7 mile. Turn right, and after passing Goldback Springs, turn right again and climb on the Tower Mountain Trail to the second junction with the Eagle Peak Loop Trail, 1.6 miles from the trailhead.

Take the Eagle Peak Loop Trail to the right and follow it to the junction with the Ridge Top Trail. Stay right and follow the Eagle Peak Loop Trail to a junction with the short Eagle Peak Trail. This path leads to the high point of the hike, with great views to the east and north. Return to the Ridge Top Trail, turn right, and follow it to the Lost Pond Trail. After a side trip to Lost Pond, return to the Ridge Top Trail and follow it to the junction with the Tower Mountain Trail, 2.6 miles from the trailhead.

Turn left on the Pond Loop Trail and follow it to East and West ponds, then return to the Pond Loop Trail and follow it to Camp Caro.

GOING FARTHER

You'll find a network of well-marked trails that climb from Camp Caro in steep but short steps through pine forest and between basalt cliffs and ravines. Pathways lead to several high points overlooking Dishman and across the Spokane River valley to the foothills of the Selkirk Mountains. Several pathways leave the Conservation Area and cross private land, including the Tower Mountain Trail and an extension of the Ridge Top Trail. In addition to the trailhead at Camp Caro, you'll find trailheads off 8th Avenue near Edgecliff Park, 16th Avenue, and Siesta Drive. These offer limited on-street parking.

89. Liberty Creek

RATING	🚶 🚶
DISTANCE	4.6 miles round-trip
HIKING TIME	2 hours
ELEVATION GAIN	500 feet
HIGH POINT	2,600 feet
EFFORT	Easy Walk
BEST SEASON	Spring; open year-round
PERMITS/CONTACT	Entry fee required/Spokane County Parks, (509) 477-4730; www.spokanecounty.org/parks
MAPS	USGS Mica Peak
NOTES	Great family walk; leashed dogs welcome

THE HIKE

Walk beside a quiet stream to a picnic area and a shady forest of giant cedars, with the option of a steeper, longer loop hike.

GETTING THERE

Take Interstate 90 east from Spokane to the Liberty Lake exit and follow Appleway Blvd. east to Molter Road. Turn right and drive 1 mile to Valley Way, which becomes Lakeside Road. Follow Lakeside Road to the south end of the lake and Liberty Lake Park. The park is gated and open from June through September, although hikers often walk into the park from the access road. The trailhead parking area is 2,060 feet above sea level. GPS trailhead coordinates: N47°37.851'; W117°03.497'

THE TRAIL

Liberty Lake has been one of Spokane's historic recreation areas for almost 140 years, with early settlers riding the rails to get to the old lakeside pavilion for dances and socials. The lake's south end has always been the more primitive area, with trails leading into the forests and hills above the lake.

The trail leading up Liberty Creek is wide and smooth, a great walk for families with young children. You'll spy a variety of birds and be serenaded by dozens more in the forest.

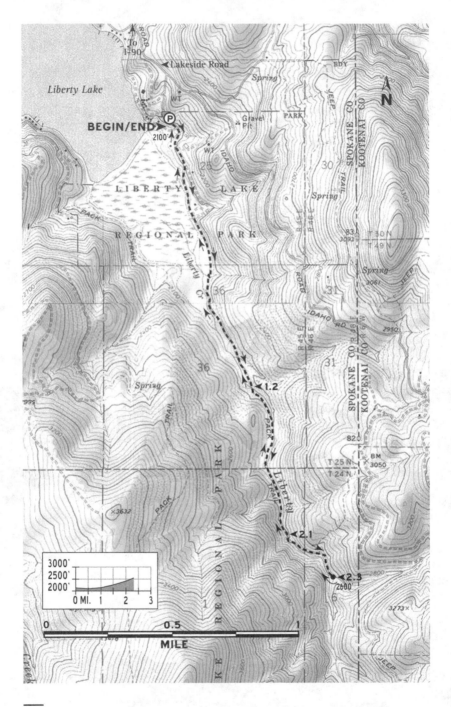

After paying your entry fee, begin by walking the flat trail beside the creek and in 0.3 mile, pass the junction with the return trail, staying left. The trail passes wetlands at the south end of the lake and crosses the creek 1.2 miles from the trailhead. Wander from open areas with views to nearby hills to forests of mixed evergreens. At 2.1 miles, you'll cross the creek again on a footbridge and find yourself in a vast cedar forest and a big picnic area.

GOING FARTHER

To extend your trip and get a more strenuous workout, cross the footbridge at the picnic area and climb in switchbacks up the forested hillside to peekaboo views of the lake. You'll pass a waterfall at 3 miles to climb to the Camp Hughes Shelter, then contour and descend to Liberty Creek, closing the loop hike 0.3 mile from the trailhead. Total distance for the loop hike is 7.5 miles, with an elevation gain and loss of about 2,300 feet.

90. Centennial Trail West

RATING	🚶 🚶 🚶 🚶
DISTANCE	7.8 miles round-trip
HIKING TIME	4 hours
ELEVATION GAIN	450 feet
HIGH POINT	1,740 feet
EFFORT	Moderate Workout
BEST SEASON	Spring; open year-round
PERMITS/CONTACT	Discover Pass required/Riverside State Park, (509) 465-5064; www.parks.wa.gov
MAPS	USGS Airway Heights, Spokane NW; state park map
NOTES	Bicyclists and leashed dogs welcome

THE HIKE

This splendid walk along the river begins with a swinging-bridge crossing and a downriver view of interesting basalt formations.

GETTING THERE

Take the Maple Street exit from Interstate 90 in Spokane and follow Maple Street north across the bridge to Francis Avenue. Turn left on Francis and follow it west, staying right at the Assembly/Driscoll intersection. Francis turns into Nine Mile Road at the junction. Continue downhill to the Riverside State Park sign, turn left, and drive three blocks to the Aubrey White Parkway; turn left again and drive to the Bowl and Pitcher entrance to the park, on your right. Elevation at the trailhead is 1,699 feet above sea level. GPS trailhead coordinates: N47°41.804′; W117°29.755′

THE TRAIL

I've visited the Bowl and Pitcher often, beginning with hikes at least five decades ago, and I still can't figure out why they call that gnarly basalt formation just downstream from the swinging bridge the Bowl and Pitcher. If you squint real hard, you might get the bowl part, and maybe Mother Nature was thinking of a pitcher without a handle. It's not a big deal—no matter what the rock formations look like to you, they are a fascinating geological display.

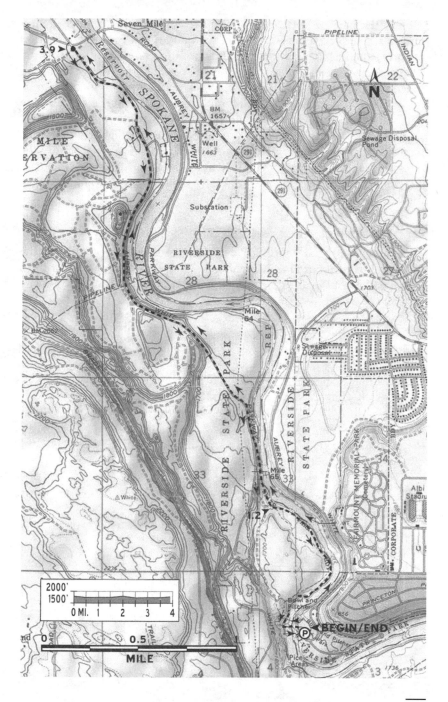

From the parking area, follow the paved trail down to the swinging bridge, where bicyclists are asked to walk and the pavement ends. Cross the bridge and look downstream to the basalt formations jutting from the river and cleaving the white water. Just across the bridge, climb to a trail junction and turn right, following the wide path downhill through a pine forest and basalt canyons. A spur trail heads to the river's edge, where you'll get a close-up view of the Bowl and Pitcher formation.

The trail continues downstream and at 1.2 miles, climbs up to a wide plateau above the river where it cuts across a field away from a wide bend in the watercourse. Beyond, it bypasses Camp Seven Mile and at 3.9 miles, crosses the Seven Mile Road, your turnaround point. Return the way you came.

GOING FARTHER

The Centennial Trail continues downstream from Seven Mile to the official start of the trail at Nine Mile Falls. If you're in the mood for a 34-mile one-way hike, you can also walk east on the trail, all the way to Idaho.

91. Centennial Trail East

RATING 🚶 🚶 🚶
DISTANCE 8.2 miles round-trip
HIKING TIME 4 hours
ELEVATION GAIN 85 feet
HIGH POINT 2,075 feet
EFFORT Easy Walk
BEST SEASON Spring; open year-round
PERMITS/CONTACT None/www.spokanecentennialtrail.org
MAPS USGS Spokane NE
NOTES Bicyclists, inline skaters, and leashed dogs
welcome; hot in summer

THE HIKE
This is a rare opportunity to hike in two states (Washington and Idaho) on the same day, along one of the prettiest stretches of the Spokane River.

GETTING THERE
Drive east from Spokane on Interstate 90 to the Harvard exit and follow Harvard north to the trailhead on the left, 2,021 feet above sea level. GPS trailhead coordinates: N47°41.644'; W117°02.920'

THE TRAIL
The biggest bull snake I ever saw lazed in the summer sun the last time I walked on this trail. It looked like an albino tire tube for a mountain bike, and it was not happy to have me shooing it off the warm pavement.

The trail ducks under Harvard Road from the trailhead, just across the river from a popular raft put-in spot, and follows the river upstream to the Idaho state line, which is the official eastern end of the Centennial Trail. Walk along above the river through mostly open country decorated sparsely by pines for about 1.6 miles, where the trail gets closer to the noise of Interstate 90. The route meanders back to the river's edge again and follows the southern bank to a wide bend at the state line. You'll cross under the freeway and climb to a monument marking the state line, then cross a pedestrian bridge to your turnaround point in Idaho.

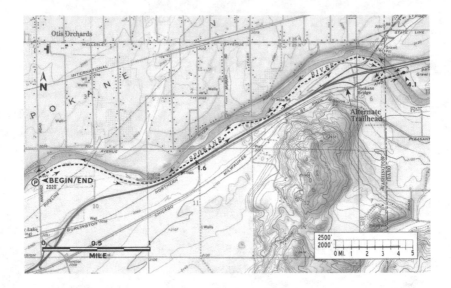

Though the distance of this walk may seem daunting, the way is mostly flat and the pavement underfoot is smooth. That makes the miles fly by, and your dogs aren't likely to bark at all.

GOING FARTHER

The Centennial Trail continues in Idaho to Post Falls and beyond, where you'll find wayside parks for picnics, with water and restrooms. You can also hike several miles downstream from the Harvard Road access, or walk south along a new section of the trail that links it with Liberty Lake.

A bench beside the Sullivan Lake trail (#85) overlooks the lake.

The Snake River near the Columbia Plateau trail (#93).

SOUTHEASTERN
WASHINGTON

The Blue Mountains, the Snake and Tucannon rivers, and the hill country around the southeastern corner of Washington yield some of the least traveled trails in the state. If it's not elk or deer season, and if the fish aren't running, you are quite likely to have the path all to yourself—except for the wild critters that live here. The wildlife will make certain you don't get too lonely. And if you're looking for blue skies and sunshine, plan to hit a trail in this neck of the woods.

The White Bluffs trail (#92) climbs toward the bluffs north of the trailhead.

SOUTHEASTERN WASHINGTON

92. White Bluffs

RATING	🚶 🚶 🚶 🚶
DISTANCE	6.0 miles round-trip
HIKING TIME	3 hours
ELEVATION GAIN	200 feet
HIGH POINT	600 feet
EFFORT	Easy Walk
BEST SEASON	Fall, winter
PERMITS/CONTACT	Discover Pass required/Washington Department of Fish and Wildlife, (509) 575-2740 ; www.wdfw.wa.gov
MAPS	USGS Locke Island
NOTES	Leashed dogs welcome

THE HIKE

Rich in wildlife and winged creatures, this part of the Columbia River is the only remaining portion unrestricted by dams, and the neighboring Hanford Nuclear Reservation is likely to keep it that way for quite some time. The trail follows ivory bluffs above the river, yielding superb views.

GETTING THERE

Take exit 137 from Interstate 90 on the east side of the Vantage Bridge and follow State Route 26 south to State Route 243. Turn right on 243 and drive 14.3 miles to the Mattawa/Highway 24 cutoff, 24SW. Drive 13.8 miles to its junction with State Route 24, and turn left. Turn right just beyond milepost 63 to the gated entrance to the Wahluke National Wildlife Refuge and drive 4 miles to an intersection; turn right and follow the road downhill 1.3 miles to the trailhead parking area. Overnight parking is prohibited, and the wildlife entrance gate closes automatically at night. The trailhead is 472 feet above sea level. GPS trailhead coordinates: N46°40.620′; W119°26.715′

THE TRAIL

The trail leads up slopes to the north of the parking area and may be difficult to follow until you crest the plateau above the bluffs. Climb through the cottonwoods to the north, where the trail becomes more

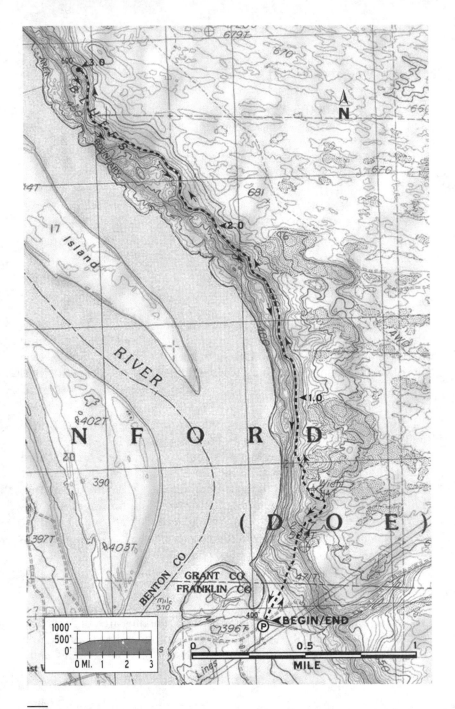

distinct and follows the crest of the bluff above the Hanford Reach of the Columbia River.

At about 1.0 mile, you'll reach a viewpoint overlooking the river and Locke Island, which splits the main stem of the Columbia River. In another mile, you'll find sand dunes rolling toward the river from the east, and in the fall, you have the best chance of spotting mule deer and Rocky Mountain elk along the trail.

You can continue another mile along the bluffs, where the trail alternately climbs and drops to viewpoints along the edge. A good turnaround point might be the broad bench overlooking a narrow bay underneath the bluff, 3.0 miles from the trailhead.

GOING FARTHER

You can walk for another mile to the northwest to the boundary of the Saddle Mountain National Wildlife Refuge, which is adjacent to the Hanford Nuclear Reservation. This area is closed to the public; trespassers run the risk of glowing in the dark or getting something definitely more than a slap on the wrist from Uncle Sam.

93. Columbia Plateau Trail

RATING	🚶 🚶 🚶
DISTANCE	6.0 miles round-trip
HIKING TIME	4 hours
ELEVATION GAIN	100 feet
HIGH POINT	700 feet
EFFORT	Moderate Workout
BEST SEASON	Spring, fall
PERMITS/CONTACT	Discover Pass required/Columbia Plateau State Park, (509) 902-8844; www.parks.wa.gov
MAPS	USGS Snake River
NOTES	Equestrians, bicyclists, and leashed dogs welcome; rough rock ballast

THE HIKE

Follow the path of a historic wagon road and railroad route under the blue skies and basalt walls of the Snake River Canyon.

GETTING THERE

From US Highway 12 in Pasco, take the Pasco-Kahlotus Road for 24 miles to the McCoy Canyon–Snake River Road. Turn right and follow the McCoy Canyon–Snake River Road to its end at the Snake River Junction, passing the junction with the Neff Jones Road on the right. Park in the new trailhead lot just beyond the junction, 500 feet above sea level. GPS trailhead coordinates: N46°23.401'; W116°40.829'

THE TRAIL

This lonely portion of the Columbia Plateau Trail, one of the state's newest rail-trail conversions, follows the Snake River to the northeast through desolate canyon steps. The grade was recently rolled and smoothed, providing much easier walking and bike-riding than in years past. Still, you'll appreciate boots with stiff soles for this walk.

Spokane, Portland, and Seattle Railway trains steamed up the Snake River here, following the route first traced by wagon trains in the mid-1800s. You'll find relics of the railroad along the way, and the path winds through the sage. Waterfowl and wildlife are abundant on this

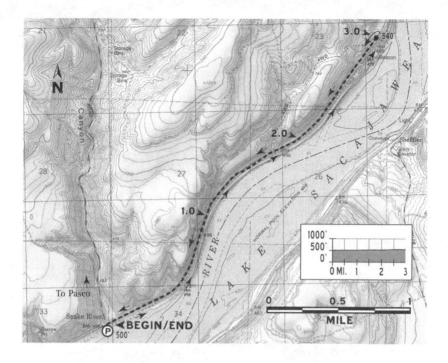

route: look for coyote and mule deer in the side canyons that climb through the basalt walls surrounding Lake Sacajawea. Raptors float on air currents above, and partridge and quail dart through the brush. Looking for a workout? Chase a chukar. Wildflowers decorate the landscape in the spring; in the frosty autumn light, the hills shine like platinum.

You can walk about 3.0 miles upstream, as the rail grade winds in gentle curves along the river. It makes a broad sweep to the east about 1.0 mile from the trailhead, then curves to the north at about 2.0 miles. You can continue for another mile to a spot where a double-track trail drops down a canyon from the north, at 3.0 miles.

GOING FARTHER
Burr Canyon is another mile to the east, which would make a round-trip hike of 8 miles. To go farther, return to the trailhead and walk to the west for up to 1.3 miles to the site of an old watering stop for steam engines.

94. Boyer Park

RATING	🚶 🚶
DISTANCE	4.0 miles round-trip
HIKING TIME	2 hours, 30 minutes
ELEVATION GAIN	100 feet
HIGH POINT	750 feet
EFFORT	Stroll in the Park
BEST SEASON	Spring; open year-round
PERMITS/CONTACT	None/Boyer Park and Marina, (509) 397-3208; www.parks.wa.gov
MAPS	USGS Starbuck East
NOTES	Bicyclists and leashed dogs welcome; great family walk; hot in summer

THE HIKE

This is a paved trail that meanders along the Snake River, serving up interesting views of the golden hillsides of the Palouse along the way.

GETTING THERE

From Colfax, follow Almota Road and State Route 194 for 15.7 miles to Granite Road, turn east, and drive 3 miles to the park and trail-head, 643 feet above sea level. GPS trailhead coordinates: N46°41.120′; W117°26.949′

THE TRAIL

This hike follows the Snake River along Boyer Park from Almota Creek to the west to the base of the Lower Granite Lock and Dam. This is splendid canyon country and remains scenic throughout the year, although spring might be the best time to hike here. The paved trail follows the river downstream to the northwest and provides views across the river of the rippled canyons of the Palouse, where hawks cruise the skies and scan the sage for a meal, and chukars dash through the brush like winged rabbits.

You can walk about 2.0 miles in each direction from the parking area at the park. The section upstream from the parking area might be the most interesting for the youngsters, with the locks and fish ladder to keep them interested.

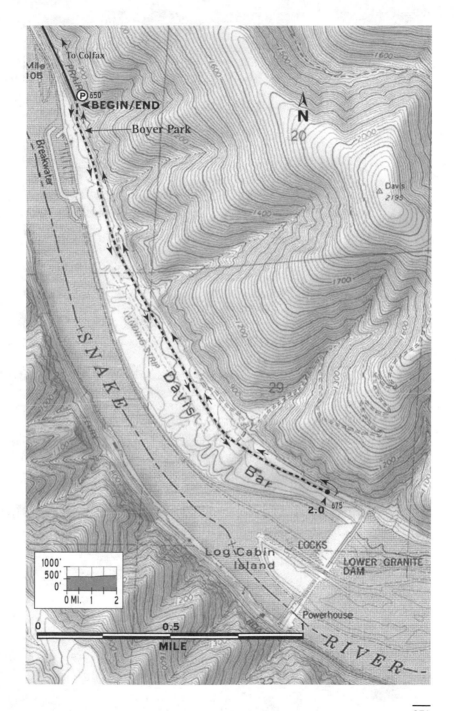

A pedestrian bridge crosses the Wenatchee River along the Apple Capital Loop trail (#99).

URBAN TRAILS

Sometimes you just don't have the time to get away from the big—or the little—city, but you'd still like to stretch the legs and get your glucosamine flowing to joints that need it. Thanks to City Mothers and Fathers and volunteer groups who make urban trails a reality, you can spend a morning or afternoon on a civilized pathway and still make that business meeting or get that roast in the oven.

Many cities and towns throughout the state serve up some sort of route intended exclusively for muscle-powered travel. They vary from gravel-surfaced single-tracks to smooth asphalt, from quarter-mile walkways along Poulsbo's waterfront to 20-mile supertrails through the heart of Seattle. Following, from west to east, are brief descriptions of what my feet and creaky old knees say are the best urban trails in Washington.

Park of the Apple Capital Loop trail (#99) passes through Wenatchee Confluence State Park.

URBAN TRAILS

95. Olympic Discovery Trail, Port Angeles and Sequim

RATING 🚶 🚶 🚶 🚶
DISTANCE 60.0 miles round-trip
EFFORT Stroll in the Park
BEST SEASON Summer; open year-round
PERMITS/CONTACT Discover Pass required
SURFACE Asphalt with timber bridges; gravel
NOTES Bicyclists, inline skaters, and leashed dogs welcome; equestrians welcome on some sections; wheelchair accessible

THE TRAIL

The Olympic Discovery Trail is part of the old Chicago, Milwaukee, St. Paul, and Pacific Railroad, with paved sections stretching from Port Angeles to Sequim, on the Olympic Peninsula. It is hoped the route will eventually link Port Townsend to the Pacific Coast.

GETTING THERE

Trailheads are located at various points along the route. My two favorites are downtown Port Angeles, just east of the Red Lion Inn, and the Railroad Bridge Park in Sequim. For maps and information, visit www.peninsulatrailcoalition.com.

THE WALK

The nicest part about the Olympic Discovery Trail is that it is located in the sunny and dry part of the wet and gray Olympic Peninsula. While it may be raining in Seattle, where it averages about 35 inches of rainfall a year, it may be sunny in Sequim, which gets half that amount.

You can get a good walk along the paved section of trail on the Port Angeles waterfront. The path heads east along the inner harbor past an old mill before turning inland and heading up the Morse Creek Valley to a trailhead and timber bridge across Morse Creek, 5.0 miles from downtown Port Angeles.

Another good paved 5.0-mile section, one-way, heads west from Railroad Bridge Park in Sequim, crosses the Dungeness River, and meanders to Robin Hill Farm Park, where you'll find a nice series of short forest trails.

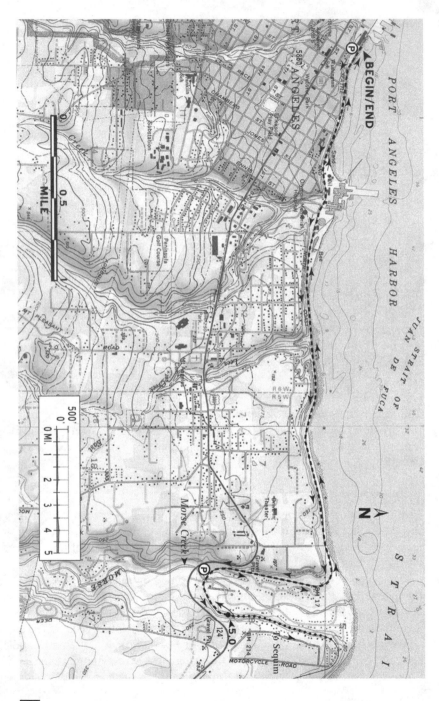

96. Chehalis Western Trail, Olympia

RATING   𝒳 𝒳 𝒳
DISTANCE   44 miles, round-trip
EFFORT   Stroll in the Park
BEST SEASON   Summer; open all year
SURFACE   Asphalt
NOTES   Bicyclists, inline skaters, leashed dogs welcome; equestrians permitted south from Fir Tree Road

THE TRAIL

This walk along a portion of the historic Chehalis Western Railroad, owned by the Weyerhaeuser Company, meanders through woodland and farms past an interesting sculpture park.

GETTING THERE

You'll find three main access points on the southern section of this trail. I'd suggest the 67th Street Trailhead, which provides an opportunity for a country walk. To get there, take Exit 109 from I-5 and drive south on College Street, which becomes Rainier Road. Continue south to 67th Ave., turn right, and follow it to the parking area at the end of the road. For maps and information on the Chehalis Western Trail, visit www.co.thurston.wa.us/parks/Trails/cw-trail.htm.

THE WALK

Parts of the Chehalis Western Trail traverse woodland and riverfront, but the one-way stretch of 3.2 miles from the 67th Street Trailhead south to the 13-mile marker offers great views of Mount Rainier and a quiet walk through farmland.

The path leads south, with mileage markers every half-mile, and you'll pass the 10-mile marker 0.2 miles from the parking area. After 11.3 miles, you'll pass the Monarch Sculpture Park on the left. Continue for another 0.7 miles to the Fir Tree Road access, a good turnaround for families with younger hikers, or continue another 1.0 mile for a longer walk.

On the return, plan a stop at the Sculpture Park, which features a summertime outdoor cafe and some interesting and whimsical statuary. Admission is free.

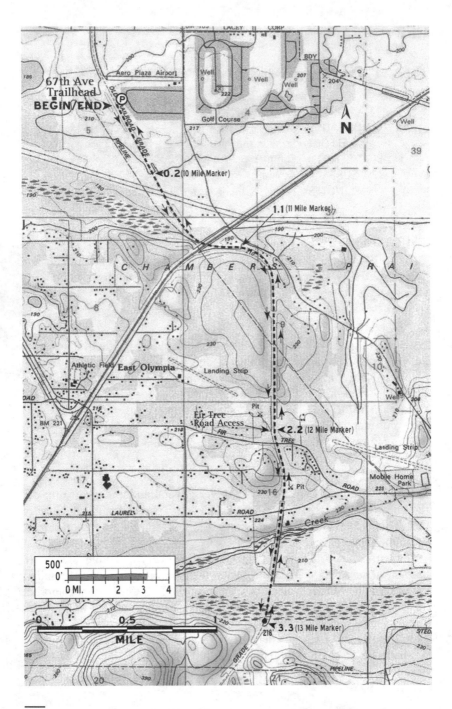

97. Burke-Gilman Trail, Seattle

RATING 🚶 🚶 🚶
DISTANCE 37.6 miles, round-trip
EFFORT Stroll in the Park
BEST SEASON Summer; open all year
SURFACE Asphalt
NOTES Bicyclists, inline skaters, leashed dogs
welcome; wheelchair accessible

THE TRAIL
Here is the Granddaddy of all urban trails in the state, a former railroad grade that winds from Shilshole Bay to Bothell, where you can add more miles on the newer Sammamish River Trail.

GETTING THERE
You'll find access points at Gasworks, Matthews Beach, and Log Boom parks, with disability access at Gasworks and Log Boom. I'd suggest the 5.1-mile one-way section north from Matthews Beach Park to Tracy Owen Station in Kenmore. Follow Sand Point Way to NE 93rd, and turn east to the park. For maps and information, visit www.ci.seattle.wa.us/parks/BurkeGilman/bgtrail.htm.

THE WALK
The Burke-Gilman is a trail of many facets, from the busy marine sections along the Lake Washington Ship Canal, past the University of Washington, and over the traffic of Sand Point Way. But if it is a quiet walk you're after, I'd recommend the nearly flat section that begins at Matthews Beach Park. It winds north to the official end of the trail at Tracy Owen Station in Kenmore.

Though close to the shore of Lake Washington, the trail winds along behind waterfront houses, so you'll get only peekaboo views of the lake. That may be one reason many bicyclists make Matthews Beach their turn-around point. Cross Lakeside Place NE at 1.6 miles from Matthews Beach and NE Ballinger Way 4.5 miles from the park. Beyond, at the end of the trail, 5.1 miles, is the Tracy Owen Station in Kenmore. *WARNING: You run the risk of replacing all the calories you've burned at a bakery, tavern,*

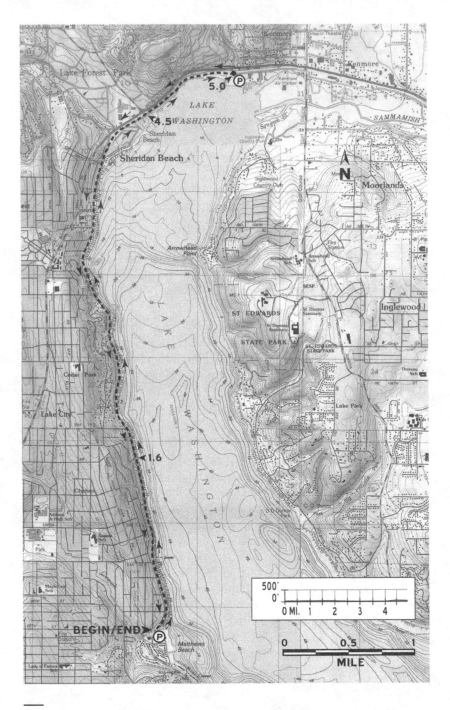

ice-creamery, or coffee store alongside the trail in Kenmore. Instead, settle on the grass of the park, watch the float planes on Lake Washington, and rest up for the walk back.

98. Boulevard Park, Bellingham

RATING 🚶 🚶 🚶 🚶
DISTANCE 4.0 miles, round-trip
EFFORT Stroll in the Park
BEST SEASON Summer; open all year
SURFACE Gravel; Boardwalk
NOTES Bicyclists, inline skaters, leashed dogs welcome

THE TRAIL
It's worth the trip to Bellingham just to watch the sunset turn Bellingham Bay crimson and paint the San Juan Islands purple from Boulevard Park.

GETTING THERE
Take Exit 250 off I-5 and follow Old Fairhaven Parkway to 10th Street in Fairhaven, then follow it around the corner to the right to Fairhaven Village Green and the trailhead. For a map and information, visit www .cob.org/services/recreation/parks-trails/trail-guide.aspx.

THE WALK
Though short, the one-way hike of 2.0 miles is a great introduction to the lively and beautiful city of Bellingham, with splendid views of Bellingham Bay and the ever-changing maritime scene. Begin at Fairhaven Village Green and walk north for 0.2 miles to 10th Street, where you'll continue less than two blocks to pick up the trail again at historic Taylor Dock and round Pattle Point on a boardwalk, 0.5 miles from the trailhead. Pattle Point offers variety on the return trip via a short nature trail that loops back to the main path. Past the point, the route crosses a trestle and continues 1.4 miles on a waterfront trail past playgrounds, picnic tables, barbecues, and beaches in Boulevard Park. Wharf Street, at the north end of the park, is a good turnaround point, although you can continue along the trail another 0.4 miles to its official end at Maple Street in downtown Bellingham.

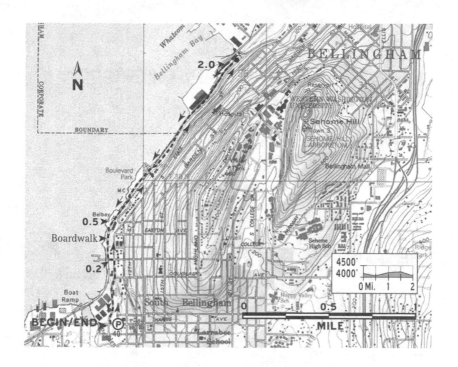

99. Apple Capital Loop, Wenatchee

RATING 🚶 🚶 🚶 🚶 🚶
DISTANCE 10.0 miles
EFFORT Stroll in the Park
BEST SEASON Spring, winter; open year-round
SURFACE Asphalt with timber bridges
NOTES Bicyclists, inline skaters, and leashed dogs welcome; equestrians welcome on east bank; wheelchair accessible

THE TRAIL

If anything good comes from hydroelectric dams (besides electricity!), it might be the outdoor recreational opportunities they create. The Apple Capital Loop Trail is such an opportunity; it is arguably the best urban trail in the state.

GETTING THERE

Trailheads are located at several points along the path. My favorite is Wenatchee Confluence State Park, which—by no serendipitous accident—is located at the confluence of the Wenatchee and Columbia rivers. For information and maps, visit www.chelanpud.org/apple-capital-loop-trail.html.

THE WALK

The walk, ride, or skate around the Apple Capital Loop is a joy at any time of year. In the spring, you start at Wenatchee Confluence State Park and walk south, crossing a pedestrian bridge over the snow-swollen Wenatchee River, then walk past downtown Wenatchee along the Columbia River for about 5.0 miles. You're in the middle of an urban environment, but it may not feel that way as you pass by the Horan Natural Area, a favorite spot for bird-watchers.

Next is Walla Walla Point Park, where there's a great sculpture of a coyote conducting a salmon tour. The path continues through Riverfront Park to an irrigation pipeline bridge at the south end of town.

Across the bridge, the trail takes on an entirely different personality: you'll walk through undeveloped sage land where marmots dig and bald eagles soar above the river. Residences are distant, and the trail

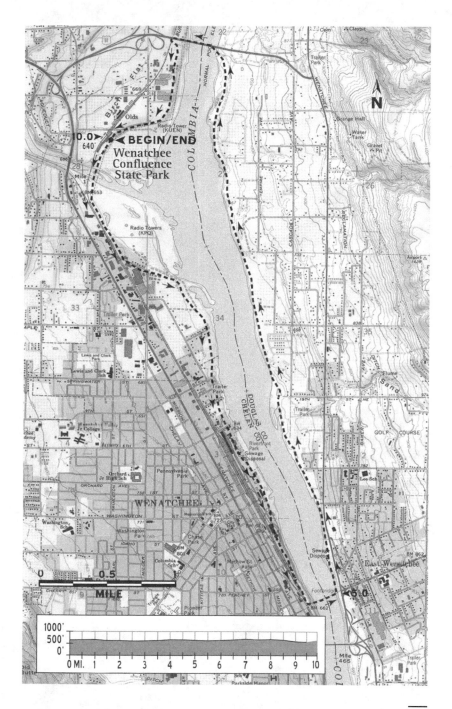

no longer feels urban, even though you can look west to the heart of the city. The path continues for 5.0 miles upriver, occasionally dipping gently to cross gullies, and crosses the Highway 2 bridge over the Columbia before turning south into Confluence State Park.

100. Yakima Greenway, Yakima

RATING   🚶 🚶 🚶 🚶
DISTANCE   20.0 miles, round-trip
EFFORT   Stroll in the Park
BEST SEASON   Spring, winter; open year-round
SURFACE   Asphalt with timber bridges
NOTES   Bicyclists, inline skaters, and leashed dogs welcome; wheelchair accessible

THE TRAIL

One of the most enjoyable urban trails in the state can be found in sunny Yakima. It's worth a trip here simply to hike the trail.

GETTING THERE

You'll find a number of trailheads along the 10-mile course of the Yakima Greenway. I'd suggest the Sherman Park trailhead, which is pink every spring with fruit tree blossoms and where you can watch the Sons of Italy playing boccie ball. For information and maps, visit www .yakimagreenway.org.

THE WALK

The noise from Interstate 82 and Highway 12 might be distracting at first, but once you're walking along the Yakima or Naches rivers, you probably won't notice it. I'd suggest walking north from Sherman Park to Sarg Hubbard Park and its natural area and fitness stations, then continuing to Rotary Lake, where you'll find wheelchair-accessible fishing platforms.

There's river access at Harlan Landing, farther north, and the trail turns up the Naches River to Myron Lake. Bicyclists take note: Goat head thorns lurk beside the paved pathway.

For a longer walk, return to Sherman Park and walk south along the trail for another 2.0 miles one-way.

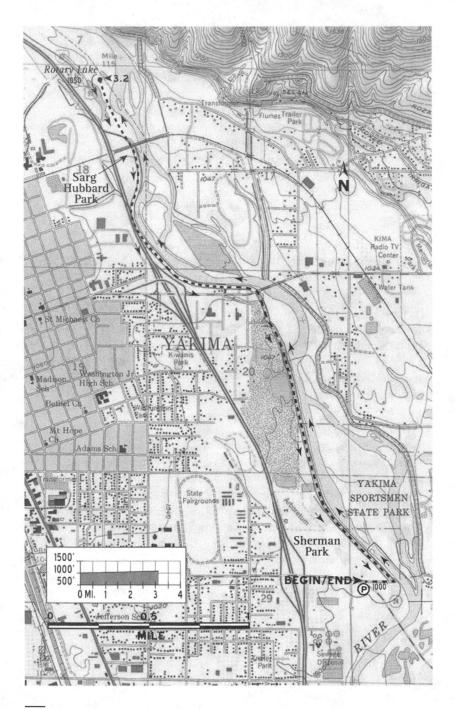

The Yakima Greenway (#100).

INDEX